CONSEQUENCES OF CLASS
AND COLOR

DAVID LOWENTHAL, a geographer and historian, has devoted twenty years to research on the West Indies. He has taught at Vassar College and has been visiting professor at a number of universities in the United States and at the University of the West Indies, where he was Fulbright Research Fellow at the Institute of Social and Economic Research (1956–57). During 1961–62 he worked in the Lesser Antilles with the assistance of a Rockefeller Foundation research grant and later received a Guggenheim Fellowship. Until 1972, he was Secretary and Research Associate at the American Geographical Society, and he is currently Professor of Geography at University College, London. His most recent book is *West Indian Societies,* a comprehensive study of the non-Hispanic Caribbean.

Lambros Comitas is Professor of Anthropology and Education, Director of both the Center for Education in Latin America and the Center for Urban Studies and Programs, and Associate Director of the Division of Philosophy and Social Sciences at Teachers College, Columbia University. He is also Associate Director of the Research Institute for the Study of Man, an institution for research and scholarship of the Caribbean. Awarded a Fulbright Graduate Study Grant (1957–58) and a Guggenheim Fellowship (1971–72), Mr. Comitas' field research was done in Barbados, Jamaica, Bolivia, and the Dominican Republic. He has written numerous articles, he was editor of *Caribbeana 1900–1965: A Topical Bibliography,* and serves as consultant or editor for several publishing projects.

Four books, edited and introduced by Lambros Comitas and David Lowenthal, provide a broad variety of material for the West Indies as a whole; each has the subtitle *West Indian Perspectives:*

> SLAVES, FREE MEN, CITIZENS
> WORK AND FAMILY LIFE
> CONSEQUENCES OF CLASS AND COLOR
> THE AFTERMATH OF SOVEREIGNTY

CONSEQUENCES OF CLASS AND COLOR

West Indian Perspectives

Edited and Introduced by
David Lowenthal and Lambros Comitas

Anchor Books
Anchor Press/Doubleday
Garden City, New York, 1973

The Anchor Books edition is the
first publication of *Consequences
of Class and Color:* West Indian
Perspectives.

Anchor Books edition: 1973

ISBN: 0-385-04402-x
Library of Congress Catalog Card Number 72–84928
Copyright © 1973 by David Lowenthal and Lambros Comitas
All Rights Reserved
Printed in the United States of America

CONTENTS

Contents

EDITORS' NOTE

The West Indies, the earliest and one of the most important prizes of Europe's New World and the first to experience the full impact of the black diaspora from Africa, were also the most enduringly colonized territories in the history of the Western Hemisphere. Here more than anywhere else masters and slaves constituted the basic ingredients of the social order; here more than anywhere else class and status were based on distinctions of color and race. Yet out of that past, here more than anywhere else societies with black majorities have emerged as self-governing, multiracial states.

This collection of four volumes—*Slaves, Free Men, Citizens*; *Work and Family Life*; *Consequences of Class and Color*; and *The Aftermath of Sovereignty*—chronicles the remarkable story, played out on the doorstep of the North American continent, of transitions from slavery to freedom, from colonialism to self-government, and from self-rejection to prideful identity.

The West Indies face a host of continuing problems—foreign economic domination and population pressure, ethnic stress and black-power revolts, the petty tyranny of local rulers and an agonizing dependence on expatriate culture. For these very reasons, the West Indies constitute an exceptional setting for the study of complex social relations. The archipelago is a set of mirrors in which the lives of black, brown, and white, of American Indian and

East Indian, and of a score of other minorities continually interact. Constrained by local circumstance, these interactions also contain a wealth of possibilities for a kind of creative harmony of which North Americans and Europeans are scarcely yet aware. Consequently, while these volumes deal specifically with the Caribbean in all its aspects, many dimensions of life and many problems West Indians confront have analogues in other regions of the world: most clearly in race relations, economic development, colonial and post-colonial politics and government, and the need to find and express group identity.

It can be argued that the West Indies is a distinctive and unique culture area in that the societies within it display profound similarities: their inhabitants, notwithstanding linguistic barriers and local or parochial loyalties, see themselves as closely linked. These resemblances and recognitions, originally the product of similar economic and social forces based on North European settlement, plantation agriculture, and African slavery, have subsequently been reinforced by a widespread community of interest, along with interregional migration for commerce, employment, marriage, and education. These volumes focus mainly on these underlying uniformities. Within the Caribbean itself, however, one is more conscious of differences than of resemblances. While each Caribbean land is in part a microcosm of the entire archipelago, local conditions—size, resources, social structure, political status —also make it in some significant fashion unique.

The range of these essays is the entire non-Hispanic Caribbean, but most of the material that is not general in character deals with the Commonwealth Caribbean, a preponderant share of this specifically with Jamaica and Trinidad. This reflects neither a bias in favor of these territories nor a belief that they are typical, but rather the fact that most recent scholarly attention has concentrated on, and literary expression has emanated from, the Commonwealth Caribbean. Close understanding of and expression in the smaller French and Netherlands Caribbean and larger but less well-known Haiti lie in the future.

In the Caribbean, a real understanding of any problem requires a broad familiarity with all aspects of culture and society. Thus the study of economic development relates intimately to that of family organization, and both of these interlink with aspects of political thought, systems of education, and patterns of speech. Consequently, the subject matter of this collection lies in the domains of history, geography, anthropology, sociology, economics, politics, polemics, and the arts. For example, essays on work and family life by economists and anthropologists are complemented by other studies tracing the historical background and sociological interplay of these with other themes. Throughout these volumes economists and geographers indicate how social structure bears on and is influenced by economy and land use, and linguists, littérateurs, lawyers, and local journalists provide insights on the impact of these patterns in everyday life.

The reader will find here not a complete delineation of the Caribbean realm but rather a sketch in breadth, with fuller discussion of significant themes, given depth and personality by picaresque flavor. He may gain a sense of what West Indians were and are like, how they live, and what problems they confront; he can see how their own view of themselves differs from that of outsiders; he will know where to look for general studies and for more detailed information. And if there is such a thing as a regional personality, this collection may enable him to acquire a sense of it.

What is currently available to most students of Caribbean affairs is woefully inadequate by comparison with most other regions of the world. A few general histories, technical analyses on particular aspects of Caribbean society or culture, and detailed studies of one or two individual territories comprise the holdings of all but the best-equipped libraries. Moreover, no book has yet been published that includes a broad variety of material for the area as a whole, and few studies transcend national or linguistic boundaries. We therefore aim to make available a wide range of literature on the Caribbean that is not readily accessible anywhere else.

Most of this collection is the work of West Indians themselves, for they contribute forty-five of the seventy-two selections. Seventeen of these are by Trinidadians, fifteen by Jamaicans, four by Guyanese, three each by Vincentians and St. Lucians, two by Martiniquans, and one by a Barbadian. Non-West Indians contribute twenty-seven selections: fourteen by Americans, ten by British writers, two by Canadians, and one by a French author. Many of the North American and European contributors either have been permanent residents in the West Indies or have worked there for long periods of time.

Editorial comment has been held to a minimum, but readers will find three levels of guidance. An introduction to each of the four volumes summarizes the general implications of the issues therein surveyed. A paragraph of topical commentary together with a few lines identifying the author introduces each selection. Finally, a selected West Indian reading list appears at the end of each volume, and a general comprehensive bibliography is appended to *The Aftermath of Sovereignty*.

The papers and documents included here have been altered only for minimal editorial consistency and ease of reference. All original titles of articles have been retained, but where none appear or where book chapter headings do not identify the contents of excerpted material, we have added descriptive titles, identified by single asterisks in the text. Series of asterisks also indicate the few instances where material is omitted. When required in such cases, we have completed some footnote references. Otherwise, only obvious typographical and other errors have been corrected. Our own two translations from French sources adhere to the originals as closely as possible, within the limits of comprehensibility.

The editors are grateful to those who have assisted them in this enterprise, both in and out of the Caribbean. We owe a special thanks to Marquita Riel and Claire Angela Hendricks, who helped with the original selections and styled the references. Miss Riel also made the original translations from the French. We are indebted to the Research Institute for the Study of Man, and its Director, Dr. Vera Rubin, to the American Geographical Society, and to Teachers College of Columbia University, and notably to their library staffs, for many facilities.

Our main gratitude goes to the contributors represented in these pages and to their original publishers, who have in most cases freely and uncomplainingly made available their work and have helped to correct errors. We are particularly obliged for cooperation from the Institute of Social and Economic Studies and its Director, Alister McIntyre, and to the Department of Extra-Mural Studies, both at the University of the West Indies, under whose auspices a large number of these studies were originally done. We are also obligated to M. G. Smith for encouragement throughout the course of selection and composition.

David Lowenthal
Lambros Comitas
March 1972

INTRODUCTION:
Cultural Expressions of Class and Color

The foundation of the West Indian social order on a colonial class-color hierarchy has had effects that remain manifest in every aspect of Caribbean culture. The focus of this volume is on the nature and style of these influences in West Indian life and thought. Another volume in this collection, *Slaves, Free Men, Citizens*, explores the structural constraints of West Indian societies as consequences of imperial goals, forced labor, and ethnic diversity. This volume examines the racial stresses within the West Indian social hierarchy, the stereotypes about race and class that the society fosters, and the acculturative media—education, language, the arts—through which social and racial attitudes and values are transmitted from generation to generation. It is through these media too, however, that traditional values are at times challenged in the search for an autonomous and self-respecting local culture.

The ascription of inferiority lies at the heart of West Indian racial problems. In the Caribbean, color is a common indicator of status, and racial identification pervades everyday life; those least favored by racial circumstance and stereotype comprise a majority that is increasingly conscious of its deprivations. West Indians are not sealed off from one another in separate worlds, like blacks and whites in South Africa or, to a lesser degree, in the United States. And because they live in societies that publicly celebrate multiracial harmony and equity, West Indians have more reason to be privately aware of how often color constrains access to status, power, and rewards.

Allegiance to Eurocentric culture and institutions likewise continues to impede social reform. Western models and experience provide the only available vehicle for most West Indian cultural expression. Denied a tradition of indigenous culture and deprived of links to African and Asian homelands, West Indians of all colors tend to identify themselves as, and with, Europeans. Black may now be politically beautiful, but the ubiquity of European forms and the general absence of African connections make a positive identification with Africa unviable for most West Indians.

Self-rule and the diminishing role of local whites in political affairs have expanded opportunities for those of other races, but deeply imbedded prejudices still persist in many areas of economic and social life. This is a consequence not merely of discrimination by white and light elites, but also of the fact that West Indians of all shades have internalized the white code of color values and its accompanying stereotypes. Fundamental social change is all the more difficult to achieve because racial position in the social structure is not wholly fixed by birth but can fluctuate with such circumstances as appearance, education, marriage, wealth, and personal associations.

Two opposing trends suffuse West Indian social relationships today. In many areas of life, racial differences are being bridged and racial inequalities overcome to an extent that would have seemed impossible under colonial regimes. But far from allaying the sense of racial injustice, progress toward social equality has engendered a keener sense of resentment against the racial and ethnic minorities —white, colored, or whatever—that have traditionally held privileged positions in West Indian society. The crucial Caribbean dilemma, as many thoughtful West Indians see it, is to overcome the residues of prejudice, to instill self-respect in the historically deprived majority, and at the same time to establish a sense of West Indian identity that will transcend racial stereotypes.

How people are taught, how they communicate, and what they create are products of their social structure; they also help to confirm that structure along with its entrenched values. The steeply hierarchical, color-conscious, status-ridden, European-focused West Indian social order was a consequence of conquest, slavery, and expatriate economic control. But that order has also been ratified by West Indians of all classes, who have accepted the framework and internalized its concomitant values. Although every institution—law, the family, religion, education, and the like—exhibits a wide range of local forms and norms, the closest approximation to whatever is believed European has traditionally been the ideal, even among subordinates barred from realizing it in practice.

The idealization of European standards has significant consequences for West Indian education, language, and the creative arts. Class-oriented upbringing emphasizes distinctions between elites and other West Indians. At the same time, everyone is exposed to a double system of culture, European and local, blended together in different ways in various social contexts. But the poles of the cultural continuum are not equivalent in value: European forms identify the user as superior, to himself and to others. Elite and folk alike have incentives to exaggerate distinctions of education, expression, and creativity, the elite to denigrate the folk, the folk to show their familiarity with the elite ways they seek to emulate. Thus everyone idealizes British, French, Dutch, or American forms of expression and behavior, even though local Creole ways are in most circumstances both more to the point and more serviceable.

The persistence of colonial educational styles, whether by choice, by habit, or by economic necessity, impedes the cultural integration local governments proclaim as their goal. The West Indian literary and artistic efflorescence of the past two decades, notwithstanding its social realism and its concern for local identity, likewise remains essentially European in style and expression. Folk themes and local forms of speech render much of this new work vivid and meaningful, and local cultural expression is increasingly acceptable even to the middle class; but the West Indian author, who writes mainly for European and American readers, like the West Indian teacher and administrator, writes mainly in French and English. Patois or Creolese writing may be an affirmation of being West Indian, but it has little currency for larger audiences. In this sense the writer's dilemma is somewhat analogous to that of the local champion of the masses who orates in patois during election campaigns but once in office reverts to standard English or French.

West Indian teachers, writers, and artists and all their audiences are torn between inherited values and new values often no less exclusive. To some, an exclusive West Indianness is the hallmark of local authenticity. But others feel that a commingling of forms and features from all over the world is more apt to be locally functional, more broadly acceptable to West Indians in all their modes of experience. This multiformity of experience and values has, in any event, stimulated an extraordinary and creative outpouring. Considering how little from the local past has survived and how rapidly anything of local origin is dispersed by export or expatriation, it is remarkable that Caribbean creative expression is so recognizably idiosyncratic, exuberant, and vivid.

The first section, "Race and Color," opens with a hitherto unpublished letter by the black leader Marcus Garvey describing the Jamaican racial scene in 1915. Garvey's principal targets—white domination and colored and black emulation of white values—were responsible for conflicts and tensions which, as the next selection suggests, have remained characteristic of the West Indies. The persistence of a hierarchy stratified by color, of black self-denigration, and of underlying aggressivity is then discussed, again in a Jamaican context. The extent of mass hostility toward the elite and middle classes is queried in the following article; and white upper-class attitudes toward the folk are the subject of the succeeding selection, highly critical of the middle class for its entrepreneurial incapacity and lack of nationalist zeal. Physical departure does not eliminate the expatriate presence; as the ensuing selection shows, a system of imperial rewards helps maintain West Indian values, with European and white ways seen as best. The two following articles debate the extent of actual, as opposed to fancied, discrimination against black Jamaicans a decade ago; and the rising temper of West Indian dialectics is apparent in the concluding selection, a 1970 black-power diatribe against all elite minorities.

The second part of the volume, "Tutelage, Expression, and Creativity," divides into three broad themes, one on education, a second on language, and a third on the arts and literature. The first opens with a description of the background of West Indian schooling as an externally oriented, class-biased system designed to produce colonial administrators and subservient helots and lays bare its defects of focus, content, recruitment, and training. Elementary schooling, with all these drawbacks, has a critical function in the fabric of West Indian life; the next selection shows how expectations and aspirations in a rural village affect parent-teacher-pupil relationships and perpetuate barriers to educational reform. Just how great the disparity is between the goals in life that most Jamaican children are taught to select and those they have the remotest chance of realizing is analyzed in the subsequent selection.

The second subsection surveys the social implications of differences between formal and folk speech patterns, first in St. Lucia, where standard English coexists with French patois, then in Haiti, where the patois and official tongues are both French-based. In each case, problems stem not merely from difficulties of communication but from the approbation of European speech and the denigration of Creolese by all speakers.

The third subsection focuses on metropolitan influences and local concepts in culture, art, and literature. The interaction of British and West Indian perspectives on the creative arts in Trinidad is the theme of the first selection. The next surveys the rise of a truly native West Indian literature and elaborates its deep concerns with folk life and national identity. There follows a critique of the search for relevance and audience that confronts the West Indian writer. Lastly, a St. Lucian dramatist offers personal testimony about the problems of creativity in a small-island society imprinted by colonial tradition.

I RACE AND COLOR

1.

This unpublished letter by Jamaica's renowned black prophet was written to an American before Garvey had ever set foot in the United States. It highlights the racial components of the Jamaican social structure. Then as now, Americans, conscious of their own color bar, were prone to view the West Indies as a region marked by interracial understanding; but as Garvey shows here, Jamaican social conditions had improved little since emancipation, partly because brown men imitated whites and successful blacks emulated both. What Garvey deplored most in Jamaica was the failure of black leadership and the absence of black racial unity against white oppression and cooptation.

MARCUS GARVEY came from a lower middle class background on Jamaica's north coast. As a radical activist, he became progressively disillusioned by his failure to get black Jamaicans to insist on their rights. In the United States, after 1916, Garvey was more successful, owing to the prevailing sense of all-Negro unity engendered by traditional white exclusion of all nonwhites. But Garvey's Universal Negro Improvement Association foundered after he was imprisoned for mail fraud and then deported. After his return to Jamaica in 1925 he had little impact on the local scene. Only since his death have the causes he championed—the return to Africa, actual or symbolic, black pride, and black power—become significant forces in West Indian life and thought.

Marcus Garvey (1887–1940) first contacted Tuskegee Institute in April 1915, when he asked Booker T. Washington for assistance on a lecture tour of the United States. After Washington died in late 1915, Garvey was informed that his successor, Robert Russa Moton (1867–1940), would be taking a vacation trip to Jamaica in late February 1916. Garvey then wrote Moton the long, informative, and impassioned letter printed here.

In a covering note accompanying this letter to Moton (called "Major" because of his post as commandant of cadets at Hampton Institute) Garvey explained that his Universal Negro Improvement Association, founded eighteen months before, was "well appreciated by the cultured white people of the country, and in a small way they have come to my assistance to help me along." Yet in spite of such assistance "from His Excellency the Governor down," Garvey found himself "engaged in fighting a battle with foes of my own all around, but I am prepared to fight on with the strength given me by Almighty God." He described the following letter as "the honest views of a true man who believes himself called to service in the interest of his unfortunate race."†

† Professor Carl S. Matthews of the Department of History, Georgia State University, has provided this background to the Garvey letter.

The Race Question in Jamaica*
Marcus Garvey

30 Charles Street,
Kingston,
Febry. 29th. 1916.

To Major R. Moton,
Head of Tuskegee Industrial Institute,
On visit to Jamaica Febry., 1916.

Dear Sir,

You, being a prominent American Negro Leader, coming into a strange country, and I, being a resident here, and one who also claims the distinction of being a race leader, I think it but right that I should try to enlighten you on the conditions existing among our people; hence I now take the opportunity of laying before you my views on the local aspect of Negro life.

Jamaica is unlike the United States where the race question is concerned. We have no open race prejudice here, and we do not openly antagonise one another. The extremes here are not between white and black, hence we have never had a case of lynching or anything so desperate. The black people here form the economic asset of the country, they number 6 to 1 of coloured and white combined and without them in labour or general industry the country would go bankrupt.

Letter to Major Robert R. Moton, 29 February 1916, Robert Russa Moton Collection; Tuskegee Institute Archives.
* [Editors' title]

The black people have had seventy eight years of Emancipation, but all during that time they have never produced a leader of their own, hence they have never been led to think racially but in common with the destinies of the other people with whom they mix as fellow citizens. After Emancipation, the Negro was unable to cope intellectually with his master, and per-force he had to learn at the knees of his emancipator.

He has, therefore, grown with his master's ideals, and up to today you will find the Jamaica Negro unable to think apart from the customs and ideals of his old time slave masters. Unlike the American Negro, the Jamaican has never thought of race ideals, much to his detriment, as instead of progressing generally, he has become a serf in the bulk, and a gentleman in the few.

Racial ideals do no people harm, therefore, the Jamaica Negro has done himself a harm in not thinking on racial ideals with the scattered Negroes of other climes. The coloured and white population have been thinking and planning on exclusive race ideals—race ideals which are unwritten and unspoken. The diplomacy of one race or class of people is the means by which others are outdone, hence the diplomacy of the other races prevent them leading the race question in Jamaica, a question that could have been understood and regarded without friction.

You will find the Jamaican Negro has been sleeping much to his loss, for others have gained on top of him and are still gaining.

Apparently you will think that the people here mix at the end of a great social question, but in truth it is not so. The mixture is purely circumstancial and not genuine. The people mix in business, but they do not mix in true society. The whites claim superiority, as is done all over the world, and, unlike other parts, the coloured, who ancestrally are the illegitimate off-springs of black and white, claim a positive superiority over the blacks. They train themselves to believe that in the slightest shade the coloured man is above the black man and so it runs right

up to white. The black man naturally is kept down at the
foot of the ladder and is trampled on by all the shades
above. In a small minority he pushes himself up among
the others, but when he "gets there" he too believes himself other than black and he starts out to think from a white
and coloured mind much to the detriment of his own people whom he should have turned back to lead out of sur-
rounding darkness.

The black man lives directly under the white man's
institutions and the influence over him is so great that he
is only a play-thing in the moulder's hand. The blackman
of Jamaica cannot think for himself and because of this
he remains in the bulk the dissatisfied "beast of burden."
Look around and see to what proportion the black man
appears a gentleman in office. With a small exception the
black man is not in office at all. The only sphere that he
dominates in is that of the teaching profession and he
dominates there because the wage is not encouraging
enough for others; and even in this department the Negro
has the weapon to liberate himself and make himself a
man, for there is no greater weapon than education; but
the educated teacher, "baby-like" in his practice, does not
think apart from the written code, hence he, himself, is a
slave to what is set down for him to do and no more.

If you were to go into all the offices throughout Jamaica
you will not find one per cent of black clerks employed.
You will find nearly all white and coloured persons including men and women; for proof please go through our
Post Office, Government Offices and stores in Kingston,
and you see only white and coloured men and women
in positions of importance and trust and you will find the
black men and women, as store-men, messengers, attend-
ants & common servants. In the country parts you will
find the same order of things. On the Estates and Plantations you will find the blackman and woman as the
labourer, the coloured man as clerk and sometimes
owner and the white man generally as master. White and
coloured women are absent from the fields of labour. The

professions are generally taken up by the white and coloured men because they have the means to equip themselves.

Whenever a black man enters the professions, he per force, thinks from a white and coloured mind, and for the time being he enjoys the apparent friendship of the classes until he is made a bankrupt or forced into difficulties which naturally causes him to be ostracised.

The entire system here is bad as affecting the Negro and the Negro of education will not do anything honestly and truly to help his brethren in the mass. Black Ministers and Teachers are moral cowards, they are too much afraid to speak to their people on the pride of race. Whenever the black man gets money and education he thinks himself white and coloured, and he wants a white and coloured wife, and he will spend his all to get this; much to his eternal misery.

Black professionals who have gone abroad have nearly all married white women who on their arrival here leave them and return home. Others marry highly coloured women and others taking in the lessons of others refuse to marry in preference to marrying the black girls. You will find a few educated black men naturally having black wives but these are the sober minded ones who have taken the bad lessons home. Our black girls are taught by observation to despise blackmen as they are naturally poor and of social discount; hence you will find a black girl willing to give herself up to any immoral suggestion of white or coloured men, and positively refusing the good attentions of a blackman at the outset.

Not until when she has been made a fool of by white and coloured before she turns back to the black man and wants him as a companion. Our morality is destroyed this way. Ninety per cent of the coloured people are off-springs of immorality, yet they rule next to the whites over the blacks.

This is shameful, but our men hav'nt the courage to stem the tide. Our ministers are funning at the "teaching of the gospel" and they have been often criticised for their inactivity in correcting vice and immorality. I am sorry I have to say this; nevertheless it is true.

The blackman here is a slave of destiny, and it is only by bold and conscientious leadership that he can emancipate, and I do trust your visit will be one of the means of helping him. I am now talking with you as a man with a mission from the High God. Your education will enable you to understand me clearly. I do not mean literary education alone, for that we have here among a goodly number of Blacks as teachers and ministers. I mean the higher education of man's appreciation for his fellowman; of man's love for his race. Our people here are purely selfish and no man or people can lead if selfishness is the cardinal principle.

One Negro here hates to see the other Negro succeed and for that he will pull him down every time he attempts to climb and defame him. The Negro here will not help one another, and they have no sympathy with one another. Ninety per cent of our people are labourers and serfs, the other ten per cent are mixed up in the professions, trades and small proprietorships. I mean the black people, not coloured or white—you look out for these carefully. We have no social order of our own, we have to flatter ourselves into white and coloured society to our own disgrace and discomfiture, because we are never truly appreciated. Among us we have an excess of crimes and the prison houses, alm houses, and mad houses are over crowded with our people much to the absence of the other classes.

Our prisoners are generally chained and marched through the streets of the city while on their way to the Penitentiary. You should pay a visit to the Prisons, Alms house, and Asylum to test the correctness of my statements. We have a large prison in Kingston and another one at Spanish Town. You will find Alms Houses all over the Island, but the Union Poor House is near to Kingston in St. Andrew.

Our women are prostituted, and if you were to walk the lower sections of Kingston after night fall you will see hundreds of Black prostitutes in the lanes, streets and alleys.

Our people in the bulk do not live in good houses, they live in "huts" and "old shanties," and you will see this as you go through the country. If you care to see this in Kingston you can visit places like Smith's Village and Hannah's Town. Our people in the bulk can't afford to wear good clothes and boots. Generally they wear rags and go barefooted in the bulk during the week, and some change their garbs on Sundays when they go to church, but this is not general.

The people have no system of sanitation. They keep themselves dirty and if you were to mix in a crowd on a hot day you would be stifled with the bad odour. You can only see the ragged and dirty masses on alarming occasions when you will see them running from all directions. If a band of music were to parade the city then you would have a fair illustration of what I mean. Our people are not encouraged to be clean and decent because they are kept down on the lowest wage with great expences hanging over them.

Our labourers get anything from nine pence (eighteen cents) 1/- (25 cents) 1/6 (36 cents) to fifty cents a day, on which they have to support a family.

This is the grinding system that keeps the blackman down here, hence I personally, have very little in common with the educated class of my own people for they are the bitterest enemies of their own race. Our people have no respect for one another, and all the respect is shown to the white and coloured people.

The reception that will be given you will not be genuine from more than one reason which I may explain later on to you.

Black men here are never truly honoured. Don't you believe like coloured Dr. Du Bois that the "race problem is at an end here" except you want to admit the utter insignificance of the black man.

It was never started and has not yet begun. It is a paradox. I personally would like to solve the situation on the broadest humanitarian lines. I would like to solve it on the platform of Dr. Booker T. Washington, and I am working on those lines hence you will find that up to now my one true friend as far as you can rely on his friendship, is the whiteman.

I do not mean to bring any estrangement between black and white. I want to have Jamaica a country of "Black and White" all living in peace and harmony but with equal rights and opportunities.

I would not advise you to give yourself too much away to the desire and wishes of the people who are around you for they are mostly hypocrites. They mean to deceive you on the conditions here because we can never blend under the existing state of affairs—it would not be fair to the blackman. ——To blend we must all in equal proportion "show our hands."

Your intellect, I believe, is too deep to be led away by "sham sentiment." If you desire to do Jamaica a turn, you might ask those around you on public platforms to explain to what proportion the different people here enjoy the wealth and resources of the country. Impress this, and *let them answer* it *for publication,* and then you will have the whole farce in a *nut shell.* When you are travelling to the mountain parts, stop a while and observe properly the rural life of your people as against the life of others of the classes.

I have much more to say, but I must close for another time.

Again I wish you a pleasant stay.

Population of Jamaica
  white 15,605; coloured
  163,201; black 630,181;
  East Indian 17,380; Chinese 2,111;
  2,905 colour not stated.

Yours in the Brotherhood,
Marcus Garvey

P.S.   Another condition that I would like you to observe is how our people attend church. The churches are generally crowded with women with an opposite absence of men. The women are of different classes but the majority of them are people of questionable morality who parade themselves in the garbs of vice for which the men have to pay.

2.

The tacit acceptance by the majority of West Indians of the patterns of racial inequality that Garvey described has had an enduring impact on personality structure, as a West Indian psychologist shows in this pioneering article. Attempts by the masses to conform to elite and middle-class standards inevitably fail, partly because West Indian society offers little opportunity to realize these standards, partly because it is in the self-interest of local elites to bar lower-class access. The frustration of ambition finds outlets in aggressive behavior, reinforcing the derogatory stereotypes of the West Indian proletariat already held by elites.

C. V. D. HADLEY was born in St. Vincent of a prominent planter family. He became well known as a clinical psychologist, social worker, and educator.

Personality Patterns, Social Class, and Aggression in the British West Indies
C. V. D. Hadley

SOCIAL CLASS AND PERSONALITY PATTERNS

Professor T. S. Simey has described[1] one type of personality pattern which has resulted from the interplay of the social forces operating in the West Indies since the emancipation of the slaves in 1834. After discussing the applicability to West Indian conditions of the concepts evolved by Dollard[2] in *Caste and Class in a Southern Town* and *Frustration and Aggression,* and by Horney[3] in *The Neurotic Personality of Our Time,* he goes on to summarise his observations in this way. 'In the light of psychological theory, it is seen to be inevitable that the West Indian should be exceedingly unsure of himself, inclined towards quarrelsomeness, and generally hypersensitive. He is, above all, exceptionally vulnerable to ridicule, which is

Human Relations, Vol. 2, No. 4, 1949, pp. 349–62. Reprinted with permission of Plenum Publishing Co., England.

[1] T. S. Simey, *Welfare and Planning in the West Indies* (Oxford: Clarendon Press, 1946), pp. 99–100.

[2] John Dollard and others, *Frustration and Aggression* (New Haven, Conn.: Yale University Press, 1937); Dollard, *Caste and Class in a Southern Town* (1937) (New York: Doubleday Anchor Books, 1957).

[3] Karen Horney, *The Neurotic Personality of Our Time* (London: Kegan Paul, 1937).

a weapon that should never, in any circumstances, be used against him. When the West Indian encounters resistance he is apt to assume an attitude of reserve, and withdraw himself into a world of his own, remote from contact with the people or classes with whom he came into collision. Administrative affairs in the West Indies accordingly tend to become submerged in a welter of conflicting personalities, until almost all traces of principles and policies are lost. The collisions between individual and individual, and social frictions generally, are so acute that even the most doctrinaire advocate of a competitive economy should be satisfied. The daily round of human existence is made difficult, and at times almost intolerable, by the struggle of one human being against another to assert himself. Man is forever claiming, questioning, demanding. A generous offer cannot be regarded as such, and thankfully accepted; there is no standard to judge it by, and the offer of much only provokes a demand for more. Even after discounting a tendency which gradually asserts itself in the mind to find aggressiveness everywhere (which is itself one of the unfortunate features of the situation), there can be no doubt that the amount of aggressiveness that is discharged is quite abnormal, and that it is often manifested in a direct sense in a physical way.'

What follows is, in part, an attempt to apply the theory of basic personality type to the class structure of West Indian society; and from this point of view to modify Professor Simey's general statement in terms of this class structure. His description applies particularly to the lower-middle class, and does not appear to apply to the same extent to the proletariat or to the established, coloured upper-middle and upper classes. It would seem that there is no single basic West Indian personality, but that there are at least three major types. These may be described as: (a) the proletarian personality pattern, (b) the personality pattern of the unestablished, emergent or lower-middle class, and (c) the personality pattern of the established, upper-middle

class. A more detailed analysis of this statement will be
attempted in this paper.

DEFINITION AND DEVELOPMENT OF THIS CLASS STRUCTURE

The term proletariat is used to describe the people engaged in agricultural field labour, in fishing, and in occupations in which wages are earned on a daily or weekly basis,
as for example, in road making and dock work. The term
would apply to the vast majority of the villagers in the
West Indies.

In the unestablished, emergent or lower-middle class,
salaries are paid, and individuals of this class are found
in such occupations as elementary school teaching, in the
junior posts in business, and in the civil service; they may
also be small landed proprietors.

The established upper-middle class is composed of individuals in the professions, or in senior posts in the civil
service or in business, and whole families usually have
behind them at least one or two generations of such status.

The historical development of this structure must now
be briefly described, since it throws light on the satisfac-
tions, frustrations, anxieties, and hostilities of members of
these three social classes.

The slave society which existed on the plantations in
the West Indies shortly before emancipation was a singularly interdependent structure. The relationship between
the slave and his owner rested on certain sanctions, embodied in custom and law, which gave the owner certain
disciplinary and coercive powers. The owner was bound
to provide his slave with the necessities of life—food,
shelter, and clothing—and in return the slave was compelled
to work on the plantation. In this social situation, with its
clean-cut roles and relationships, certain traditional attitudes developed on the part of both slave and slave
owner—to each other, to work, property, and, indeed, to
all values of life.

From Mrs. Carmichael's account[4] we can gather the content of a number of these attitudes and realise that the behaviour trends and habits of present day West Indian proletarian society are, in many respects, very similar to those which characterised the slaves in the earlier period. One problem, therefore, is to explain the survival of these patterns, with scarcely any modification, in a large section of the population over a subsequent period of more than a hundred years. Customary behaviour, individual or social, is developed as an adaptive response to the particular environmental circumstances with which the individual has to deal. Prior to 1834 those environmental circumstances were the state of society which obtained under slavery; after 1834 the environmental circumstances were those which obtained under the type of capitalist economy then almost universal in western societies. Since the experience was that behaviour developed as an adaptive response in the first situation possessed survival value in the second, the obvious conclusion seems to be that for large numbers of West Indians the emancipation altered in very little degree the normal circumstances of their lives as they had experienced them under slavery. It could, indeed, be said that one sort of slavery was, apparently, exchanged for another.

The individual, habituated to institutional life, for example, or to the conditions of military service, finds it more and more difficult, in proportion to the length of time of the habituation, to adjust to a less autocratic society when released, and may in fact seek to return to the mode of life to which he has been conditioned. In a similar way, slaves in a slave society, habituated to dependence and unaccustomed to self-reliance, self-direction, and initiative, found it difficult to adjust themselves after emancipation to what is potentially a very different mode of life.

[4] Mrs. A. C. Carmichael, *Domestic Manners and Social Conditions of the White, Coloured and Negro Population of the West Indies* (2 vols.; London: Whittaker, Treacher and Co., 1833).

Having been accustomed to authority in a personal form in the guise of a manager, overseer, or driver, and having, therefore, been frequently subject to a considerable amount of arbitrary control, the freed slaves were unaccustomed to law as a socially sanctioned and impersonal directive. They were accustomed to a mode of life in which forms of sexual and parental behaviour, which appear strange and irresponsible in our eyes, had been forced on them, especially on the men; in the women the biological bonds of motherhood qualified this irresponsibility. In this connection it has to be remembered that the slave-owner had taken care to safeguard the health and lives of the children. According to Mrs. Carmichael, 'Children who are too young to be employed are all brought up by women whose sole office is to take care of them . . . Their food is given by the manager to the nurse. . . . They return to their parents at night but not till then. . . . The woman who has the care of them keeps them together all day in a building, appropriated for them, out of the sun. It is her business to keep them clean. . . . Every mother has time allowed her in the morning to wash, dress and suckle her infant—that is when she again returns from her confinement to work. The nurse keeps the baby and attends upon the mother from three to four weeks, as may be requisite. One or more nurses are required for the estate, according to the number and ages in the nursery.'

In the slave society, work had been regarded as an imposition and a burden, to be avoided as much as possible. It bore no particular relation to securing the necessities of life; and money, used mainly to buy luxuries, did not relate to purchasing such necessities. Self-expression came through dancing, singing, dressing up, i.e., through emotional release, rather than through constructive activities directed to economic and social ends, since such activities were denied to them.

The slaves were accustomed to a social stratification in which everything "white" had high prestige value, and in which, therefore, "colour" was of great importance—not, of course, that prestige value was attached to the mere fact of "whiteness," but rather that whiteness was, in the then scheme of things, indissolubly associated with power; to be white meant to be powerful. The slaves were unlettered, and largely untutored in the moral restraints required by an internal discipline such as an accepted religious ethic, being accustomed to a morality which was almost wholly external and in which their chief concern was, therefore, "not to be found out," i.e., in psychological terms, an extra-punitive type of morality. As a consequence they possessed a character structure in which there was little obvious development of a social conscience or a personal morality. Such slaves, freed without preparation into a society of free competition, might, indeed, find their psychological equipment woefully inadequate to deal with their new environment. For this environment could be mastered only by a quite different set of psychological tools from those which, as slaves, they had been accustomed to use. Moreover, their emancipation had not resulted from their own efforts. It was a gift, in the sense that they got it for nothing. It had no relation to their own striving and participation, but was brought about through the efforts of others who represented groups with independent goals, and from impersonal causes connected with general economic developments in western society.

Work—and unfortunately for the freed slave, estate work —became almost the sole means of securing the necessities of life, whereas before, these necessities had been provided either directly by the planter or through the gift of a "ground". With regard to this point Shephard says[5]: 'The conditions regulating the allocation and cultivation of estate gardens and provision grounds were altered by the Act of Emancipation. The planter was thereby relieved of the obligation to provide his labourers with rations, housing, and provision grounds; but he could no longer compel them either to work as and when required, or to

[5] C. Y. Shephard, *Peasant Agriculture in the Leeward and Windward Islands* (Ms.), Ch. 11, par. 18.

remain in his employment. He endeavoured to retain a
large and elastic supply of labour by offering labourers
task work and the perquisite of a plot of land. The labourer
could be deprived of his provision ground if he failed to
work to the satisfaction of his employer. Thus, the use of a
provision ground which had been secured to the slave by
law, now became subject to the arbitrary decision of the
employer. The labourer had no legal security of tenure
and was not entitled to compensation on eviction.'

Successful adaptation to a competitive, capitalist society
rests on the ability to accept the values which are the
dynamics of such a society. One of the essential "incentives"
in a society of this sort is the ability to regard "work" as
the chief means of securing the necessities of life, of rising
up in the world, and of acquiring such other embellish-
ments of life as social comforts, position, and prestige. As
Simey says[6]: 'The compelling social tendencies of the present age give as the dominant aim of modern (western)
society the acceptance of middle-class patterns of conduct
by the whole population, and this is as true in the West
Indies as anywhere else.' To do this must have been extremely difficult for the majority of the ex-slaves; only
those slaves who had already, before emancipation, gone
some distance along the road of acculturation, of acquiring
"white" or middle-class values and standards, would be
in a position to make a serious effort to do so after emancipation. The fact remains that 115 years after emancipation
there are large numbers of West Indians who have never
successfully made this adjustment, and who, to a large
extent, retain much the same psychological attitudes as
did their forefathers under slavery; they exist in economic
circumstances which, from the point of view of social
security, are certainly little better and, if anything, worse
than those which obtained under slavery.

[6] Simey, *op. cit.,* pp. 99–100.

FACTORS AFFECTING FAILURE TO ADJUST

The question still remains to be answered, however, why the present day West Indian proletariat have in so many instances failed to acquire the psychological adjustments necessary to successful adaptation to a competitive society. A genetic argument, sometimes put forward by members of the established middle class, states simply that they are too "stupid" or "worthless" to do so. It is believed that "stupidity" and "worthlessness" are inherited characteristics which preclude the possessors from successful adjustment in modern society, and that the position of the proletariat is the inevitable social result of such handicaps. This belief represents a typical defensive rationalisation of a type commonly put forward by an uncertain social group in such circumstances. Similar attitudes and arguments concerning the working class of that day were developed, for example, in Victorian England, and in more modern times the rationalisations with which the Nazis defended their attitudes to subject-peoples were of a similar nature. Such defensive attitudes are maintained in face of the fact that members of the West Indian proletariat who have emigrated in the past to such places as Panama, Cuba, and the U.S.A., and more recently to Trinidad, Aruba, Curacao, and America, have successfully adjusted themselves to the conditions of work experienced in these places, and have often acquired considerable affluence and position.

But if the general arguments are valid, first, that successful adaptation to a modern competitive society means that the individual must be able to acquire the motivations which are the dynamics of the society, and, secondly, as Professor Simey contends, that '. . . the acceptance of middle-class patterns of conduct by the whole population is the dominant aim of modern society,' then the problem under consideration reduces itself to the question why so many West Indians do not find it possible to accept these values and to develop the motivations which would lead to the acceptance of middle-class patterns of conduct.

For an ex-slave suddenly (or even gradually) to change his whole mental attitude to work and labour—from an attitude which regarded work as an imposition and a burden, bearing no close relationship to the procurement of food, shelter, and clothing, to an attitude which regarded it as the sole means of honestly attaining these things—compelling reasons would be needed; and these compelling reasons could only reside in the opportunities provided by the society in which he lived for the realisation of these ambitions; i.e., for a demonstration of the practical achievement of these values and of the successful operation of the motivations derived from them.

The fact, however, is that since emancipation West Indian society has never provided the conditions by means of which the vast mass of the proletariat could possibly hope to achieve through work any rise or improvement in their status. It is irrelevant at the moment to consider whether this was due to factors outside the control of West Indian society—such as prices in world markets, poverty of natural resources, etc.—or to factors within West Indian society itself, or to both. No human being is likely to adopt the values of a society and to acquire the motivations which derive from and maintain such a value system, if, at the same time, this society does not provide the means which its value system lays down as the only possible way of achieving satisfaction of these values. There is a manifest inconsistency in suggesting that working hard for wages is the only legitimate and praiseworthy manner of getting on in the world and of acquiring middle-class standards, if at the same time the only kind of work and wages open to those concerned make it practically impossible for them to do so. If the values and modes of a society demand that the barefoot man must acquire boots, then reasonable means for procuring boots must be provided, or alternatively, that society will inevitably be perceived as hypocritical in its values. Such a situation existed in other forms in the mass unemployment in the United Kingdom in the 1930's. It is small wonder that many West Indians give up the unequal struggle, and retain or adopt patterns of behaviour which serve to compensate them for repudiation of the values of the society in which they live.

It is probably for reasons of this nature that so many of the behaviour patterns of slavery persist to this day in the West Indian proletariat, as for example, concubinage of various degrees of permanency, which is very largely the basis of family life among them. In slavery, marriage of the conventional pattern—in those years largely patriarchal in type—was obviously impossible, for no slave owner could possibly share or dispute the control of a female slave and her children with a slave-husband. Hence the casual type of sex relationship which obtained in slavery was the way in which the slaves accommodated their sexual needs and interests to the conditions under which they lived; that accommodation is still an adaptive response under present day conditions. The slave owner has gone, and there is no apparent reason why marriages should not take place. The reasons why they are not the general custom are probably complex, and systematic investigation is lacking. The financial aspect is important, but there is another which is not often discussed: observation suggests the probability of the view that many of those under discussion do not get married simply because they see no point in it. They have to a great extent given up any struggle to acquire middle-class status and standards, and therefore do not feel any necessity or compulsion to abide by those standards. They have evolved a mode of life which is satisfactory in that it is shared by a large number of people, and is not likely to give rise to endo-psychic conflict as long as there is no striving for middle-class status. Again, it is probable that the present norm of social behaviour in this respect may have compensatory advantages of its own. The individual who, in his economic and other relationships with his environment, is in the position of one beset by forces of which he understands little, and over which he can exercise little control, achieves through promiscuous sex relations the experience of a certain mastery over a portion of this environment, namely the woman. In his relations with women at least he is dominant, and in this freedom to pick and choose, to cast off or to keep, he is acting as an individual whose "will" has some relevance to—and in reality in—his behaviour. There are psychological reasons to suggest that similar considerations are connected with the wide occurrence of gambling.[7] Attitudes towards work, responsibility, and authority, etc., betray this same repudiation of middle-class standards.

From the point of view of the frustration-aggression hypothesis,[8] proletarian culture in the West Indies can be regarded, therefore, as an attempted solution of a conflict situation which arose through the emancipation of the slaves from a situation which was one of almost complete dependence to a situation of severely handicapped free competition and individual responsibility. The necessity for such a solution was brought about by the fact that the society into which the slaves were freed did not provide the means whereby the dynamic of the society could become operative in the vast majority of individual cases. It is in this sense that the statement that the proletariat have repudiated middle-class standards must be understood, and not in the sense of conscious repudiation.

EXISTING PROLETARIAN PERSONALITY PATTERNS

The personality pattern which resulted from this situation has given rise to that stereotype of the negro which

[7] These views are supported by Arthur Geddes, "The Social and Psychological Significance of Variability in Population Change" (*Human Relations*, Vol. 1, No. 2 [November, 1947] p. 198), who provides observations from India which suggest a connection between "loveless promiscuity" and "despair, frustration, and anger."

[8] Dollard and others, *op. cit.*

pictures him as a happy-go-lucky irresponsible, indolent, childlike creature who is always laughing and happy in spite of his poverty. This stereotype is, of course, an exaggeration; but the personality pattern which in fact resulted —that of the non-aggressive (i.e., from the point of view of class or race-directed aggression), dependent, accommodating, and deferential negro who "knew his place" and stayed in it, was a real one; and it can be regarded as the basic proletarian personality pattern which is still to be found among the rural proletariat of the West Indies. This basic proletarian personality pattern is, however, undergoing change, especially in the direction of an increase in overt aggression. This is apparently due to the stress of modern conditions, particularly the results of participation in two world wars; of emigration to countries more advanced industrially and culturally than the West Indies; of the introduction of the cinema and radio; of trade union organization; and particularly through the activities of such Governmental agencies as the Colonial Development and Welfare Organization. The modern West Indian proletarian is becoming increasingly unwilling to tolerate what he was formerly accustomed and, indeed, expected to accept.

If the above analysis is correct, it is seen to be inevitable that efforts to better the proletarian's position, if successful, must result in an increase in overt aggression on his part unless the frustrations which intensify the aggression are dealt with equally and simultaneously. Since the frustrations are likely to be slow in moving, such efforts must persuade the proletarian to accept the dynamic of his culture, to strive for middle-class status and for greater identification with the culture in which he finds himself; it must induce him to try to improve his position and to get on in the world; and this, inevitably, will produce frustrating situations with resulting aggressions similar to those which proletarian culture was evolved, in the first instance, to circumvent. The final success of these efforts will depend almost entirely on the ability to guide this aggression into

socially constructive channels. We can also understand, if
this analysis is correct, the source and nature of the apathy
which characterises so much of rural life in the West Indies.
(Such "apathy" is here regarded as a withdrawal from
social life, with an accompanying inhibition of feeling, in
order to avoid the pain of severely frustrating social relationships.)

It is an important conclusion that welfare efforts in the
West Indies, if they are to be successful, must largely concern themselves, at least in the short run, with the difficult
problem of providing constructive channels for aggression
which has been aroused by those efforts. We must now
turn to the situation of the middle classes.

THE PERSONALITY PATTERN OF THE UNESTABLISHED LOWER-
MIDDLE CLASS

The coloured man who is just emerging from the proletariat and who has had the influences of a wider society
brought to bear on him is liable to be much more aggressive in his behaviour than is the long-established, coloured,
middle-class individual, or the proletarian. The true proletarian, as we have already suggested, has no desire to
aspire to, or to compete for, middle-class standards, he has
made certain compromises with his environment which
have resulted in his retaining or adopting modes of behaviour which originated under slavery, and which, it is to be
presumed, also possess compensatory value under present
conditions.

In West Indian circumstances, the only direction in
which the proletariat could express class-instigated or class-
directed aggressiveness is upwards, that is, against the class
or classes above it. The expression of aggressiveness depends on the nature of the related frustrations and the
extent to which they occur. It has been assumed, however,
that most members of this proletarian group are not class-
conscious to the extent which would bring them into col-

lision with the members of the established middle and upper classes owing to their repudiation of any striving or competition for middle-class standards. That is to say, they have accepted the existence of a "social distance" which they make no attempt to cross and, this being so, this group, as a class, will display little aggressiveness which could be said to arise out of their class situation *vis-a-vis* the other classes. This is still largely true of the rural proletariat of a small island such as St. Vincent. Such aggressiveness as they do display tends to be as individual reactions to individual circumstances within their group.

But when an individual of this class has started to improve his social status by the acquirement of middle-class standards, he has become class-conscious. He now deliberately recognises the existence of a group or class of persons who have qualities, possessions, privileges, to which he aspires and which he does not himself possess; he recognises, therefore, that he is different, and that certain people are regarded as "better" than he is. This "recognition" does not necessarily take place at a fully conscious level; most of it appears to be carried on at subconscious levels. The opportunities for "frustrations" to arise in this type of individual are great. He is self-assertive—striving upwards, unsure of himself, and uncertain as to what reception his self-assertiveness will encounter in his contacts with established middle-class people and with the upper classes. It is in this group that there are found examples of what in the West Indies the upper classes refer to as "a bumptious nigger". Conscious of his proletarian origin, frequently of illegitimate birth, and facing a future of considerable uncertainty in the social field, an extreme sensitivity and touchiness is developed, the individual is perpetually on the outlook for possible slights and insults, and frequently, by his own manner, succeeds in provoking them. It is obvious that in such a situation the possibilities of frustration are great; and, as a corollary, the opportunities for displays of aggressive behaviour are increased. The man of recent proletarian origin who, on entering a

crowded Council Chamber, finds all of the seats occupied
except one, which he is informed is being kept for the wife
of the white Administrator, and orders his own coloured
wife to sit in it, is exhibiting the type of aggressive behaviour
which will frequently result from the conditions described
above.

The emerging middle-class individual, by reason of his
new orientation, that is, by reason of his new set of goal-
responses, is inevitably brought into situations with many
more possibilities of frustration than the proletarian who
has not made this re-adjustment. This change in behaviour
is clearly demonstrated by men who have been to Aruba,
Curacao, Trinidad, or U.S.A., and who have acquired
some money. On their return this change is evident in their
dress, their speech, and in their general attitude to life.
They are apt, as the West Indian saying goes, 'to show a
lot of form'! In this group the "Saga-Boys" are to be
found—flamboyantly dressed men with exaggerated manners and mannerisms and somewhat aggressive tendencies.
They now have goal-responses which include seats "up-
stairs" in the cinema, car hire, good clothes, opportunities
to show off, and, if at all possible, girl friends of a lighter
complexion and better social status than themselves. It
would seem safe to draw the conclusion that the emergent,
or lower-middle class, individual is, by reason of his class-
position, more liable to experience frustrating situations
and therefore more liable to overt aggression, especially of
a class-conscious nature, than individuals of any other
group or class in the West Indies. He is liable to feel
threatened or frustrated by claims made on him by the
group from which he is emerging, claims which remind
him of previous identification with the group, e.g., illegitimate children; he is also liable to be frustrated by individuals of the group above—the upper-middle-class group, who
may refuse to accord him the recognition of a social status
which he desires. To an even greater extent he is also
frustrated by the feelings of insufficiency and inadequacy,
related to the colour situation, which he would have been

a fortunate and exceptional West Indian to have escaped. He is, therefore, very liable to be an exceedingly aggressive person.

Difficulty in dealing with the local ex-service men has been experienced in the West Indies by the committees appointed to re-absorb demobilised West Indian personnel into civilian life. These men, the majority of them from the proletariat—middle-class youth for various reasons seldom joined the Caribbean Defence Force—proved to be difficult to handle. Their mode and manner of life had been raised, and their social status increased by being in the army, and on demobilisation they were apt to seek roles which were out of proportion to their knowledge, abilities, or previous experience, and which were all directed to enhancing their previous social status. For the most part they wanted to be clerks, road overseers, lorry drivers, mechanics, or shopkeepers. Most of them had the feeling that the community was not adequately fulfilling its obligations to them by offering lesser roles, and they were inclined to be rather aggressive in consequence.

In this lower-middle-class group, overt aggressiveness is sometimes replaced by an attitude of aloofness or withdrawal. This attitude of aloofness which is clearly a less external form of the apathy seen in proletarians is, of course, a self-protective one as it reduces the possibilities of frustrations by reducing the number of social contacts which could produce them. It sometimes takes interesting forms as, for example, in the development of a carefully formal and somewhat exaggerated politeness. One has the feeling here that the individual who is protecting himself in this way is determined that in the event of the occurrence of any "unfortunate" social situation he, at any rate, will never be the one who is "in the wrong".

Conversely, in personal relationships, a hearty, expansive attitude is sometimes developed, involving excessive friendliness, familiarity, and the use of Christian names. The function of this attitude is apparently to create a situation in which, from the very beginning, conditions of equality and easy familiarity are established and taken for granted, so that no possibility or even suspicion could ever arise that the person being subjected to this "friend-liness" could possibly be the cause of frustrations. Unlike the attitude of withdrawal, which reduces the number of frustrations by reducing the possibilities for their occur-rence, this attitude offers reassurance by assuming boldly that frustrations simply do not occur. It has much the same transient or inadequate psychological value to the individ-ual as talking loudly in a dark room has to the somewhat timid and frightened child; it attempts to reassure in a social context which without the reassurance might be somewhat menacing to underlying fears.

These two types—the withdrawn, defensive type, and the expansive, emotional, friendly type, represent the two poles between which the coloured middle class personality pattern oscillates.[9]

The emerging or lower-middle-class individual is on many occasions a most difficult person to deal with. He is apt to be very verbose, for like Mr. Polly he is very fond of big words; and he is apt to be somewhat lacking in ob-jectivity and in the capacity for analytical thought. He is "difficult" because his manner and general attitude create frustrating situations for himself. The general aggressive-ness which some West Indian and other colonial students appear to display in London is due very largely to the expectation that they will be "discriminated against" in the "white man's country". They react to this expectation by an increased aggressiveness, and, in so doing, probably succeed in provoking "discriminations" which they might otherwise have avoided, and which, whatever may have been the circumstances, are likely to be interpreted as due to "colour". There is, of course, more to it than just this; but, in point of fact, individuals of this type do on occasions succeed in making life much more difficult for themselves

[9] H. Powdermaker, "The Channeling of Negro Aggression by the Cultural Process" in Clyde Kluckhohn and H. A. Murray, eds., *Personality* (New York: Knopf, 1948).

and for other people than the objective situation by itself would normally warrant. In terms of practical social work, it is often extremely difficult for individuals of this class to act together as a group. The normal self-assertiveness of each individual makes it difficult for him to accept leadership or direction from another individual of the same class —even one he may have elected himself—and he is extremely sensitive to any suspicion, real or imagined, that such an individual may be attempting to "show off on him" by ordering him around or by giving him directions. In consequence, as Simey says, 'principles and policies tend to become submerged in a welter of conflicting personalities'.

One of the weaknesses in the social structure of a West Indian island, especially a small island such as St. Vincent, for example, is the paucity of the middle class as a whole, with a preponderance, among such middle-class families as do exist, of families of the emergent type, and a relatively small number of families of the upper or established middle-class type. The West Indian middle class has not yet been able to produce in any numbers individuals with those qualities of objectivity, disinterestedness, and rationality which are so necessary for dealing with public affairs.

An attitude which grows out of the general sensitivity to criticism, either overt or implied, of the lower-middle and middle-class individual, is the necessity to "save face". The compulsion to "save face" is an obvious imperative when we consider the equally compulsive imperative to assert and maintain social status; these two attitudes are complementary to each other. A coloured middle-class West Indian is usually reluctant to exercise disciplinary measures which will have the effect of "showing up" another coloured middle-class individual in some delinquency; his tendency is to try to cover the matter up and smooth it over, "to give him a chance". The motive behind this attitude would appear to be a general reluctance to do anything which would bring discredit on coloured West Indians as a group or class, by advertising or publicising the fact that a coloured West Indian had failed to act according to the required white standards; the obvious—perhaps largely unconscious—fear being that this failure would be attributed to the fact that the individual had failed because he was a coloured person. This interpretation is illustrated by the following incident. The author, remonstrating with a good friend of his on the latter's failure to clear himself of a certain charge by placing the fault where it really lay, namely at the door of another individual, was told, 'Well, you see, old man, we are all black people together!' The decisions of juries have, on occasions, been such as to cause suspicion that they were moved largely by this consideration. The reluctance to exercise disciplinary measures, due to this "face-saving" imperative, quite obviously leads to difficulties in maintaining standards and discipline, especially in public affairs.

THE PERSONALITY PATTERN OF THE ESTABLISHED OR UPPER-MIDDLE CLASS

The coloured individual who belongs to the established or upper-middle class is not as a rule as overtly aggressive as the lower-middle-class individual. His position in the process of acculturation is a much more advanced one. He has had at least a generation or two of established middle-class security and status behind him, and in consequence, his place, and that of his family, in the community is an assured one; and he has the confidence and the sense of security which comes from such a background. It does not follow, of course, that he will be satisfied with his position as a member of a dependent and subject people, or that he will necessarily be free from all the resentments and antagonisms which consciousness of "colour" brings in its train, especially in those colonies in which membership of certain clubs and residence at certain hotels are contingent on the absence, or the degree, of pigmentation of one's skin; but his reactions to these matters will be much more self-conscious, discriminating, and subtle than those of the lower-middle-class individual. He is capable in many cases of a much greater objectivity and rationality in his attitude. The established, or upper-middle-class person is usually a professional man—a doctor, lawyer, etc.— or he is a member of the Civil Service, or holds some responsible position in business, or he may be a planter; and, in point of fact, there is no difference culturally between him and the average white member of the same class; as frequently as not the advantages culturally, if any, will lie with the coloured person.

Since there is no aristocracy in any real sense of the word in the West Indies—there are merely people with more or less money—the upper-middle-class individual we have been describing is, for all practical purposes, at the top of the social tree in the West Indies, and the manner in which he deals with any "frustrations" which may arise as a result of racial or colour snobbery will depend largely on his temperament and character.

SUMMARY

The proletarian personality pattern has been evolved because of the necessity to solve a conflict situation which has arisen through the fact that West Indian society, after emancipation of the slaves, did not provide the means necessary to achieve the ends which its value system lays down as the desirable objectives of human endeavour. Such a situation would have been an intolerable one if no solution to it could have been found. The proletariat have attempted to solve this conflict situation by refusing to accept the dynamic of the culture, that is by refusing to strive for the improvement of class status and associated goals. The benefits or gains which accrue from this, lie in the greater freedom for impulse gratification and in the avoidance of frustrating situations which, in turn, lead to the absence of aggression of a class- or race-instigated nature.

The integration of the proletariat into the dominant culture of which they form a part is necessary if the West Indies is ever to take its place as a democratic community among the nations, and will inevitably result, at any rate in its initial stages, in a recrudescence of aggressive behaviour, since it will be necessary for the proletariat to accept the dynamic and the value system of the culture in which they exist. This hypothesis is supported by the behaviour and personality pattern of the emergent or lower-middle-class individual who has set about the process of identifying himself with the prevailing culture, by the acceptance of the cultural dynamic and value system; this has been accompanied by a recrudescence of overt aggression in this personality pattern.

The upper-middle-class individual represents the end product of this process of acculturation, and his personality pattern tends to be similar to that of any integrated individual, white or coloured, within the culture.

3.

A Jamaican educator and creative artist here explores the social and psychological dimensions of residual racial prejudice. Black political power and increasing access to high-status positions notwithstanding, the system of color stratification deplored by Garvey and explicated by Hadley survives to this day. Jamaica's official multiracial creed camouflages the conviction of the black majority that the country does not really belong to them and conceals their ingrained equation of blackness with inferiority. Mass despair and self-denigration can only be overcome, the author contends, by major social and economic reform.

REX NETTLEFORD, himself of rural background, is a striking exception to most of the consequences he perceives. He followed a degree in history at the University of the West Indies with a Rhodes Scholarship at Oxford in politics; on returning to the West Indies he became a Resident Tutor, then head of the Trade Union Education Institution in the University's Department of Extra-Mural Studies, of which he is now Director. In addition to his work in social science, trade unionism, adult education, and university administration, he is co-founder, director, choreographer, and principal dancer of Jamaica's world-renowned National Dance Theatre Company. *Mirror, Mirror: Identity, Race, and Protest in Jamaica* and *Roots and Rhythms* are his most recent books.

National Identity and Attitudes to Race in Jamaica
Rex Nettleford

The need for roots and the attendant quest for identity are said to be natural to peoples everywhere. The phenomenon may be said to inhere in a people's desire to collate and codify their past collective experience as well as to lay foundations for the realisation of future aspirations. New nations usually give large portions of their creative energy to what may be termed the 'identity problem' and the mid-twentieth century with its flux of emergent countries in Africa, Asia and the Caribbean is particularly noted for this aspect of nation-building. In Jamaica, a Caribbean country which attained independence from Great Britain in August 1962, the search for identity has been the focus of attention for some time. It is indeed difficult to determine what exactly is meant by the term 'the Jamaican identity'.[1] It is variously expressed as 'things Jamaican' or 'the Jamaican image'.[2]

Race, Vol. 7, No. 1, July 1965, pp. 59–71. Reprinted with permission of the Institute of Race Relations, London, and the author.

[1] M. G. Smith, 'Our National Identity and Behavior Patterns' (Lectures on Jamaican National Identity, Jamaica: University of the West Indies, Radio Education Unit, n.d.), reprinted in *Race*, Vol. 7, No. 1 (1965).

[2] After 307 years as a British colony, Jamaica gained her independence on 6 August 1962. A strong Jamaican nationalism had shown itself from the thirties, when labour disturbances

There are, however, ways of approaching the problem. The question 'What *are* we?' entails the desire of 'what we *want* to be'. And if what we want to be must have any practical significance for Jamaica, there should be some concordance between the external *conception* of the island's 1.6 million people on the one hand, and Jamaicans' own *internal perception* of themselves as a national entity on the other.[3] This is presumably one certain way of being saved from a schizoid state of existence. The postulate seems more reasonable when one remembers that Jamaicans are a people who are constantly exposed to external influences, whose economic system traditionally depends on the caprice of other people's palates, whose values are largely imported from an alien set of experiences, and whose dreams and hopes have, at one time or another, been rooted either in a neighbouring Panama, Cuba or Costa Rica, in big brother America and sometimes in Canada, a Commonwealth cousin. Of late, they tend to be rooted in father Africa and more so in mother England.[4]

---

and middle-class clamour for self-government characterized the political scene. But from the late forties there was a slight shift of emphasis to West Indianism in the plans for a Federation of the British West Indies which was actually established in 1958. Jamaica withdrew in 1961 by referendum from the Federation and decided to 'go it alone'. Since then the 'Jamaican image' has become a positive goal for different efforts in the country.

[3] This approach is suggested by a paper presented in the U.W.I. Extra-Mural Sunday morning lecture-series, and entitled 'Our National Identity and Behavior Patterns', by Professor M. G. Smith of the University of California (U.C.L.A.), *op. cit.*

[4] This refers to the external influences on Jamaica. As a primary-producing agricultural country, the economy is dependent on the outside market. This is also true of bauxite which is shipped in its raw state or as alumina to North America. Jamaicans have also been a migrating people ever since the late nineteenth century when the first Panama Canal project was started. Between the 1880s and 1920, net emigration from Jamaica amounted to about 146,000—46,000 went to the U.S.A., 45,000 to Panama, 22,000 to Cuba (to work in sugar), and

The multi-focal nature of Jamaican life and history is often said to be the greatest obstacle to a real national identity. And the object of this article is to relate the resulting quest to Jamaicans' attitudes towards race.

There are obvious difficulties in any such task. For one thing, data drawn from attitudes, revealed or scientifically observed, do not usually solve the problem of the transition from attitude to behaviour. For another, there is need for a social psychology of West Indian race relations. What is more, race presupposes a biological purity which is difficult to justify. This makes the concept an extremely difficult one with which to work. The fact is that claims to such biological purity are not absent from Jamaican society and these claims have traditionally served to underline, rather boldly, the social stratification, thus making the matter of race more than yeast for the dough. If one assumes that the Jamaican identity must entail a measure of national unity, though not uniformity, among all the differentiated sectors of the society, then one can pose the question of whether the phenomenon of racial consciousness or non-consciousness is an obstacle to national unity. This is the measure of the internal problem. Since race is an important determinant in people's assessment of each

other countries like Costa Rica (for railroad building and banana cultivation) drew some 33,000 (George W. Roberts, *The Population of Jamaica* [Cambridge: Cambridge University Press, 1957], p. 139). Some 10,000 went to Britain during the Second World War for war work, while some 48,000 went to the U.S.A. in the Farm Work Scheme. The postwar period saw migration largely to Britain where nearly 200,000 Jamaican first generation now live. Emigration to Africa is the dream of some Jamaicans, who endow their sentimental attachment with religious fervour in the 'Back to Africa' movement. But West Africa has benefited from the skills of Jamaican and other West Indian migrants who went to Nigeria, Sierra Leone and the old Gold Coast as engineers, teachers, lawyers, civil servants and missionaries. See Don Mills, 'Migration—Where Do We Go Next?' (Lecture presented for the Extra-Mural Sunday Seminar on 'External Relations and the Jamaican Economy', Jamaica: U.W.I., Radio Education Unit, n.d.).

other in the outside world, it is of particular relevance to know if what we think of ourselves racially as a nation coincides with what others think of us in this particular. Racial attitudes, especially when they are accompanied by national or individual schizophrenia, are therefore important. The Jamaican Mental Health Association could well do a serious study of the factor of race attitudes in its records of mental illness. Paranoiac experiences some-times turn on a patient's frustrated aspirations of being 'white'. In this context being 'white' means little more than being privileged and rich. But the fact remains that even today one is still able to have 'whiteness' connote privilege, position and wealth and, of course, purity which is in-grained in Christian mythology. This attitude is particularly evident among many who form the large majority of the population and who happen to wear that colour of skin long associated with poverty, manual labour, low status and ignorance. The *in-betweenness* and *half-identification* result-ing from these attitudes is probably one of the positively distinctive features of Caribbean communities emerging from a plantation and colonial system. It does mark us off from many of the developing countries of Asia and Africa, as can be seen in fundamental differences in attitudes to certain aspects of social and political organization.

For example, it is difficult to find the kind of logic that would justify the renunciation of the Queen of England, as the head of the Jamaican State, in favour of a 'son of the soil'. Quite apart from the fact that any such sugges-tion would be confronted with letters of horror from con-scientious Jamaican 'monarchists', one would have to ask who are the real sons of the Jamaican soil. Is it Sir Clifford Campbell, Sir John Mordecai, Hubert Tai Tenn Quee, Dr. Varma, Edward Seaga or Bruce Barker?[5] In fact they

[5] These are names of well-known Jamaicans of different racial origin. Sir Clifford is the Governor-General and of African stock; Sir John is a distinguished civil servant of Afro-European stock; the Tai Tenn Quees are a Chinese family and prominent in the mercantile community; Dr. Varma is an East

are none of them 'sons of the soil' in the sense that Tunku Abdul Rahman is of Malaya, Jomo Kenyatta is of Kenya, Nkrumah is of Ghana or Nehru was of India. No Jamaican can seriously make claims to Arawak ancestry. In a real sense, we are all of us immigrants—most of us of long-standing, but immigrants, nevertheless! We have had to work out ways and means of distributing power internally as a result of our uprootedness. Over the centuries this has been done by a certain amount of piecemeal political engineering. One significant thing about the progressive assumption of civic status is that the people receiving their share of power at the different stages of development came from groups distinguishable largely by their racial origin and were in fact so described. So, if it were the white planters and their managerial aides who first received control of representative government in the late seventeenth century,[6] it was the 'free coloureds' who next shared in the citizenship rights in 1832;[7] and although they both joined with the blacks to encourage the takeover of the Constitution by white honest brokers at the Colonial Office after the chaos of 1865,[8] it was the whites and free coloureds whose wealth, influence and social position qualified them for participating in the nominated legislatures of the Crown Colony system. It was not until 1944,[9] following

Indian; Edward Seaga is of Syrian stock who is Minister of Development and Welfare in the government which has been in power since independence; and Bruce Barker is of European stock who, from his letters to the press, seems to disapprove of the idea of nationalism and is seen by many of his opponents as a representative of traditionalist white upper class Jamaica.

[6] Anton V. Long, *Jamaica and the New Order 1827–1847* (Jamaica: University of the West Indies, I.S.E.R., 1956), pp. 15–16 (monograph).

[7] Bryan Edwards, *History of the West Indies* (London, 1807), Book 1, Chapter 3.

[8] E. B. Underhill, *The Tragedy of Morant Bay* (London: Alexander & Shepheard, 1895); and S. H. Olivier, *The Myth of Governor Eyre* (London: The Hogarth Press, 1933).

[9] Jamaica Constitution Order in Council 1944 (London: H.M.S.O., 1944).

the disturbances of the late thirties, that the blacks who form the vast majority of the populace were given the right to share in the political cake. Despite the potential power of the black vote which followed universal adult suffrage, one still hears that the upper echelons of governments and the centres of influence do not reflect the racial composition of the country. The Queen, despite the way she looks, therefore fits into the landscape as head of state. It is fair to say that she is generally preferred to a black President, though a black representative of the Queen manages to hit a very comfortable medium. The feature makes Jamaica an autonomous Commonwealth entity resembling Canada, Australia and New Zealand inhabited by Britons overseas, more than Ghana, India, Nigeria, Malaya or Tanganyika which are autochthonous entities. Jamaicans have earned the name, understandably, of 'Afro-Saxons' among some Africans at the United Nations.

Jamaica's apparently peculiar position is usually explained along lines somewhat like this: 'We are neither Africans though we are most of us black, nor are we Anglo-Saxon though some of us would have others to believe this. We are *Jamaicans*! And what does this mean? We are a mixture of races living in perfect harmony and as such provide a useful lesson to a world torn apart by race prejudice.' The harmony based on tolerance is the thing which is supposed to make Jamaicans distinct from such countries as (Southern) Rhodesia, South Africa, and parts of the United States of America. In other words, Jamaica is a non-racial nation and the non-racialism, besides being a distinctive feature, is an essence of the Jamaican identity. Jamaican leaders make non-racialism into an important national symbol by declaring at home and abroad that Jamaica and the West Indies are 'made up of peoples drawn from all over the world, predominantly Negro or of mixed blood, but also with large numbers of others, and nowhere in the world has more progress been made in developing a non-racial society in which also colour is not psychologically significant'.[10] This was a report of a speech made by a prominent Jamaican leader in April 1961 to an American audience. It was, therefore, somewhat reassuring to read subsequently in a Jamaican newspaper that the Jamaican Government had admitted to the Secretary General of the United Nations that 'racial discrimination has yet to be entirely eliminated from the island'.[11] The Report was, however, soon spoilt by the assertion that any problem of racial discrimination still existing in Jamaica was due in part to the fact that Jamaica was a small country which received large numbers of visitors from abroad and that some 'of these visitors bring with them prejudices they acquired in societies less tolerant than Jamaica's'.[12] This betrays a somewhat smug pride in what is assumed to be tolerance and we still look outside of ourselves for the foreign bogey which should take some, if not all, of the blame. One has cause to wonder how it is that visitors find it so easy to practise discrimination when they visit Jamaica. The question could be asked whether there is a cradle ready and waiting to receive the bad seed? Or, is it that there are certain visitors who believe in the old injunction—when in Rome, do as the Romans do.

With a bit of charity one could assert that the tendency of Jamaicans to deny their own shortcomings in the matter may indeed stem from a genuine desire to free our national unity and identity of a disruptive racial differentiation. The motto is almost daily invoked in sermons—secular and religious—to make into a fact what is as yet an aspiration.[13] Unfortunately, it is the 'many' in the motto and not the 'one' which tends to get the emphasis. So against a background of unemployment, and disparities of economic wealth and educational opportunities, the 'many' too often

[10] N. W. Manley, Premier of Jamaica, Speech made to the National Press Club, U.S.A., April, 1961. Report in *New York Times*.

[11] Jamaica, Report to the United Nations on Racial Discrimination. Reported in *Daily Gleaner* (October 9, 1964).

[12] *Ibid.*

[13] The national motto is 'Out of Many One People'.

connotes a differentiation according to how people look. In the minds of many Jamaicans, it is still a poor black, a middle-class and privileged brown man, and a rich or wealthy white man. This is the traditional colour-class correlation.[14] Chinese and East Indian Jamaicans are marginal to this structure, having come to Jamaica after the classifications were long determined in society. They tend to be assessed by the mass of Jamaicans largely on their economic position rather than on their racial origin. The peasant Indian hardly has significance outside of his membership of the lower class where he marries and still lives and has his being. Significantly, no one makes a mistake about to what section of the society the Bombay merchants and their sari-clad wives belong. The Chinese have grown in stature since the early days when terms like 'Madam' and 'John' expressed attitudes of disrespect or even contempt for the men and women, in what has always proved to be a self-contained and restrained minority group. They, the Chinese, chose to stay out of the society as long as they could and now enter the society at the top on the basis of their wealth and education. When the commercial banks yielded to pressure to employ Jamaicans of colour the Chinese were among the first to be used to break tradition. They provided a gradual and smooth transition for the more recent developments in those very commercial banks.

Yet both the Indians and the Chinese intermarried, or rather cohabited, with the blacks quite extensively to produce a new group of Jamaicans numbering some thirty-six thousand.[15] This new development bolstered an attitude long evident among the middle-class people of mixed African and European blood. This attitude is expressed in the idealization of mixed blood. As an integrating force

[14] F. Henriques, *Family and Colour in Jamaica* (London: Eyre & Spottiswoode, 1953), pp. 33–63; and Madeline Kerr, *Personality and Conflict in Jamaica* (London: Collins, 1963), pp. 93–104.

[15] *West Indies Population Census, Jamaica 1960* (Kingston, Jamaica: Dept. of Statistics), Bulletin No. 20, Vol. II, Part A.

in the national life of Brazil this phenomenon has reputedly helped that country to find and project an identity generally accepted at home and abroad. Indeed, it can probably be said that the objective norm in the minds of many Jamaicans (both black and coloured) who choose beauty queens is the hybrid or the miscegenated person.[16] The trouble with this solution to our race differentiation problems is that if the hybrid is the norm, then the vast majority of pure blacks must be the aberration. It therefore invests the mixed blood idealization with a middle-class unction which is unacceptable to the lower-class blacks. The implications are also a source of great irritation to a growing body of middle-class black opinion which insists that, despite the virtues of a mixed-blood ideal in Jamaica, it is the 'African' which is the constant in the racial complex and all other racial strains are variables among the majority of the people.

The 1960 census bears this out by padding the categories into which people are placed. These are African, European, East Indian, Chinese or Japanese, Syrian, Afro-European, Afro-East Indian, Afro-Chinese, and Other (meaning, no doubt, odd admixtures).[17] The prefatory remarks in the provisional report give something of a clue to our racial attitudes. For it declares that the 'intention of the first five categories should contain persons who appeared to be racially pure and the following three, various mixtures'. This betrays a certain sensitivity to universally

[16] Beauty contests are held frequently for the selection of 'queens' from all sections of the community. Traditionally 'Miss Jamaica' tended either to be near-white or to have coffee-coloured European features and straight ('good') hair. This fact sparked off controversy in the press from time to time until in 1955 the island's evening newspaper—*The Star*—sponsored a 'Ten Types One People' contest giving the titles to Jamaican women who span the colour spectrum from 'Ebony' (black) through 'Mahogany' (coloured), 'Lotus' and 'Satinwood' (Chinese and East Indian), and 'Pomegranate' (Mediterranean type, Syrian-Jewish), to 'Appleblossom' (Caucasian). The event received wide international press coverage.

[17] *West Indies Population Census, Jamaica 1960, op. cit.*

accepted norms which classify races into Caucasoids, Mongoloids and Negroids, usually in that order. But the Jamaican classification betrays also a sensitivity to the realities of the local situation. It not only puts the Negroid group first, it gives a detailed breakdown of groups of persons who in the wider world would be termed simply 'coloured'. The preface further informs us that enumerators were 'instructed to include in the group "African", persons of pure African descent, that is those who were classified as "black" in 1943'.[18] This is a clear indication of the growing refinement in attitudes since the term 'black' has long been considered an epithet of opprobrium in the country and not suitable for use in official circles. It has in a sense now changed places with the term 'African' which once meant 'primitive' and 'uncivilized' in the vocabulary of Jamaicans. The enumerators were also instructed to include in the term 'European' persons usually listed as English, French, Spanish, German, etc.[19] Could this mean that attitudes which once marked off the English as a privileged group among whites have changed? It certainly makes for easier census-taking, if nothing else. The same cannot be said, however, of the group that used to be classified 'coloured' in previous censuses. The Jamaican census restricts the term to Afro-European though the outside world would include Afro-Asians as well. Small wonder, then, that the resultant large areas of doubt as to people's descriptions of themselves led the census organizers to omit the racial classification of Jamaicans out of the final census reports.

This does not, however, prevent racially conscious black Jamaicans from keeping their eyes glued to the census figures. For although the blacks cannot claim prior discovery of Jamaica (the Jews were here before) nor effective occupation (the economy is still said to be in the hands of the white and half-white groups) they make strong claims for more influence on the basis of their numbers.

[18] *Ibid.*
[19] *Ibid.*

For of every 100 Jamaicans, 76.8 are of pure African descent, 0.8 are pure European or White, 1.7 are East Indian, 0.6 are Chinese, 0.1 are Syrian, 14.6 are Afro-European, 1.7 are Afro-East Indian, 0.6 are Afro-Chinese and other mixtures add up to 3.1.[20] If we add together all the persons of obvious African descent (pure or mixed) we get some ninety-one persons out of every hundred with the 'tarbrush'. It is this obvious fact which apparently leads to the external conception of Jamaica as a *coloured country*—a conception which does not coincide with the current internal perception which is one described usually in terms of *multi-racialism*. Now this implies a number of things. It gives to the hybrid groups a positive racial quality which in terms of external classifications they should not have. There is nothing necessarily wrong with the claim, however, since it further implies a robust and even healthy refusal on the part of some Jamaicans to bow to the rather arbitrary and crude classification of human beings into coloured and white. Such Jamaicans prefer to see the world in terms of greys and 'in-between colours', each shade and hue deserving of its own individual identity. This taken to its logical conclusion produces in practice a denial of that half of the racial ancestry which is regarded as inferior and a corresponding exaltation of the other half which happens to be respectable in the sight of the world at this particular time. This comes out in many Jamaicans' attitudes towards Great Britain and the white world in general and to the black world and emergent Africa in particular.

The historical antecedents of slavery, the plantation system, and colonialism which are responsible for this, are too well known for detailed recapitulation.[21] But the conscious choice by some Jamaicans and the projection by

[20] O. C. Francis, *The People of Modern Jamaica* (Kingston, Jamaica: Department of Statistics, 1963).

[21] J. H. Parry and P. M. Sherlock, *A Short History of the British West Indies* (London: Macmillan and Co., 1960); and L. J. Ragatz, *The Fall of the Planter Class in the British Caribbean, 1763–1833* (New York: Century Co., 1928), esp. chapter on 'Caribbean Society'.

those Jamaicans of civilized 'whitedom' over primitive 'blackdom', result from the firmly rooted attitudes of a plantation society of a perfect pyramid with white masters at the apex and black labour at the base. The free coloured buffer between the two extremities developed out of widespread miscegenation and formed a natural middle class. This middle class became the target as well as the expression of all the pressures and psychological problems of a society that depended for its rationale in the long run on theories and attitudes of superiority on the part of a white governing and ruling class over an inferior black labouring group. The free coloureds had to pay for their African taint by suffering indignities in the early stages but they were later to benefit from their European blood-strain through the acquisition of wealth and inheritances and of culture through exposure to tolerably good education both in Jamaica and in England. As the pure white population dwindled, the free coloureds became the heirs to the European position and power and regarded themselves as the rightful sons of the Jamaican soil since they, of all groups in Jamaica, were the ones that came directly out of the peculiar circumstances and conditions of early Jamaican society. After all, the argument seemed to go, the blacks can look to Africa, the whites to England, the Chinese to Formosa or Hong-Kong, the Indians to India and the Syrians to Lebanon. But they, the coloureds (*mullatos*), must look to Jamaica.[22] This 15 per cent of Afro-Europeans form the core of the middle class and

[22] The problem is succinctly expressed in a Trinidadian calypso which carries the following refrain:

> You can send the Indians to India,
> And the Negroes back to Africa,
> But will somebody please tell me,
> Where they sending poor me, poor me?
> Six of one, half a dozen of the other,
> If they serious 'bout sending back people in tru—
> They're going to have to split me in two.

'The Mighty *Dougla*' (*Dougla* in Trinidad vernacular means an Afro-Indian).

persist in attitudes which bolster the motto, reprimand the Rastas for turning the clock back, and indulge in a strange love-hate relationship with the whites of both local and expatriate vintage who threaten their claim to the inheritance from Britain. They regard themselves as the true heirs to the governing class despite their small numbers if only because they were the first to display a capacity to assimilate completely the ideals of the masters. They could be as good as, if not better than, the whites. John Hearne in his essay on 'The European Heritage' discusses this group's striving towards the European image—an effort which was further aided by the system of boarding and grammar schools in which some 'five generations of this new brown ruling middle-class learned by rote all the attitudes, patterns of behaviour and values taught to English contemporaries.'[23] These are the people who dominate the trading classes and exert influence in the taking of decisions of national moment.

The assertion by Ras Tafari cultists[24] that since 1938 there has been a series of 'brown-man governments' therefore makes sense in the light of Jamaican history.[25] And the further assertion that these people are really white in attitude is merely another way of describing what the sociologists call the 'white bias' in a society with a population, 76 per cent of which is black. The incongruity has led Jamaican commentators to declare that Jamaica will never know what she really is until she accepts the fact

[23] John Hearne, 'The European Heritage and Asian Influence', *Our Heritage* (Jamaica: University of the West Indies, Extra-Mural Affairs Pamphlet, 1963).

[24] The 'Ras Tafari' are a Jamaican cargo cult whose doctrines of social rejection postulate a promised land in Africa in general (and Ethiopia in particular) where their earthly deliverer and leader Haile Selassie lives. They see repatriation as an ultimate necessity since there is no hope for them in Jamaica from which they are alienated. See M. G. Smith, Roy Augier, and Rex Nettleford, *The Ras Tafari Movement in Kingston, Jamaica* (Jamaica: University College of the West Indies, Institute of Social and Economic Research, 1960).

[25] *Ibid.*

that she is a *black country* and projects a black personality. This is a counter-claim to the unspoken but eloquent claim by the brown middle classes that the Jamaican image should root itself in this group of Jamaicans who are the very embodiment of the tensions set up by the counter-point relationships in the twin heritage from Europe and Africa. A well-known Jamaican journalist and political commentator once said that 'the most obvious bar to integration of our society is the white bias that assaults and degrades the sense of self-respect of the vast majority of the Jamaican people. If everything worthwhile is to be associated with white—goodness, beauty, even God—and if the society as a whole accepts these standards without question, then you are condemning the non-white groups in our society to a permanent and perpetual inferiority since they are inexorably outside the pale of whiteness.'[26] This plea for a fundamental change will have to be seen in a wider context. The Jamaican's conception of his own racial rank is going to be determined partly by the conception of racial segmentation in the world at large. It is significant that with the rise of black Africa, greater confidence has developed among the black people of the society. And many a black middle-class professional need no longer carry around with him a protective hostility to the group he has left behind. He can even marry a black woman of class and thus save her from lifelong spinsterhood in the confines of the teaching, social welfare or nursing professions which Professor Fernando Henriques once observed as havens of black unmarryable spinsters.[27] Many Afro-Europeans of the middle class are even now discovering the beauty of the blacks among them and there are several places now in the sun for Jamaican young women of all shades through the fetish of the beauty contest. These have even received minis-

[26] Frank Hill, "Racial Integration in Jamaica" (Lecture delivered at the University of the West Indies, February 10, 1963).
[27] Henriques, *op. cit.*

terial blessing. Such harmless terms as 'bad hair' and
'good hair', meaning African kink and European straight
respectively, are still being used and one can still hazard
the guess that certain mothers will prefer a white Glasgow
carpenter to a Jamaican flag-black civil servant, for their
daughter.[28] The latter alternative might just mean hardships for everybody concerned. The *Daily Gleaner,* Jamaica's only daily newspaper, could carry without fear of
contradiction a leader, the first paragraph of which read:
'Many people in Jamaica still boast that they have never
entertained a negroid person in their homes. They do not
say it openly but that is their boast nevertheless. Every
change in our society that has enabled the people really to
live like the nation's motto is pain and distress and
"disaster" to them'.[29] A letter to the editor published subsequently commented on the inconsistency between this
view and what is often proclaimed as the island's attainment of racial harmony.[30]

If we look at the expressed attitudes of people on the
Jamaican Government's plans to make a national hero out
of the late Marcus Garvey, we find the anxieties and
emotionalism that exist among many Jamaicans on the
matter of race.[31] It is more than coincidental that it

[28] 'Flag-black' alludes to the symbolism behind the colours
in the Jamaican flag, which are green, gold and black. The
black symbolizes 'hardships' and this was criticized as a further
example of Jamaican attitudes to that colour. Significantly, the
argument sometimes ran, the black in the Trinidad flag symbolizes strength.

[29] Editorial, *Daily Gleaner* (May 6, 1964).

[30] Letter to the Editor, *Daily Gleaner* (June 24, 1964).

[31] Marcus Garvey is to some African and American Negro
leaders the greatest 'black prophet and visionary' since Negro
emancipation. His 'Back-to-Africa' movement won enormous
support from some six million American Negroes in the early
1920s, and his advocacy of the dignity of the black man and
his rightful place in the world made him a *bête noire* to European rulers at the time. His Universal Negro Improvement
Association (U.N.I.A.) was designed as a 'social, friendly, humanitarian, charitable, educational, institutional, constructive

should be a white Jamaican who took the trouble to chronicle the misdemeanours which Garvey reputedly committed during his lifetime.[32] One could indeed have predicted the sharpness of the replies in the press. They all expressed people's belief in the importance of African consciousness in Jamaican development. Here is a typical argument against the fuss that was made over Garvey: it is in a letter to the *Daily Gleaner:* 'Certainly, transporting of Negroes from America to Africa does not in the least affect the welfare of Jamaica. To my way of thinking we do not have in Jamaica any Negroes, Chinese, Syrians or English; we have Jamaicans and certainly if we are to spend thousands of pounds on a monument to honour someone, let it be spent to honour a Jamaican who has contributed tangibly to the development of the nation.[33] This was doubtless written with the best intentions, but this may well be mistaking a wish for the facts! There are indeed all the racial groups which the writers claimed not to exist. There are people 'Negro' enough to feel a sense of personal affront when reports of discriminatory acts against a black American college student are reported in

---

and expansive society' founded for the general uplift of the Negro all over the world. He was convinced that given the time, opportunity and self-confidence, the Negro could equal the whites in all the latter's intellectual, cultural and technological attainments. He even set up a provisional Government of Africa complete with himself as President and a court of titled men and women. Bad business management put paid to the scheme. His involvement in Jamaican local government politics was not successful and he went to England, where he died in 1940. His remains were brought back to Jamaica early this year and placed in a shrine as Jamaica's first National Hero. See George Padmore, *Pan Africanism or Communism* (London: Dobson, 1956), pp. 22ff.; Marcus Garvey, 'Philosophy and Opinions: Declaration of the Aims of the U.N.I.A.' (speech delivered at the Convention, August 1, 1920); Amy Jacques Garvey, *Garvey and Garveyism* (Kingston, 1963); and D. Cronon, *Black Moses* (Madison: University of Wisconsin Press, 1955).

[32] Letter to the Editor, *Daily Gleaner* (September 10, 1964).
[33] *Ibid.* (September 22, 1964).

the local press. There can hardly be any difficulties of identification. There are people 'Syrian' enough to want to return to Lebanon for a spouse. The bond among the Chinese of Jamaica may be said to be a racial Chinese one and not a sophisticated Jamaican one. And there are 'English' or white people who are English or white enough to want to help out people who look like themselves when it comes to the matter of a job. Whether this kind of differentiation is strong enough to rend the society apart is doubtful outside the framework of purely private individual relationships. But this is where the shoe pinches, and a localized pain can affect the entire body. The scores of letters from middle-class citizens clearly indicated further that Garvey's championing of the dignity and self-respect of the black man is a very tangible contribution to the development of a nation which is 91 per cent of African descent.

Yet for all Garvey's work, one might say that attitudes among the black-skinned masses still exist which betray a self-contempt and a lack of self-confidence. Herein lies the greatest danger to attempts at finding an identity in terms of race. For a people who do not believe in themselves cannot hope to have others believing in them. The insecurities of this important racial grouping persist with a vengeance. A poor peasant is indeed glad to have her children rise above the peasantry, marry brown, and forget the roots. A bright young university graduate must suffer praise for a barely tolerably competent speech because of no other reasons than he 'use the white people dem word good good'. People like the Ras Tafari and their neighbours in West Kingston are still convinced that there is some dark conspiracy to keep 'black people down' and although Millard Johnson's coarse *negritude*[34] was re-

[34] Millard Johnson, a Jamaican barrister, attempted to base his campaign on racism by invoking the name of Garvey during the 1962 (April) General Elections. His People's Progressive Party (P.P.P.) polled 12,616 votes with no seats while the People's National Party (P.N.P.) now in opposition polled

jected the leadership of two bona fide political parties are sometimes identified with the brown middle class. A maid insists that she would never work 'for black people'; and well she might not, for the bad treatment meted out to servants by coloured and black middle-class housewives is usually a topic for conversation among some visitors to the island. A watchman in a private compound coldly informs a black-skinned university student that he could not proceed on the compound for the authorities had instructed him (the watchman) not to let 'any black people pass there after six o'clock'. A black doctor goes into stores in Kingston and fails to receive the civil attention due to every citizen until he pulls rank and invokes his status. A worker in an industrial plant finds it impossible to have any interest in the plant because 'there is no hope for the black man' and he resents the black supervisor in authority. The black supervisor in turn abuses his unaccustomed power in dealing with his own and toadies to the white boss. A black young woman destroys a photographic print of herself because it is printed too black; and an older black woman insists that she is giving her vote to a white candidate 'for no black man can help me in this yah country these days'. The examples just cited are based on actual occurrences and betray an interesting ambivalence on the part of these people in their attitudes to race. It also betrays a signal lack of self-confidence.

This happens to coincide with the attitudes of coloured and near-white Jamaican group-attitudes towards the blacks. So when a black-skinned official replaces the white official at the old colonial governor's mansion some middle class verandahs sighed sighs of disapproval and even apprehension. The Afro-European middle classes seem to be fighting on two fronts. For they are beginning to experience competition from a growing group of newer white expatriates who are felt to be without caste since they speak

---

279,771 votes and the ruling party, the Jamaica Labour Party (J.L.P.) polled 288,130 votes out of a total of 580,517 votes cast (i.e., 72.88 per cent of registered voters).

with the wrong accents and betray no sensitivity for the finer things.[35] The trouble is that these people come in and take their traditional place of privilege in the white bias structure: they drink in the right bars and hotels and even get into the right kinds of brawls. The coloured middle class resent the pretensions and even object to their children 'picking up cockney intonations from certain expatriate children'.[36] It might very well turn out that the coloured middle class will be the ones to find greatest satisfaction in the new act designed to limit the employment of expatriates.[37] The resentment of the Jamaican blacks to this group of people and indeed to white visitors in places like hotels may very well be an extension of their dislike for the Jamaican high browns who have long been the symbols of wealth, influence and privilege in the society.

The important thing about all this is that the black-skinned Jamaican senses that he must compete on the same ground as his brown, Chinese and white compatriots. In many a case he has to work twice as hard because of the handicap of being years at the base. Psychologically, he does not possess too strong a racial memory of great cultural achievements as these European, Chinese and Indian compatriots. The Africans, of all the groups which came to the New World, came as individuals and not as part of a group which maintained identity through some great religion, or activity through age-old recognizable customs. *The obvious answer for the African or black Jamaican is to sink his racial consciousness in the wider greater aspirations to acquire education and other means of mak-*

[35] Shirley Maynier-Burke, 'The Jamaican Civil Rights Dilemma', *Daily Gleaner* (October 2, 1964).

[36] The view of a coloured Jamaican housewife in interview with the author.

[37] The Foreign Nationals and Commonwealth Citizens (Employment) Act, commonly called the Work Permits Act, came into force in Jamaica on April 1, 1965, limiting the employment of aliens only to those jobs which cannot be suitably filled by Jamaicans.

ing himself economically viable. Of course, if he sees no chance of doing this he is bound to fall back on the religion of race which is the one thing which he will feel makes him distinctive and which is aided and abetted by the rise of black Africa and the increased stature of the black man in the world at large.

It could indeed be argued that there is nothing necessarily wrong with stratification based on racial consciousness *per se.* But there is everything wrong with racial stratification which has no compensatory responsibilities to complement it. In other words, each racial group must be assured of such things as adequate educational opportunities, of accessibility to rewards for efforts and of an environment which provides incentives to even greater efforts. Only with these will there follow an accelerated social mobility, which is yet another compensatory responsibility. Such compensatory responsibilities do indeed exist in Jamaica and this is frequently the cause of the hyperbolic expressions of the virtue of racial harmony in Jamaica, but in fact they are extremely limited. However, where attempts might be made to plough more money and planning into the black groups, as the Malayan people did among the Malays, there is fear that accusations will be made that blacks are being favoured at the expense of other racial groups in the society—colour prejudice in reverse. And this is so even if politicians are able to justify their actions with the democratic argument of the greatest good for the greatest number. The truth of the matter is that while in Malaya the Malays are the accepted indigenous sons of the soil and the foundation of the Malayan image, in Jamaica the blacks are not regarded as the desirable symbol for national identity. The fact is that we are still enslaved in the social structure born of the plantation system in which things African, including African traits, are devalued and primacy is given to European values in the scheme of things. The developments of the twentieth century are putting pressures on the structure but most people seem to prefer to remain with the known evil rather than accept the uncertain good. As I have said elsewhere, the parboiled state of our national identity will continue to be just this until adjustments are made in the society in bold economic and social terms.[38] People who look like Africans will then no longer have evidence to support their much-repeated claim that their poverty, destitution and loss of hope is somehow organically linked with the fact that they are of a certain ethnic origin in a country controlled by people of another ethnic origin who think themselves superior.

[38] Rex Nettleford, 'The African Connexion', *Our Heritage* (University of the West Indies, Department of Extra-Mural Studies, Public Affairs Pamphlet, 1963).

4.

The distinctions of race and class explored in the preceding selections engender widespread mistrust and animosity. An American sociologist here describes the Jamaican elite stereotype of mass hostility as an outgrowth of relationships stemming from slavery. The author's interviews of a sample drawn from the urban proletariat, however, lead him to believe that these stereotypes are erroneous: most poor blacks express admiration rather than anger toward the elite. It is only the self-fulfilling quality of some elite fears, he suggests, that prevents Jamaican class tensions from diminishing. But in the light of recurring outbreaks of violence in Jamaica, middle-class and elite Jamaicans might well be reluctant to assume that emulation characterizes the masses more than hostility, whatever the conclusions of visiting social scientists. Often the expression of hostility is real and vivid.

JAMES MAU took his doctorate, based on field work under a Social Science Research Council grant in Jamaica, at the University of California, Los Angeles. He is presently Associate Professor of Sociology at Yale. His *Social Change and Images of the Future* expands some of the themes in this article.

The Threatening Masses: Myth or Reality?[1]
James A. Mau

In 1965, Jamaicans will mark the centennial of the Morant Bay Rebellion. It was an incident hardly deserving the name "rebellion": it was not part of a general insurrection, nor was it an uprising against the white oligarchy. A militant band of St. Thomas hill-people, intent on airing their grievances, marched to Morant Bay to confront the administration. In the rioting that followed, a handful of the black rioters and perhaps 21 other persons were killed. The official reaction to the incident by the Gover-

The Caribbean in Transition: Papers on Social, Political and Economic Development; eds., F. M. Andic and T. G. Mathews (Río Piedras: Institute of Caribbean Studies, 1965), pp. 258–70. Reprinted by permission of the author and the Institute of Caribbean Studies. Copyright 1965 by the Institute of Caribbean Studies, University of Puerto Rico.

[1] Revised version of a paper presented at the Second Caribbean Scholars' Conference, Mona, Jamaica, April, 1964. These data are also reported in James A. Mau, "Social Change and Belief in Progress: A Study of Images of the Future in Jamaica" (Ph.D. Dissertation, University of California, Los Angeles, 1964). I should like to express my thanks to the Carnegie Corporation which financed part of my fieldwork, and to the Social Science Research Council for a Pre-doctoral Training Fellowship during the years 1961–63. I am indebted to Wendell Bell for his suggestions and criticism throughout the project, and to Leo Kuper and Raymond J. Murphy for their helpful comments. I also wish to thank Phillip E. Hammond for his comments on an earlier draft of this paper.

nor, Edward John Eyre, was brutally vengeful. Six hundred "rebels" were flogged and nearly as many killed.[2] This violent reaction effectively "pacified" the parish of St. Thomas, but probably did little to allay the fears of the ruling minority.

In April, 1963, Jamaicans heard by radio broadcast of another "uprising", this time involving six Ras Tafarians on the North Coast of the island. Reminiscent of the Morant Bay disturbance of 1865, the nature of the incident was misjudged. It was most certainly not an uprising, yet the misnomer was quickly applied. The repressive official reaction in the hours and days that followed, although less severe, was also reminiscent of Governor Eyre and Morant Bay. The Prime Minister called out the Chief of Staff of the Jamaica Defense Force; troops, armed police, armored cars and Cabinet Ministers rushed to Montego Bay. Hundreds of persons, some Ras Tafarians, others simply black men with beards, were imprisoned or denied their freedom temporarily.[3] Reports of police brutality during this roundup were frequent.[4] Yet, this was occurring even while it was known that the six "Rastas" involved in the incident had either been killed, captured, or were elsewhere in the district. One can only surmise that this repressive reaction to a purely local incident grew out of fear and the belief that others among the depressed and poor might heed the example given by some criminals in the "lunatic fringe". What other reason could explain the mass arrests? Vengeance? Probably not. Rather, the reaction was probably intended to intimidate any others who might be a threat to order and stability, and to put to rest the easily aroused fears of many Jamai-

[2] J. H. Parry and P. M. Sherlock, *A Short History of the West Indies* (London: Macmillan and Company Ltd., 1957), p. 241.

[3] *The Daily Gleaner* (April 13, 1963), p. 1; *Newday*, Vol. 7 (April, 1963), p. 14; *Spotlight*, Vol. 24 (April–May, 1963), p. 17; *The Star* (April 13, 1963), p. 12.

[4] *Public Opinion*, Vol. 27 (June 7, 1963).

cans who view the lower social orders as malevolent and barbaric.

To many Jamaicans, this popular image of the black masses as hostile would not seem unreasonable or unfounded. It is an image supported by objective conditions of social and economic life in Jamaica. Who should be more aware of the improvements in levels of living than the burgeoning middle and upper classes to whom the benefits of Jamaica's development have accrued? But some of them are also aware of the vast disparities in the distribution of those benefits. While the lessening of inequalities of minimum rights of all Jamaicans has been an important trend of social change, it remains clearly evident that gross inequalities of opportunity and achievement are widespread. The level of living among the lower classes is certainly not desirable. The maldistribution of income, the level of unemployment, the rising cost of living, the lack of educational opportunities, the lack of adequate housing, and inadequate social services are only a few of the acknowledged deficiencies. Moreover, these shortcomings are magnified in the urban areas by the pressure of sheer numbers. Awareness of these conditions obviously buttresses the middle and upper-class Jamaicans' belief in the hostility of his less fortunate countrymen.

In addition to these objective conditions of deprivation of the lower classes, support for the belief that they are at war with the middle and upper classes may be found in the styles of thought concerning social relationships among the various social classes. For example, a government officer publicly declared that the condition of the lower classes "constituted a peril that might erupt at any time." Comparable sentiments have been expressed by a writer who remarked that "nervous people sipping Scotch by the poinsettias on their patios have asked one another how long they will be safe in their beds."[5] Also, it has been in vogue among middle and upper class persons discussing

[5] Marjorie Hughes, The Fairest Land (London: Victor Gollancz, Ltd., 1962), p. 12.

Jamaica's development to lay heavy stress on the problen
of the "revolution of rising expectations among th
masses." Similarly, it was fashionable to point to the cor
servatism of organized labor, especially among thos
workers called by one Jamaican economist, "the labc
elite." These more prosperous workers seem to establis
their self-identification with the middle class by moraliz
ing about the behavior of the less fortunate masses, an
negating any association with them.[6] These people fee
on and foster the stereotype of the masses as harborin
dangerous animosity toward the rest of society.

Another facet of this phenomenon may stem from an
important influence in the heritage of modern social an
political thought; namely, Marxism and the radical tradi
tion. This tradition of thought promotes an interpretatio
of history and a definition of the current situation tha
supports the belief that the lower classes are in conflic
with the middle and upper classes. Even the loudest anti
communists among Jamaican politicians view the lowe
classes with an eye on their revolutionary potential. Ja
maica's confrontation with the experience of Haiti an
other republics in and around the Caribbean basin lend
credibility to their fears of lower class antagonism. A fea
of *fidelismo* and any other movement of an ideologica
nature directed at the lower orders has resulted.[7]

In brief, the stereotypes conveyed by the press, th
styles of thought regarding the relations between classes

[6] M. G. Smith, "The Plural Framework of Jamaican Society," *The British Journal of Sociology,* Vol. 12 (September
1961), p. 261.

[7] On more than one occasion my presence in some areas o
West Kingston at odd hours was not too subtly probed by members of the security police. It is interesting to note that I was
most often forewarned because the officers were quite well
known in the area. Norris has suggested that persons showing
an interest in the masses are liable to be suspected of being
Communists. See Katrin Norris, *Jamaica: The Search for an
Identity* (London: Oxford University Press for the Institute of
Race Relations, 1962), p. 69.

and the objective conditions of the lower classes all contribute to the maintenance of an image of the masses which is marked by virulent hostility and animosity. In this paper we shall explore the prevalence of this view among a systematically drawn sample of public leaders in Jamaica. The universe of leaders was made up of persons who were influential in policy formulation and implementation in relation to West Kingston, the largest area of urban lower-class residence. These leaders included Members of Parliament, Cabinet Ministers, Parish Councillors, civil servants, clergymen, and some prominent solicitors and businessmen. All of these leaders were persons who had a reputation for playing an important role regarding the urban lower-class area and the problems of the people there. Depth interviews were conducted with 54 such leaders. In addition, some comparable data collected in 132 interviews with a 25 per cent random sample of heads of households in a selected squatter-housing area of West Kingston allow a partial verification of the image of the threatening masses. Is it myth or reality?[8]

Whether founded on myth or reality, the image of the hostile masses can be very real in its consequences. Just as pessimism can facilitate the failure it anticipates,[9] so

[8] The universe of leaders under consideration was defined by the reputational or "power attribution" approach. Of the 66 leaders who received three or more nominations, 82 per cent were interviewed, including 90 per cent of the 50 top-ranked persons. The data were collected between August 7, 1961, and September 21, 1962. A complete discussion of the findings and methodology of the larger study from which these data are drawn will soon be available. See James A. Mau, "Social Change and Belief in Progress: A Study of Images of the Future in Jamaica," in Wendell Bell, ed., *The Democratic Revolution in the West Indies: Studies in Nationalism, Leadership, and the Belief in Progress* (Cambridge, Mass.: Schenkman Publishing Company, 1967).

[9] For example Sanford and associates have concluded that "the pessimist, belittling the likelihood of appreciable or significant progress, by his attitude adds obstacles to practical

also the belief that the lower classes are hostile may moti-
vate or engender a style of behavior on the part of the
middle and upper-class persons that could further estrange
members of the lower classes. This may be particularly
true if the view that the masses are hostile is held in official or quasi-official circles. Such an image of the masses
may result in repressive legislation and action conducive
to mass reaction, rather than more positive integrating
measures. As one Jamaican columnist has observed:

> Already we spend four million pounds on internal
> security in the army and the police force. Much of it
> could be better spent on feeding people instead of pre-
> paring to shoot them when they become too hungry to
> care.[10]

Writing about the need for a change in thinking about the
dissident groups in Jamaica, another journalist stated, "And
if we think only in terms of repression, eventually we shall
have a movement not far removed from the Mau Mau."[11]

As part of a discussion of the people and problems of
West Kingston, the Jamaican leaders interviewed in this
research were asked, "What would you say the people of
West Kingston think of the middle and upper-class people
of Jamaica?" This question and the conversational probes
that followed elicited detailed statements about the *typical*
or *majority* view of the urban lower-class people. The content of these responses was analyzed to determine whether
the leaders perceived the typical attitude to be one of
hostility toward the more privileged classes in Jamaica.
The leaders' perceptions of lower-class attitudes were:

---

accomplishment and facilitates the very failure he anticipates."
R. Nevitt Sanford, Herbert S. Conrad, and Kate Franck, "Psychological Determinants of Optimism Regarding Consequences
of War," *The Journal of Psychology*, Vol. XXII (1946), p.
235. See also Robert K. Merton's discussion of social fatalism
in "The Self-fulfilling Prophecy," *Social Theory and Social
Structure* (rev. ed.; Glencoe, Ill.: The Free Press, 1957), pp.
421–436.

[10] *Public Opinion*, Vol. 27 (June 7, 1963), p. 13.
[11] *Ibid.* (May 11, 1963), p. 2.

The lower classes are hostile	61 %
They are not hostile	39 %
TOTAL	100 %
Number of cases	(51)
No answer	(3)

The majority of these leaders would have agreed with the nineteenth century West Indian colonial governor who wrote that he was ". . . convinced that the spirit of discontent is anything but extinct, it is alive as it were under the ashes."[12] And with a recent writer: "So one might sum up all the information on Jamaica today: the island is littered with the remnants of a fire that is liable to flare up again. Jamaica is still branded by the institution of slavery."[13]

One question of immediate interest is whether the Jamaican leaders were correct in their assessment of the sentiments of the urban lower classes. Were the majority of the urban lower-class people hostile toward the middle and upper classes of Jamaica as 61 per cent of the leaders believed them to be? The findings of the survey in the selected urban lower-class area of Kingston clearly indicate the mythical nature of the leaders' image of the hostile masses. The attitudes toward the privileged classes actually expressed in interviews with the urban lower-class respondents were:[14]

[12] Quoted in Ruth Glass, "Ashes of Discontent: The Past as Present in Jamaica," *Monthly Review*, Vol. 14 (May, 1962), p. 24.

[13] *Ibid.*

[14] Because one might expect reticence of the lower-class respondents to express hostility, it should be noted that in analyzing the responses any indication of hostility by indirect statement or even mode of expression was classified as a hostile response; also, the interviewing was done by two black or dark-skinned Jamaicans. It should be noted that 59 per cent of the lower-class respondents answering this question were women, and as might be expected they were somewhat less likely to express hostility in the interviews than were the men. The phi correlation coefficient for the relationship between sex and expression of hostility was .22.

Hostility	20 %
Indifference	12 %
Emulation	56 %
Friendship (mutual respect)	11 %
Mixed	1 %
TOTAL	100 %
Number of cases	(120)
No answer	(12)

One-fifth of the lower-class respondents in West Kingston expressed hostility toward the middle and upper classes of Jamaica, whereas these sentiments of enmity and animosity were believed by 61 per cent of the leaders to be characteristic of the majority. The typical lower-class attitude was found to be one of emulation or aspiration to the standards of life and behavior exhibited by the privileged classes. As Henriques has said, commenting on the relations between segments of Jamaican society, ". . . the majority of the people, are constantly striving by every means in their power to emulate and imitate the European."[15] Indeed, more than half of the lower-class respondents indicated this desire to emulate the practices of the privileged classes. Only 11 per cent of the leaders reported such an attitude to be typical of the people of West Kingston.

Although one might wonder how widely accepted this mythical hostility of the lower classes is among the more socially distant middle and upper-class population, the question of overriding significance turns upon the need to explain the leaders' remarkably inaccurate perceptions of the views of the people of West Kingston. All of these leaders were persons whose acknowledged social and civic responsibilities lie to some extent in West Kingston. All of them, because of their official positions or their public activities were more or less influential in the planning and implementation of policy directed to the solution of the problems of West Kingston and the people there. Yet,

[15] Fernando Henriques, *Jamaica: Land of Wood and Water* (London: MacGibbon and Kee, 1957), p. 128.

despite their concern and involvement with the area, the majority of these leaders asserted, apparently incorrectly, that resentment and animosity were the dominant sentiments of the people. We should like to know why the majority of the leaders were mistaken in their acceptance of the myth of the hostile masses. What differentiated those leaders who perceived lower-class enmity and hostility from those who did not accept this view?

A partial answer to this last question may be found in Table 1 where the percentage of Jamaican leaders who

TABLE 1

PERCENTAGE OF JAMAICAN LEADERS WHO PERCEIVE URBAN LOWER-CLASS HOSTILITY BY SELECTED SOCIAL CHARACTERISTICS

Selected Characteristic	Percentage Who Perceive Hostility	No. of Cases on Which the Per Cent is Based
Age		
50 and over	55	(20)
40–49	60	(20)
39 and under	73	(11)
Education		
University or college graduate	56	(16)
Some university or college	88	(8)
Secondary school or less	56	(27)
Race-color		
White	42	(12)
Brown	62	(13)
Black	69	(26)
Occupational Rating		
1 (Highest)	58	(24)
2–4 (Lowest)	63	(27)
Religious Preference		
Anglican	43	(14)
Other Protestant	73	(15)
Roman Catholic	67	(6)
Jewish	—	(1)
Political Party Preference		
Jamaica Labour Party	58	(12)
Peoples' National Party	62	(26)
Other	62	(13)

perceived hostility is shown by selected social characteristics. Briefly, it was found that the oldest group of leaders less often reported the lower classes to be hostile than did the intermediate or younger age groups. Nearly three-quarters of the leaders 39 years of age and under perceived lower-class hostility compared to 55 per cent of the oldest leaders. In addition to age, the clearest differences to emerge were by race-color, religion, and political party preference. Those leaders who were white, members of the Anglican Church, and who preferred the Jamaica Labour Party, were the groups least likely to perceive hostility. Those leaders with the highest occupational rating,[16] were also less likely to report the lower classes to be hostile than those leaders in lower rated occupations, though this difference was quite small. The educational level of the leaders presented a curious relationship with the perception of hostility. Those leaders who were in the intermediate category with some college or university training were the most likely to report the lower classes to be hostile.

Additional information about the leaders is presented in Table 2. There the percentage of the leaders who perceived hostility is shown by the type of elite position they held.[17] Members of the clergy, officers and staff of the Jamaica Social Welfare Commission, and the Parish Councillors were the groups of leaders who were likely to accept the image of the hostile masses in West Kingston. Although

[16] The measure of occupational rating was adapted by Wendell Bell for use in Jamaica from W. Lloyd Warner, Marchia Meeker, and Kenneth Eells, *Social Class in America* (Chicago: Science Research Associates, Inc., 1949), pp. 140–141; and Carson McGuire, "Social Status, Peer Status, and Social Mobility," a mimeographed memorandum for research workers based on procedures used in studies for the Committee on Human Development, University of Chicago, Chicago, Ill., 1948.

[17] Leaders holding more than one such elite position were classified according to that position which was most relevant to their role in dealing with the urban lower classes and West Kingston.

these data on social characteristics and types of positions held by the leaders would seem to offer little help by way of interpreting or explaining the variation in the perception of lower-class hostility, they do importantly provide the descriptive backgrounds of the leaders.

TABLE 2

PERCENTAGE OF JAMAICAN LEADERS WHO PERCEIVE URBAN LOWER-CLASS HOSTILITY BY TYPE OF ELITE POSITION

Type of Elite Position	Percentage Who Perceive Hostility	No. of Cases on Which the Per Cent is Based
Politicians	55	(20)
Members of Parliament	50	(12)
Parish Councillors	63	(8)
Government Officers	60	(15)
Civil Servants	56	(9)
Jamaica Social Welfare Comm.	67	(6)
Non-Governmental Community Welfare Leaders	69	(16)
Clergy	88	(8)
Other	50	(8)

We have seen that the majority of these Jamaican leaders incorrectly accepted the stereotyped hostility of the people of West Kingston. Most of the leaders confirm one of Eric Hoffer's many aphorisms. He wrote: "There is a tendency to judge a race, a nation or any distinct group by its least worthy members."[18] The myth of the hostile masses in Jamaica would seem to be based on just such a tendency suggested by Hoffer. There can be no denial that one encounters hostility among the people of West Kingston. This is particularly true of some members of the Ras Tafari cult and others who don their symbols. Overt manifestations of hostile attitudes are more likely to be highly visible than those of indifference, friendship, or

[18] Eric Hoffer, *The True Believer* (New York: New American Library, 1951), p. 29.

the desire to emulate others. Hostility gains attention more readily because of its association with threats to one's security. Reports of "incidents" and violent expressions of illiterate resentment rapidly gain in significance and detail with the momentum of exaggeration. To focus attention on these incidents is to foster an incomplete conception of the views of the people of West Kingston toward the privileged segments of Jamaican society. From the data reported here one must insist that *hostility is far from the typical response to the better-off segments of society*.

In exploring the reasons for the prevalence of this myth among the leaders, we might suggest that those who accepted the veil of these misconceptions, in some sense, lacked access to the complete "reality" of West Kingston. Either by preference or circumstances, or both, many of these leaders were limited in the range and intensity of their involvement with West Kingston and the problems of people. In contrast, those leaders who rejected the myth of the hostile masses possessed greater access to the people of West Kingston, and had a broader scale of activity concerning the problems of the urban lower classes.[19] In the analysis to follow we shall examine the relationship between the leaders' perception of hostility and three variables which may be broadly interpreted as indicators of the leaders' actual or preferred degree of involvement with the urban lower-class area and the problems of the people there. These three variables, the leaders' attitudes toward equality, their relative knowledge of the complaints and discontents of the people of West Kingston, and their relative power in public affairs concerning West Kingston are shown to differentiate between those leaders who per-

[19] See Godfrey and Monica Wilson, *The Analysis of Social Change* (Cambridge, England: Cambridge University Press, 1954); and Charles C. Moskos, Jr., "The Sociology of Political Independence: A Study of Nationalist Attitudes and Activities Among West Indian Leaders," in Bell, ed., *op. cit.*

ceived lower-class hostility and those who rejected that
view.

The role of the ideology of egalitarianism would not be
unanticipated in its effect upon the perception of lower-
class hostility. A person's views of his society are conditioned to some extent by the ideas and attitudes to which
he subscribes. "That is to say, men have various ide-
ological or judgmental views of different parts of their
society, and these views may give them a 'false' or 'distorted' picture of their social world."[20] So among these
leaders it was found that their attitudes toward equality
induced selective perception of the views of the urban
lower classes.[21] Attitudes toward equality are here equated
with expressed preference for the maintenance or reduction of status differences and ascriptive barriers which limit
participation in the social process. The Jamaican leaders
were asked:

> Do you think it is advisable that any barriers to full in-
> teraction of people in Jamaica should be broken down,
> or are there some status differences which should be
> maintained?

Those leaders who favored the reduction of such barriers
to participation were categorized as egalitarian. Leaders
who did not clearly favor the reduction of these limitations,
or who gave equivocal answers were classified as inegalitarian. Two respondents who said there were no barriers in
Jamaica were also classified as inegalitarian. In this manner 60 per cent of the leaders were found to be egalitarian.
The remainder did not favor the extension of social equal-

[20] Bernard Barber, *Social Stratification* (New York: Har-
court, Brace and Company, 1957), p. 187.
[21] For a somewhat comparable finding see Donald R.
Matthews and James W. Prothro, "Southern Racial Attitudes:
Conflict, Awareness, and Political Change," *The Annals of the
American Academy of Political and Social Science*, Vol. 344
(November, 1962), pp. 108–121.

ity and were classified as inegalitarian, with the exception of two respondents for whom there were insufficient data.

The effect of the leaders' attitudes toward equality upon their perception of lower-class hostility is shown in Table 3. About half of the egalitarian leaders perceived hostility compared to three-quarters of the inegalitarians. Those leaders who favored the incorporation of all social, economic, and racial groups into meaningful participation in Jamaican society were less likely to view the lower classes as hostile than those leaders who did not assert the importance of extending equality to all Jamaicans. This finding is consistent with our earlier suggestions that the leaders' attitudes toward equality served to limit their access to the reality of West Kingston, or induced partial perception of that reality.

TABLE 3

PERCENTAGE OF JAMAICAN LEADERS WHO
PERCEIVE THE URBAN LOWER CLASSES
TO BE HOSTILE BY EGALITARIANISM

Egalitarianism	Percentage Who Perceive Hostility	No. of Cases on Which the Per Cent is Based
Egalitarian	52	(29)
Inegalitarian	75	(20)

A second indicator of the Jamaican leaders' range and intensity of interaction with the people of West Kingston and their problems is the leaders' relative knowledgeability concerning the specific discontents and complaints of the people. These leaders were all, in some measure, responsible for the betterment of the social and physical milieu of West Kingston. Consequently, we might expect them to be aware of the various shortcomings of the area which the residents desire to have corrected. However, Oscar Lewis has suggested that the elite in most developing countries do not usually have much knowledge of the poor or the subculture created by poverty.[22] To what extent was this true in Jamaica, and more importantly, how

TABLE 4

PERCENTAGE OF JAMAICAN LEADERS WHO PERCEIVE THE URBAN LOWER CLASSES TO BE HOSTILE BY THE INDEX OF KNOWLEDGE

Index of Knowledge	Percentage Who Perceive Hostility	No. of Cases on Which the Per Cent is Based
Most knowledgeable	45	(31)
Least knowledgeable	85	(20)

did the possession of knowledge affect the likelihood that the leaders would accept or reject the myth of the hostile masses?

The measure of the leaders' knowledgeability is based on the accuracy and completeness of their knowledge of the complaints and discontents of the lower-class people who reside in West Kingston. Both the leaders and the lower-class respondents were asked to list the most important complaints and sources of discontent in West Kingston. Each leader's list was scored according to the extent of agreement with the discontents reported by the lower-class people themselves. In the resulting distribution of leaders according to their level of knowledge, 63 per cent of the leaders were classified as most knowledgeable about the needs and problems of the people of West Kingston; the remaining 37 per cent were relatively less knowledgeable. Although this index does not purport to measure the leaders' knowledge of the problems of the urban lower classes in any absolute sense, it does provide an indication of their knowledge relative to one another. As shown in Table 4, the leaders' relative level of knowledge concerning the complaints and discontents of the West Kingston people was closely related to the percep-

22 Oscar Lewis, *Five Families* (New York: Basic Books, Inc., 1959), p. 2.

tion of hostility as the typical attitude of the lower classes. Those leaders with the least knowledge were also the most likely to perceive hostility. Forty-five per cent of the knowledgeable leaders accepted the stereotyped hostility of the lower classes, while 85 per cent of the leaders with little knowledge expressed the conviction that the people of West Kingston were hostile toward the middle and upper classes. This finding would also tend to confirm our contention that widespread enmity of the lower classes is indeed mythical.

Another dimension of the leaders' scale of activity in relation to West Kingston is their relative power in the councils of decision affecting the area. Those leaders capable of exerting greater social pressure in policy formulation and implementation directed at the solution of the problems of the urban lower classes would also have somewhat greater range and intensity of involvement with the area and the problems of its people. Consequently, we should expect the relatively more powerful leaders to less often express belief in the hostility of the people of the area. In order to determine the relative power of each leader a two-factor index of power was constructed on the basis of responses to the following question:

Now, I'd like you to tell me the names of the people you think are most important in determining and carrying out policy in relation to the problems of West Kingston.

The first factor in the Index of Power is a reputational influence score for each individual based on the number of nominations he received in response to the above question. The second factor is a score representing the accuracy and completeness of the leaders' awareness of the influence of other leaders. Thus, the measure of relative power includes both the leaders' reputation for effective action, and their degree of integration into, or awareness of the system of power relations relevant to the issue-area in question.[23] These two components were averaged for each leader and the resulting distribution of scores was dichotomized at the median interval. Again, it should be noted that this measure of power, like the measure of knowledge presented earlier, indicates only the relative power of the leaders, and is restricted to the issues concerning the people of West Kingston.

Following our earlier line of reasoning, we should expect the leaders who were relatively less powerful to be more often convinced of the hostility of the people of West Kingston than those more powerful leaders. This expectation is fulfilled by the data presented in Table 5 where the percentage of leaders who perceived hostility is shown by their relative power. Sixty-eight per cent of those leaders who were less powerful accepted the stereotype of the masses as hostile toward the more privileged classes. Among the more powerful leaders, 56 per cent expressed the belief that the West Kingston people were hostile to those who had received more of the benefits of Jamaica's growth and development.

TABLE 5

PERCENTAGE OF JAMAICAN LEADERS WHO
PERCEIVE THE URBAN LOWER CLASSES TO
BE HOSTILE BY THE INDEX OF POWER

Index of Power	Percentage Who Perceive Hostility	No. of Cases on Which the Per Cent is Based
Most powerful	56	(25)
Least powerful	68	(25)

[23] This use of the knowledge of the power of others is not unlike that of Foskett and Hohle in their community power research. See John M. Foskett and Raymond Hohle, "The Measurement of Influence in Community Affairs," *Proceedings of the Pacific Sociological Society, Research Studies of the State College of Washington,* Vol. XXV (June, 1957), pp. 148–154.

We have seen that each of three variables, egalitarianism, the leaders' knowledge of the problems of the West Kingston people, and their relative power in public affairs of the area was correlated with the differential perception of lower-class attitudes. We should now simultaneously examine the effect of all three of these variables upon the perception of lower-class hostility. Unfortunately, the number of cases on which the analysis is based prohibits the presentation of the four variable table. Therefore, a composite index of the three variables was constructed which would allow the simultaneous elaboration of the relationship between these variables and the perception of lower-class hostility.[24] Scores of zero or one were given to the leaders on each of the three variables. Zeros were assigned to leaders with inegalitarian attitudes, little knowledge, and less power. The categories given a one point value were conversely, egalitarian attitudes, and relatively high knowledge and power. The sum of these three assigned values is the total score on the composite index. These scores range from zero to three.

Having constructed the index, we may now examine the cumulative effect of this composite indicator of the leaders' scale of activity in relation to West Kingston upon their perception of hostility. The percentage of leaders who perceived hostility as typical of the urban lower classes is presented by this composite index in Table 6. Thirty per cent of the leaders who were egalitarian, most knowledgeable, and most powerful (score 3) expressed the belief that the people of West Kingston were hostile to the privileged classes. At the other extreme, 100 per cent of those leaders who were assigned scores of zero on the composite index perceived the lower classes to be hostile. That is, all of the leaders who were inegalitarian, less knowledgeable, and less powerful, viewed hostility as the

[24] See Herbert Hyman's discussion of the deliberate creation of a configuration, which though synthetic, allows more complex and refined analysis; *Survey Design and Analysis* (Glencoe, Ill.: The Free Press, 1955), pp. 271–272.

typical urban lower-class sentiment toward Jamaica's middle and upper classes.

In general, the findings reported here indicate that the sentiments of hostility believed by the majority of these Jamaican leaders to be typical of the urban lower classes toward the privileged classes of Jamaica are not borne out by the attitudes actually expressed by a sample of lower-class persons in West Kingston. Whereas 61 per cent of the leaders reported the majority of the urban lower-class persons to be hostile, far less than a majority of the lower-class persons sampled indicated such hostile attitudes. Further, it was found that those leaders who by their attitudes toward equality indicated a preference for maximizing the breadth and intensity of social relations, and were also more knowledgeable and capable of exerting greater social pressure in public affairs of West Kingston, were most likely to reject the myth of the hostile masses as an unrealistic view of the relations between

TABLE 6

PERCENTAGE OF JAMAICAN LEADERS WHO PERCEIVE THE URBAN LOWER CLASSES TO BE HOSTILE BY THE COMPOSITE INDEX OF EGALITARIANISM, POWER AND KNOWLEDGE

Composite Index Scores	Percentage Who Perceive Hostility	No. of Cases on Which the Per Cent is Based
3 (Highest)	30	(10)
2	62	(21)
1	73	(11)
0 (Lowest)	100	(6)

classes in Jamaica. Those leaders, who by preference or circumstances were limited in their involvement with West Kingston were most likely to perceive inaccurately the sentiments of the urban lower classes toward the privileged classes.

The implications of this inaccuracy and the conse-

quences of the behavior it might engender are fearsome.
Some of the implications of the belief that the masses represent a threat were suggested by the disproportionately
strong reaction to the Coral Gardens "uprising" in April,
1963. Another hint of this tendency to resort to repressive
action was given only a few days prior to the Coral Gardens incident. The Unemployed Workers' Council had
planned a march and demonstration in Kingston on March
31, 1963. The Government's immediate action was a display of force with the intention of intimidating the dis-
senters. The march was banned and "armored cars rum-
bled through the streets of Kingston," in Jamaica's version
of what used to be called "gunboat diplomacy."[25] The
significance of such action in the face of any opposition
demonstration lies in the threat to democratic processes,
and in the kind of behavior it may generate in return. In
these few instances the stage has been set for the vicious
circle of the self-fulfilling prophecy in which ill-founded
fears give rise to their own spurious confirmation.[26] The
belief that the lower classes in Jamaica are hostile may be
conducive to a style of behavior on the part of the government and the middle and upper-class people which could
give truth to their initially false definition of the situation.

We have shown that the majority of these Jamaican
leaders had accepted a false definition of the sentiments of
the urban lower-class people, a definition which could
clearly assume the character of a self-fulfilling prophecy.
However, our findings also suggest that the fatalistic
prophecy might not, and certainly need not be fulfilled.
Obviously there is discontent among the people of West
Kingston, but it need not result in hostility and overt aggression unless these are provoked by unenlightened leadership. The prophecy might not be fulfilled because the
knowledgeable and powerful leaders, guided by their commitment to the ideology of equality have rejected the

[25] *Spotlight,* Vol. 24 (March, 1963), p. 10.
[26] Merton, *op. cit.*

myth of the hostile masses. If these leaders do not deny their ideology and their responsibility, "the tragic circle of fear, social disaster, and reinforced fear can be broken."[27]

[27] *Ibid.*, p. 436.

5.

The West Indian middle class has inherited many of the privileges and prerogatives of expatriate and local white elites. But there is great disparity between what the middle class has been brought up to expect and what is now expected of it. C. L. R. James here indicts the West Indian middle class as ill-prepared for the role of leadership. Excluded from the productive arena by elite solidarity and by its own concept of gentility, it lacks experience in the management of economic affairs. Trained to a hierarchical view of society, the West Indian middle class, in James's view, must reeducate itself to work for the broader national interest.

C. L. R. JAMES, born in Trinidad in 1901, is teacher, journalist, novelist, revolutionary, Socialist, pan-Africanist, and cricket devotee. He played a major role in anti-imperialist activities in England during the 1930s and 1940s and returned to Trinidad in the late 1950s to serve as editor of *The Nation*, the organ of the People's National Movement, only to break with that party's leader a few years later. He currently teaches in New York and Washington.

The Middle Classes
C. L. R. James

OUR MIDDLE CLASSES, UNPREPARED, MISEDUCATED PEOPLE
SUDDENLY FACED WITH THE ENORMOUS MESSES THE IM-
PERIALISTS ARE LEAVING BEHIND.

The middle classes in the West Indies, coloured peoples,
constitute one of the most peculiar classes in the world,
peculiar in the sense of their unusual historical development and the awkward and difficult situation they occupy
in what constitutes the West Indian nation, or, nowadays,
some section of it.

Let me get one thing out of the way. They are not a
defective set of people. In intellectual capacity, i.e. ability
to learn, to familiarise themselves with the general scholastic requirements of Western civilization, they are and for
some time have been unequalled in the colonial world. If
you take percentages of scholastic achievement in relation
to population among the underdeveloped, formerly colonial, coloured countries, West Indians would probably
be at the head and, I believe, not by a small margin either.
What they lack, and they lack plenty, is not due to any
inherent West Indian deficiency. If that were so we
would be in a bad way indeed. I set out to show that
the blunders and deficiencies of which they are guilty are

Party Politics in the West Indies, San Juan, Trinidad: Vedic
Enterprises, 1962, pp. 130–39. Reprinted with permission of the
author.

historically caused and therefore can be historically corrected. Otherwise we are left with the demoralizing result: "That is the way West Indians are," and closely allied to this: "The man or men who have brought us into this mess are bad men. Let us search for some good men." As long as you remain on that level, you understand nothing and your apparently "good" men turn rapidly into men who are no good. That is why I shall keep as far away from individuals as I can and stick to the class. I am not fighting to win an election.

For something like twenty years we have been establishing the premises of a modern democratic society: parliamentary government, democratic rights, party politics, etc. The mere existence of these is totally inadequate—the smash-up of the Federation has proved that. We now have to move on to a more advanced stage. To think that what I say is the last word in political wisdom is to make me into just another West Indian politician. I am posing certain profound, certain fundamental questions. Their urgency lies in the fact that our political pundits and those who circulate around them, consistently ignore them, try to pretend that they do not exist.

Who and what are our middle classes? What passes my comprehension is that their situation is never analysed in writing, or even mentioned in public discussion. That type of ignorance, abstinence, shame or fear, simply does not take place in a country like Britain. There must be some reason for this stolid silence about themselves, some deep, underlying compulsion. We shall see.

Our West Indian middle classes are for the most part coloured people of some education in a formerly slave society. That means that for racial and historical reasons they are today excluded from those circles which are in control of big industry, commerce and finance. They are almost as much excluded from large-scale agriculture, sugar for example. That is point number one. Thus they as a class of people have no knowledge or experience of the productive forces of the country. That stands out painfully in everything they do and everything they do not do. Mr. Nehru talks about India's new steel mills, President Nasser talked about his dam which caused a war, President Nkrumah talked and preached about his Volta Dam for ten years before he got it. A West Indian politician talks about how much money he will get from the British Government or from the United States. It is because the class from which he comes had and has no experience whatever in matters of production. It is the same in agriculture. They have never had anything to do with the big sugar estates. Banking is out of their hands and always has been. There is no prospect that by social intermixing, intermarriage, etc., they will ever get into those circles. They have been out, are out and from all appearances will remain out. That is a dreadful position from which to have to govern a country. In Britain, France, Australia, you have capitalist parties, men who represent and are closely associated with big capital, big agriculture, finance. You have also labour parties. In Britain a hundred members in the House of Commons are placed there by the union movement. The Labour Party members are the heads or connected with the heads of the union movement, of the Labour Party, of the Cooperative Movement; thus, apart from Parliament, they have a social base. In the West Indies some of the politicians have or have had posts in the labour or union movement. But as a class they have no base anywhere. They are professional men, clerical assistants, here and there a small business man, and of late years administrators, civil servants and professional politicians and, as usual, a few adventurers. Most of the political types who come from this class live by politics. All personal distinction and even in some cases the actual means of life and the means of improving the material circumstances of life, spring from participation, direct or indirect, in the government, or circles sympathetic to or willing to play ball with the government. Thus the politicians carry into politics all the weaknesses of the class from which they come.

They have no trace of political tradition. Until twenty years ago they had no experience of political parties or of government. Their last foray in that sphere was a hundred and thirty years ago, when they threatened the planters with rebellion of themselves *and the slaves* if they were not permitted to exercise the rights of citizens. Since then they have been quiet as mice. On rare occasions they would make a protest and, the ultimate pitch of rebellion, go to the Colonial Office. They did not do any more because all they aimed at was being admitted to the ruling circle of expatriates and local whites. More than that they did not aspire to. It is most significant that the father of the anti-imperialist democratic movement is a white man, A. A. Cipriani, and the biggest names are Alexander Bustamante who spent a lot of his life in Spain, Cuba and the United States, and Uriah Butler, a working man: not one of them is a member of the ordinary middle class. Sir Grantley Adams may appear to be one. He most certainly is not. After being educated abroad, he came back to Barbados, which alone of the West Indian islands had an elected House of Representatives. He neglected what would have been a brilliant and lucrative profession at the bar to plunge himself into politics. Middle class West Indians do not do that.

Knowledge of production, of political struggles, of the democratic tradition, they have had none. Their ignorance and disregard of economic development is profound and deeply rooted in their past and present situation. They do not even seem to be aware of it. For several generations they have been confined to getting salaries or fees, money for services rendered. That is still their outlook.

For generations their sole aim in life was to be admitted to the positions to which their talents and education entitled them, and from which they were unjustly excluded. On rare occasions an unexpected and difficult situation opened a way for an exceptional individual, but for the most part they developed political skill only in crawling or worming their way into recognition by government or big business. When they did get into the charmed government circles or government itself, they either did their best to show that they could be as good servants of the Colonial Office as any, or when they rose to become elected members in the legislature, some of them maintained a loud (but safe) attack on the government. They actually did little. They were not responsible for anything, so they achieved a cheap popularity without any danger to themselves.

Thus the class has been and is excluded from the centres of economic life, they have no actual political experience, they have no political tradition. The democracy and West Indianisation was won by mass revolt. Even this revolt was led by men who were not typically middle class. When, after 1937–38, the democratic movement started, it was a labour movement. Gradually, however, the British Government, felt itself compelled to make the Civil Service West Indian, i.e. middle class. By degrees the middle class took over the political parties. The Colonial Office carefully, what it called, educated them to govern, with the result that the Federation is broken up and every territory is in a political mess.

Let us stick to the class, the class from which most of our politicians come, and from which they get most of their views on life and society.

All this politicians' excitement about independence is not to be trusted. In recent years the middle classes have not been concerned about independence. They were quite satisfied with the lives they lived. I never saw or heard one of them around the politicians who was actively for independence. Their political representation faithfully reproduced this attitude. I can say and dare not be challenged that in 1959 one man and one only was for independence, Dr. Williams. I do not know one single West Indian politician who supported him except with some noncommittal phrases. You cannot speak with too much certainty of a class unless you have made or have at your disposal a careful examination. But of the politicians I am absolutely certain. Independence was not an integral part of their politics. The evidence for this is overwhelming and at the slightest provocation I shall make it public. The drive for independence now is to cover up the failure of the Federation.

If you watch the social connections of the politicians and the life they live, you will see why their politics is what it is. I do not know any social class which lives so completely without ideas of any kind. They live entirely on the material plane. In a published address Sir Robert Kirkwood quotes Vidia Naipaul who has said of them that they seem to aim at nothing more than being second-rate American citizens. It is much more than that. They aim at nothing. Government jobs and the opportunities which association with the government gives, allows them the possibility of accumulating material goods. That is all.

Read their speeches about the society in which they live. They have nothing to say. Not one of them. They promise more jobs and tell the population that everybody will have a chance to get a better job. They could not say what federation meant. They are unable to say what independence means. Apart from the constitution and the fact that now they will govern without Colonial Office intervention, they have nothing to say. They are dying to find some Communists against whom they can thunder and so make an easier road to American pockets. What kind of society they hope to build they do not say because they do not know.

Their own struggle for posts and pay, their ceaseless promising of jobs, their sole idea of a national development as one where everybody can aim at getting something more, the gross and vulgar materialism, the absence of any ideas or elementary originality of thought; the tiresome repetition of commonplaces aimed chiefly at impressing the British, this is the outstanding characteristic of the West Indian middle class. The politicians they produce only reproduce politically the thin substance of the class.

Let us stay here for a while. These people have to know

what they are. Nobody except our novelists is telling them.

We live in a world in the throes of a vast reorganization of itself. The religious question is back on the order of discussion. Two world wars and a third in the offing, Nazism, Stalinism, have made people ask: where is humanity going? Some say that we are now reaching the climax of that preoccupation with science and democracy which well over a hundred and fifty years ago substituted itself for religion as the guiding principle of mankind. Some believe we have to go back to religion. Others that mankind has never made genuine democracy the guiding light for society. Freud and Jung have opened depths of uncertainty and doubt of the rationality of human intelligence. Where the West Indian middle class (with all its degrees) stand on this, who is for, who is against, who even thinks of such matters, nobody knows. They think they can live and avoid such questions. You can live, but in 1962 you cannot govern that way.

Are they capitalists, i.e. do they believe in capitalism, socialism, communism, anarchism, anything? Nobody knows. They keep as far as they can from committing themselves to anything. This is a vitally practical matter. Are you going to plan your economy? To what degree is that possible, and compatible with democracy? To West Indian politicians a development programme is the last word in economic development. They never discuss the plan, what it means, what it can be. If they feel any pressure they forthwith baptise their development programme as "planning".

Where does personality, literature, art, the drama stand today in relation to a national development? What is the relation between the claims of individuality and the claims of the state? What does education aim at? To make citizens capable of raising the productivity of labour, or to give them a conception of life? West Indian intellectuals who are interested in or move around politics avoid these questions as if they were the plague.

Some readers may remember seeing the movie of the

night of the independence of Ghana, and hearing Nkrumah choose at that time to talk about the African Personality. This was to be the aim of the Ghanaian people with independence. Is there a West Indian personality? Is there a West Indian nation? What is it? What does it lack? What must it have? The West Indian middle classes keep far from these questions. The job, the car, the fridge, the trip abroad, preferably under government auspices and at government expense, these seem to be the beginning and end of their preoccupations. What foreign forces, social classes, ideas, do they feel themselves allied with or attached to? Nothing. What in their own history do they look back to as a beginning of which they are the continuation? I listen to them, I read their speeches and their writings. "Massa day done" seems to be the extreme limit of their imaginative concepts of West Indian nationalism. Today nationalism is under fire and every people has to consider to what extent its nationalism has to be mitigated by international considerations. Of this as of so much else the West Indian middle class is innocent. What happens after independence? For all you can hear from them, independence is a dead end. Apart from the extended opportunities of jobs with government, independence is as great an abstraction as was federation. We achieve independence and they continue to govern.

It has been pointed out to me, in a solid and very brilliant manuscript, that the accommodation of the middle class to what is in reality an impossible position is primarily due to the fact that, contrary to the general belief, it is in essence a position they have been in for many years. They or their most distinguished representatives have always been in the situation where the first necessity of advance or new status was to curry favour with the British authorities. The easiest way to continued acceptance was to train yourself to be able to make an impact as British and as submissive as possible. Now they have political power their attitude is the same only more so. Where formerly they had to accommodate themselves to the Governor and all such small fry, today they deal directly with the British Colonial Secretary and British Cabinet Ministers, with foreign business interests themselves instead of only their representatives abroad. The strenuous need and desire to accommodate, the acceptance of a British code of manners, morals and economic and political procedures, that is what they have always done, especially the upper Civil Servants. They have had to live that way because it was the only way they could live. That new combination of a West Indianised Civil Service and a West Indianised political grouping are a little further along the road, but it is the same road on which they have always travelled. The man who has worked out something usually finds the aptest illustration of it. In conversation with me the author of this really superb piece of insight and analysis has said: "If they had had to deal with, for instance, Japanese or even German businessmen they would act differently. They would have been conscious of a sharp change. With the British they are not conscious of any break with the past. Accustomed for generations to hang around the British and search diligently for ways and means to gain an advantage, they now do of their own free will what they formerly had to do."

Having lived, as a class, by receiving money for services rendered, they transfer their age-old habits to government. But as this recent analysis shows, the very objective circumstances of their new political positions in office have merely fortified their experiences out of office.

It is such a class of people which has the government of the West Indies in its hands. In all essential matters they are, as far as the public is concerned, devoid of any ideas whatever. This enormous statement I can make with the greatest confidence, for no one can show any speech, any document, any report on which any of these matters —and the list is long—are treated with any serious application to the West Indian situation. These are the people from whom come the political leaders of the West Indies. The politicians are what they are not by chance.

What is the cause of this? A list of causes will be pure

empiricism allowing for an infinite amount of "on the one hand" and "on the other hand". The cause is not in any individual and not in any inherent national weakness. The cause is in their half-and-half position between the economic masters of the country and the black masses. They are not an ordinary middle class with strong personal ties with the upper class and mobility to rise among them and form social ties with them. From that they are cut off completely. And (this is hard for the outsiders to grasp, but it is a commonplace in the West Indies) for centuries they have had it as an unshakeable principle that they are in status, education, morals and manners, separate and distinct from the masses of the people. The role of education in the West Indies has had a powerful influence here. The children of an aristocracy or of a big bourgeoisie take education in their stride. Their status is not derived from it. But where your grandfather or even your father had some uncertain job or was even an agricultural labourer, a good education is a form of social differentiation. It puts you in a different class. Twenty years is too short a time to overcome the colonial structure which they inherit, the still powerful influence of the local whites, still backed by the Colonial Office. The Civil Service open to them fortifies this sentiment. It is not that no progress has been made. Writing in 1932 and analysing the political representatives of the coloured people, I had this to say:

"Despising black men, these intermediates, in the Legislative Council and out of it, are forever climbing up the climbing wave, governed by one dominating motive—acceptance by white society. It would be unseemly to lower the tone of this book by detailing with whom, when and how Colonial Secretaries and Attorneys-General distribute the nod distant, the bow cordial, the shake-hand friendly, or the cut direct as may seem fitting to their exalted highnesses; the transports of joy into which men, rich, powerful and able, are thrown by a few words from the Colonial Secretary's wife or a smile from the Chief Justice's daughter. These are legitimate game, yet suit a lighter

hand and less strenuous atmosphere than this. But political
independence and social aspirations cannot run between
the same shafts; sycophancy soon learns to call itself mod-
eration; and invitations to dinner or visions of a knight-
hood form the strongest barriers to the wishes of the
people.

"All this is and has been common knowledge in Trinidad for many years. The situation shows little signs of
changing. The constitution is calculated to encourage
rather than to suppress the tendency."[1]

That has been overcome. A black man of ability and
influence can make his way. In personal relations, in
strictly personal relations, the political types meet the white
economic masters with a confidence and certainty far removed from the strange quirks of thirty years ago. But
their ancestry (as described above) is bad. They are political *nouveaux-riches*. And all such lack assurance (or are
very rude in unimportant matters). This middle class with
political power minus any economic power are still politically paralysed before their former masters, who are still
masters. The only way of changing the structure of the
economy and setting it on to new paths is by mobilising
the mass against all who will stand in the way. Not one of
them, even the professed Communist Jagan, dares to take
any such step. They tinker with the economy, they wear
themselves out seeking grants, loans and foreign invest-
ments which they encourage by granting fabulous advantages dignified by the name of pioneer status. (It is impossible to conceive any people more unlike the pioneers
who extended the American nation than these investors
of little money with large possibilities.) Here is the hurdle
against which the Federation broke its back. Sitting un-
easily on the fence between these two classes, so changed
now from their former status, the middle classes and the
middle class politicians they produce saw federation as
everything else but a definitive change in the economic

[1] C. L. R. James, *The Life of Captain Cipriani* (Nelson,
Lancashire, England: Coulton, 1932).

life and the social relations which rested upon it. The economy lives for the most part on a sugar quota granted by the British Government. In a society where new political relations are clamped upon old economic relations, the acceptance of the quota system appears to give an impregnable position to the old sugar plantation owners. This reinforces the age-old position of the classes and fortifies the timidity of the middle classes. They therefore are frantic in building more roads, more schools, a hospital; except where, as in Jamaica, it cannot be hidden, they turn a blind eye to the spectres of unemployment and underemployment, in fact do everything to maintain things essentially as they were. It is no wonder, therefore, that they discuss nothing, express no opinions (except to the Americans that they are anti-Communist), keep themselves removed from all the problems of the day, take no steps to see that the population is made aware of the real problems which face it, and indeed show energy and determination only to keep away or discredit any attempts to have the population informed on any of the great problems which are now disturbing mankind. They know very well what they are doing. Any such discussion can upset the precarious balance which they maintain. Any topic which may enlarge the conception of democracy is particularly dangerous because it may affect the attitude of the mass of the population. How deeply ingrained is this sentiment is proved by the fact that nowhere in the islands has the middle class found it necessary to establish a daily paper devoted to the national interest. In fact in Trinidad when it became obvious that this was not only possible but everyone expected it, the political leadership was indifferent when it was not actively hostile. After twenty years nowhere have they felt it necessary to have a daily paper of their own. The obvious reason for that is that they have nothing to say. They want to win the election and touch nothing fundamental.

It is obvious to all observers that this situation cannot continue indefinitely. The populations of the islands are daily growing more restless and dissatisfied. The middle classes point to parliamentary democracy, trade unions, party politics and all the elements of democracy. But these are not things in themselves. They must serve a social purpose and here the middle classes are near the end of their tether. Some of them are preparing for troubles, trouble with the masses. Come what may, they are going to keep them in order. Some are hoping for help from the Americans, from the Organisation of American States.

Without a firm social base, they are not a stable grouping. Some are playing with the idea of dictatorship, a benevolent dictatorship. But different groupings are appearing among them. Those educated abroad are the most reactionary, convinced as they are of their own superiority. The lower middle class locally educated are to a large degree ready for political advances—they are socially very close to the mass. There are also groupings according to age. Those over fifty have grown up with an innate respect for British ideals. They welcome in the new regime positions of status from which they were formerly excluded, but they accommodate themselves easily to authority. But the younger generation has grown up with no respect for any authority whatever; even some from abroad who have gone into good government jobs bring with them from Europe and the New World the scepticism prevailing there of any particular doctrine or social morality. Independence will compel the posing of some definite social discipline. The old order is gone. No new order has appeared. The middle classes have their work cut out for them. Their brief period of merely enjoying new privileges after three hundred years of being excluded is about over.

The West Indian middle classes have a high standard of formal education. They are uneducated and will have to educate themselves in the stern realities of West Indian economic and social life. Independence will place them face to face with the immense messes the imperalists are leaving behind. The economic mess is the greatest mess of all, and the other messes draw sustenance from it. It is not insoluble. Far from it. Economic development on the grand scale is first of all people, and history has endowed us with the potentially most powerful and receptive masses in all the underdeveloped countries. The effects of slavery and colonialism are like a miasma all around choking us. One hundred and fifty years ago, when the Non-conformists told the slave-owners, "You cannot continue to keep human beings in this condition," all the slave-owners could reply was, "You will ruin the economy, and further what can you expect from people like these?" When you try to tell the middle classes of today, "Why not place responsibility for the economy on the people?" their reply is the same as that of the old slave-owners: "You will ruin the economy, and further what can you expect from people like these?" The ordinary people of the West Indies who have borne the burden for centuries are very tired of it. They do not want to substitute new masters for old. They want no masters at all. Unfortunately they do not know much. Under imperialism they had had little opportunity to learn anything. History will take its course, only too often a bloody one.

6.

Prestigious rewards doled out by imperial and local governments are vital in assuring West Indian acceptance of metropolitan standards and patterns of local stratification. Here a Trinidadian casts a bleak eye on his fellow countrymen who continue to preach that British is best and to peddle or accept imperial titles. In several independent West Indian states, local honors now replace imperial ones; whether this promotes the sense of nationhood and local purpose more than it perpetuates the old social structure and standards of prestige remains to be seen.

ADRIAN ESPINET is a Trinidad-born journalist and political activist. He served as the first editor of *Moko*, the official organ of Trinidad's United National Independence Party, and later as editor of the political journal *Tapia*.

Honours and Paquotille
Adrian Espinet

One of the results of the post-war growth of nationalist movements among former colonies all over the world has been a broadening and deepening of our understanding of colonialism.

The lead in this understanding has not always come from nationalist leaders themselves. For one thing, they are more or less forced to spend a great deal of time and energy in simply keeping politically—sometimes even physically—alive; and for another, they tend to form a breed notoriously prone to simple and uncomprehending drives to personal glory—which too often limits their radicalism to a shifting of personnel within the inherited structure of authority.

Hence the existence today of ex-colonies where nationalist movements have petered into the thin trickle of sickly new but essentially colonial concoctions—Pakistan, Jamaica, Nigeria and so on.

Hence too, the supreme importance of those non-political figures—the social scientists, historians, creative writers and artists of every kind—to the new societies striving for independence and identity. For it is these cool observers, standing outside the dusty bullring of personal political ambition, on whom we have more and more to

New World Quarterly, Vol. 2, No. 1, Dead Season, 1965, pp. 19–22. Reprinted with permission of the author and the *New World Quarterly*, University of the West Indies, Jamaica.

depend for giving nationalist movements their true force and direction. They help to identify the real enemy by creating the *consciousness* which is the only real weapon of small-country nationalism, the only means by which such people can free themselves from colonialism and their only claim to independence.

In the post-war wave of ex-colonial nationalism writers and artists have played increasingly more significant roles. It explains why they have tended to mushroom all over the undeveloped world—not least in the West Indies—articulating, defining, pinpointing. The novels of men like R. K. Narayan and Khushwant Singh, the films of Satyajit Ray, have disbanded Stalky & Co., Mowgli, and all the old noisy paraphernalia of Kipling's India, to reveal a new India underneath, teeming, not with trick animals and loutish coolies, but with sensate human people no different, in essentials, from the people the cosy British housewife read and felt about in *Woman and Home*.

The objectives of such art are not narrowly nationalistic, of course. In Japan the spread of brash and brassy Americanism is combatted by the clean and beautiful art-films of directors like Akira Kurosawa, but Kurosawa also happens to be one of the earliest and greatest exponents of the new cinema art, the current revolution against the long, debilitating stranglehold of the Hollywood stereotype.

What people like Kurosawa, Narayan, Satyajit Ray have done, essentially, is to provide the world with new vantage points for gaining insights into the behaviour, not only of their own peoples, but of man in general. They have played a very important part in dispelling some of the webs of colonialism, political or cultural. But it would be a mistake to suppose that they provide the only kind of insights useful to an ex-colonial people in search of a sense of identity. Other useful insights, generally of a very different kind, have for years been provided, for instance, by scoffing and unsympathetic English writers who have managed, time and again in the past, to point accurate fingers at one essential aspect or another of the colonial mentality.

The American "Rochester" and Uncle Tom images—
which are only stereocast projections of the White American's conviction of superiority—have no value as art and
offer no insights. But a book like Ronald Firbank's unin-
hibitedly malicious study of social ambition in Jamaica
(*Prancing Nigger*, 1921) is something altogether different.
Here, indeed, is both art and insight into West Indian
behaviour which, despite the malice, we ought to regard as
valuable. For Trinidad, Miss Honor Tracy has done something quite as brutal, but in a different way, in her recent
novel *A Number of Things*.

And then there was that remark of Trollope's about the
West Indian Negro "burning to be a white man and a
scholar, and puzzling himself with fine words" which drew
such indignant nationalistic fire from Dr. Williams. Why,
for God's sake, when a century or so after that remark was
made, there is still evidence all around us that it contains
some relevant insight into certain intellectual and psychological effects of colonialism?

It is true that Trollope's intention was malign. It is
true that he was talking, not about the limitations of
colonialism, but about the limitations of black men. But
need we be unduly troubled by that? In so far as an artist
is an accurate observer truth will out, no matter what his
own prejudices. What is important to us, therefore, is not
the motives or prejudices behind Trollope's observation,
but the observation itself as a matter of relevant fact. And
the relevant fact here—regardless of what Trollope
thought—was a fact about certain psychological effects of
colonialism supported by African slavery in the West
Indies.

The evidence that Trollope, Firbank, Miss Tracy, and
similar writers have all touched on vital weaknesses in the
West Indian character is scarcely clearer anywhere than it
is in our absurd attitudes to honours and pointless privileges conferred by the British government. One of the
things we have certainly learned in the last twenty years—
if we did not know it before—is the system of petty bribery

by which metropolitan imperialism has managed to maintain fifth columns within the colonial societies, ensuring "stability"—that is, a clash of local interests profitable to the metropolitan ruler. It is those imperial powers which made fullest use of these systems of bribery—of which "education" has been a major factor—that have generally succeeded best in their colonial enterprises.

And it should be obvious that of all the *paquotille* traditionally employed by the British for taming the colonial natives the most intrinsically worthless is that of the Honours award system—an idea that is in itself puerile and public schoolish anyway.

It is true that if lack of actual value were all that could be charged against the system there might actually be arguments in favour of retaining our adherence to it—political arguments, mainly, such as the expediency of humouring the whims of economically useful associates, the undesirability of risking diplomatic offences (in much the same way as we agree to take off our shoes on entering a mosque) and so on.

But there are positive destructive, and peculiarly odious, effects of the system which outweigh such arguments. In Trinidad it causes middle-aged "social workers" with big bosoms and M.B.E.'s to say "sixpence" instead of "twelve cents". It has put me in a terrible personal predicament about how to address my friend's mother—after calling her Mrs. X from childhood—now that her brilliant husband has been knighted.

These may seem trivial, but are they? The fact is that, in essence and intention, the system is one founded upon a concept of social inequality—a Tory idea. Any serious socialist government in England with a real understanding of the practical benefits of egalitarianism would abolish it in that country tomorrow. In Trinidad or Nigeria or Jamaica it is no more nor less than the uninterrupted continuation of the colonial principle—infiltratory, divisive, socially and psychologically corrupting.

In England nowadays nobody takes this system "seriously"—though it is in fact a rather serious matter, like the House of Lords—and in most cases the Honours are cynically reserved for their therapeutic value in treating tired Tory Office officials, passé politicians and powerful Canadian businessmen with inferiority complexes about not being British.

To understand this is further to understand the nature of such awards to "good" West Indians—yes, Sir Uncle Tom. It is true that in places like Trinidad and Jamaica the awards are no longer nowadays made on the recommendation of the British Governor. But the new system, whereby we ourselves administer the handouts, looks rather worse, if anything, for it implies full acceptance of the ascribed role.

But there is an even more socially evil aspect of this affair, and that is where real merit is involved. Why should Mr. Frank Worrell—who everybody agrees is, or has been, a superb cricketer—wish (or for that matter *agree*) to be henceforth known as Sir Frank? The answer is that the title confers a certain formal status and privilege in the society. And it is harmful precisely because it has translated a real achievement into a formal privilege—which is a debasement. Since the formal title is intrinsically irrelevant to merit as a cricketer it can hardly be expected to do anything but detract attention from the true nature of that merit, thereby detracting from the total social value of the achievement. Worrell—who is really a far more important and valuable person—has been sold up to Sir Frank. One only has to listen to the public utterances, in London and Trinidad, of another famous Knight-Cricketer to get a stark illustration of the principle.

It is a maddening—but not surprising—fact that, lashed and flooded as we are by the huge breakers of American culture, the West Indies and the Caribbean in general seem to be receptive only to the worst—the pinball and chewing gum and jukebox—aspects of that culture. Instead of Tom Paine we get only Dr. Kildare. One would suppose that an ex-colonial society might have some of the emotional repugnance for formal ascriptions of privilege that is one of the few redeeming features of the American character.

But it was no doubt too much to expect from a society thick with the sort of people that Trollope and Firbank and Miss Tracy, in their different ways, have described. What we have certainly done consistently is to select the worst of two worlds—British snobbery and American vulgarity.

So what we can expect—any minute now—is that they will make him 'mightier yet!' Hail, Sir Sparrow, and goodbye to our best calypsonian!

7.

A YOUNG JAMAICAN NATIONALIST here ascribes racial inequality in West Indian society to government favoritism
toward expatriate interests and to the failure of blacks to
articulate their own rights. Like Garvey before him, the
anonymous author finds multiracial equality a myth in Jamaica of 1960, where the black four fifths of the population occupied only a handful of high positions. Though
exhorted to advance, blacks in general found few avenues
of advancement open to them and were held back even
from these because they themselves had been brainwashed
to accept failure as their lot. To redress the balance, the
author urges the government to require expatriate firms
and investors to place black West Indians in managerial
positions.

Realism and Race
A Young Jamaican Nationalist

The controversy on race that is currently disturbing not merely the minds and hearts of all thinking people on a world-wide scale but also, and nearer home, the soul of the Jamaican society, has now been raging on the local scene for close on a year. It is directly connected in spirit with the ferment which has gripped Africa and its outcome in the field of practical politics must to some extent run a parallel course with what happens on that great continent. It appears that the time may have arrived when there should be an attempt at an interim assessment of the situation. By tying together the loose ends of thought and expression and relating them to the realities of social, political and economic structure and development, it may be possible to point the way to a solution of the dilemma of race which now besets this island in particular and the West Indies in general.

SOCIAL UNREST AND RAS TAFARI

It may have been quite coincidental that the events which put the spark to the Jamaican powder keg, now somewhat dampened, were connected with the Ras Tafari movement and were almost simultaneous with the coming of inde-

pendence in the Congo. The spirit let loose in both case:
created an unrest, the end of which is not yet in sight
either on the local scene or in the wider field of world
affairs; and in both cases the situation has been abused
for political ends by those opposing forces whose main
object is to foster or perpetuate their own self interest
In Jamaica the myth of social and racial integration has
been pretty nearly exploded and we are being treated to
the spectacle of the myth-makers and myth-users running
around, attempting patching operations with solutions of
weak paste. Where those measures fail, a hammer is sometimes raised threateningly, as it were, to knock some awkward corners back into place.

What emerges from all this is the fact that there is an
alignment of forces on either side, each resolute in its
determinations to repel by arguments, relevant or irrelevant, the contentions of the other side. And as in all con-
troversies which question the structure of a society, one of
the protagonists is in almost complete support of the Establishment. 'There is nothing wrong with it', say the entrenched interests, with the approval of government. The
leading spokesmen for this view represent the most influential groups in industry and politics in the country.
They point with emotion to the development of the country
as an economic and political unit over the past ten years,
though with less assurance than formerly, and ask if we
would threaten or destroy all that has been built up so
laboriously. Of course no one on the other side has so
much as threatened to destroy anything except what they
regard as an iniquitous social and racial structure.

The other side, who have been labelled racialists, say
that there is nothing sacrosanct about an establishment
in which the accepted passport to preferment seems to be
a physical appearance as near to that of the average European as possible; that there must be something vitally
wrong with a society which is disposed to accept a situation where almost every comment and observation on
public matters made by visitors from abroad particularly if

they are from the United Kingdom is considered oracular, while identical comments from a member of the local community without obvious European connections are treated with scant regard. Since this argument has coincided with the stir of social unrest it is easy to hold, as the functionaries of the establishment have contended, that it is the racialists who are stirring up the people.

Some of us may prefer to think that this in common with most demonstrations of social ferment is an organic growth and that it is necessary for those who desire to lead a society first to understand it. In the confusion that has followed the first spasm of discontent, the Government of Jamaica has been alarmed to discover the truth in the elementary axiom of practical politics, that it is necessary in order to retain leadership to go in the same direction as the mass of their followers. Having found itself with only an apathetic following despite its impressive Development Programme, the Government has sniffed the political air and concluded that the Development Programme is not going fast enough, is not benefiting enough people, is not reaching deep enough into the economic needs of the people. The cry goes out 'Everyone will get his share in time'. The solution to all needs therefore, is an economic one.

It is upon this premise that the Jamaican Government now proposes to embark upon a new drive in labour intensive development, to be financed, presumably, by increased rates of taxation. This new tax rise will inevitably be borne by those who in the past have borne most of the tax impositions. This must be regarded as a great pity, since it is the considered opinion of many that the Jamaican Government is wrong in its assessment. Though there is need for continued economic development, there is a graver need, and this merits closer enquiry.

Much of the reasoning which has been used by defenders of the status quo to bolster their case turns on the proposition that it is not to be wondered at that while the majority of the members of other races in the society, with the exception perhaps of East Indians, are fairly well

established economically, the majority of those of Africa
descent are not. The explanation, they say, is simply tha
over ninety per cent of the population are of predomi
nantly African origin. And since in any country the major
ity of the people are poor, it must follow that the majority
in Jamaica who are of African descent should not expec
to have it otherwise. However, a more honest answe
would seek to explain why members of other races do no
appear to be poor in equal proportions. The reasons fo
this do not always reflect on others so much as on those o
African descent, as will be shown later.

Before the troubles of the past year began, it was custom
ary in influential circles to dismiss the Ras Tafari brethre
merely as the lunatic fringe of the Jamaican society. Bu
then, this society has hitherto been singularly lacking i
social conscience, a direct result of the fact that its leader
were previously drawn from an environment totally ou
of sympathy with the deeper aspirations of the broad mass
of the population. They have looked to other societies fo
their models and sought only to impose these models or
to the local social structure. The result to a large exten
was predictable and has had its extreme demonstration i
the total rejection of the values of an alien culture by the
cult of the Ras Tafari. It should not for a single mo
ment be considered odd that the more rational of the
Ras Tafari creeds has the support of many of the more
well educated among the young people of the country.
This merely indicates that they too have rejected the basic
premises of the present social structure, since they contain
nothing which offers them deliverance from their present
status.

AMBITION AND LOW CEILINGS

The pages of history are filled with examples which should
provide a guide to those perplexed by the present situation.
By lifting the lid which previously confined the bleak frus-

tration of the mass of the people the Government's education and other policies have merely created a new awareness of social limitations. Nor are those same social policies geared to promote an appreciation of any cultural values. The result is a chaos in moral discipline, an abnegation of the fundamental loyalties which are needed to hold any society together. There will be very little difference therefore within the general social context in the impulses which inspire wild-cat strikes among the regular employees in industry and the government services, and the vociferous rantings of the inarticulate Ras Tafari: workers organized in trade unions will inevitably express their frustrations in economic terms. The institutional pattern of their organisation leaves them little choice. This may explain why no amount of appeals to economic reason will placate them, since they express not economic, but social disaffection. The result which is being currently witnessed in Jamaica despite the feeble and unconvincing protests of the government spokesmen, is galloping inflation driven on by relentless wage demands. The Ras Tafari are not an economic force and, less well organised for pressure, express their social protest in spasmodic demonstrations of violence.

For a realistic appraisal of the situation some reference should be made to limitations, real or imagined, which induce these exhibitions of frustration. It should always be remembered that, as with individuals so with groups, there is seldom ever an objective assessment of the capacity in the party concerned to play the part or do the job sought. It is therefore a rather pointless and facile argument to declare as some leaders of the establishment have done, that certain executive and managerial jobs are available in industry and commerce, but there is a grave shortage of local people qualified to fill the posts. Obviously the training of managerial and executive staff cannot in any industry or in any country depend alone on the accident of personal ambition. This must be the effect of well laid plans, resulting from conscious policy on the part of both

industry and government. If therefore a particular sta
exists, in which local personnel or people of a particula
pigmentation are not found in certain categories of sta
in industry, commerce or government controlled enterpris
it will be obvious to the most stupid person that it is so as
result of conscious and calculated policy on the part c
those in control. Nor will the motive be far to seek. Con
trary to the suggestion that the staffing of these categories i
the result of the failure of personal capacity and ambitio
in local persons, the fact is that these people do not pursu
ambitions to qualify themselves for such posts becaus
these posts are regarded as closed to them. It would b
manifest folly on the part of native Jamaicans to go t
great expense to train themselves or otherwise develo
capacities when they are likely to be excluded from post
for reasons unconnected with their abilities to do a goo
job. Those who contend that this is not the case in a wid
range of executive, managerial and secretarial posts, clearl
underestimate the intelligence of their audience. Apar
from the Civil Service and its Local Government counter
part there is hardly an avenue of business enterprise whic
does not at this moment apply these exclusions, completel
or with subtle modifications. This is the world which ou
young people freshly out of school after a perfunctor
education have to face. This is the world that the greate
part of modern Jamaica appears clearly to have rejected
It provides their ambitions with the prospect of low ceil
ings in personal achievement, and that they will not have

NEGATIVE ARGUMENT

One of the arguments levelled against the so-called racial
ists seeks to ridicule their proposition that more obviously
coloured persons should be placed in positions of leader
ship in industry and commerce. Of course the origina
proposal ignores the fact that economic and sometime
social organisation is usually served by exclusive enclave

reflecting social prejudice, and that from these limited circles are drawn the persons who are to fill the vacancies as they arise. In social institutions as in commerce and industry there is no such thing as the career open to talent. In most cases each organisation, each firm, each industry knows precisely from which social and racial category it proposes to recruit staff for each particular level of its operations. Presumably, the existence of this state of affairs will not be denied by those who support the establishment since it is they who hold out the awesome if unrealistic prospect to this effect, that claims for equal or proportional representation of all races in business enterprise may lead those business leaders and capitalists who belong to races other than African to take their business enterprise elsewhere. And then what would the poor, unenterprising coloured population do? Those arguing in support of this assertion apparently do not merely admit that such a situation of exclusion as described above exists, but endorse it. And if they do, no more need be said on the point.

However it is important to note the fallacy in their argument. The history of economic development since the Industrial Revolution in England is a record of massive flows of capital over long periods from one country or continent to another for the purpose of development. In most instances these capital flows coincided with periods in which immigration into the developing countries took place on a comparatively large scale. Immigration occurred during the nineteenth and early twentieth centuries principally from Europe into the American continents, Australia and Africa as part of what the history books euphemistically describe as the expansion of Europe.

In those days of rampant European nationalism it was an implicit condition of capital financing that a representative if not preponderant section of the new country should belong to the same national stock as that from which the capital came. There were, of course, exceptions, such as several South American nations whose railways and other engineering industries were often financed and built by the

British. One of the more powerful inducements to th
provision of capital for the development of the Unite
States by British interests, was the fact that during th
nineteenth century the population of the United State
was almost entirely British in descent; that is, excludin
Negroes who have never been allowed more than a mino
role in the economic development of that great country

It is clear then that the proponents of the arguments a
to the inclinations of those capital-owners among the mi
nority races in Jamaica are contemplating these facts out
lined as inexorable truths, and would say that they argue
from the economic facts of life. It is of no significance ap
parently that it makes nonsense of their myth of racia
tolerance and integration existing in the Jamaican an
West Indian society. They ignore, moreover, a new an
important development in the trend and character of in
ternational finance which has taken form since the end of
the Second World War. The pattern of economic devel
opment for example, in India, Pakistan, Ghana and cer
tain South American countries such as Venezuela is clearly
not along the previously established lines. Many new coun
tries today are drawing much of their capital for develop
ment from a pool of international capital. This frees them
from the need to submit to the influence and coercion of
any single nation or power block, or to their representa
tives within their borders. The spirit that inspires this trend
is an open opposition to the devious and reactionary views
of those who hold to the proposition that Jamaicans should
watch their words lest they drive away foreign capital.

Finally, it would be interesting to hear from those who
argue it, just what they suggest is the rational basis for the
proposition that the capital provided by the members of a
particular racial group has to be administered by persons
drawn from that group. This is to all appearances an ir
rational if not altogether anti-social view and operates in
practice in denial of all the best instincts which the leaders
of any country should seek to promote in laying the foun
dations for common loyalties. For it is the establishment

of common loyalties to a national ideal that must supersede all the pretence which has spawned the illusion of our much-touted racial tolerance.

TRADITIONAL VALUES

It may reasonably be asked who are those who would seek to perpetuate a myth when the evidence of its truth and validity is so slight and superficial, and why do they try to do this. To answer this question one should first enquire into the traditions of the society under observation and find a measure for the social values held dear. In a country in which the views of outsiders, visitors and plain tourists are courted and cherished, it can be the source of little wonder that all that is considered necessary is, that these charming folk should be impressed. Any traveller knows that among the first things that strike one about a country visited for the first time, or even infrequently, are the points at which it contrasts with one's native land. And this is more or less what happens when casual visitors from the American, African and European continents comment on the West Indian society. They remark on the degree of racial integration observed, simply because it has achieved a higher level than in most places abroad. In contrast with the southern states of the United States of America, South Africa and indeed all the countries of Africa still subject to European control, the degree of racial tolerance is unusual. There is however no reason why the West Indies should congratulate itself and be smug, merely because by comparison with the very low standards of racial tolerance in European led societies, they are not doing badly. While they were an obviously European controlled society they were in no better case.

The views of many West Indians about their society and their attitudes towards that society are thus still oriented outside of the West Indies. This state of mind effectively puts a brake on any thinking which might promote a more liberal and progressive approach to social policy even among otherwise enlightened political leaders. Unless they can escape from the trammels of this mental condition the society will be restricted to a place dictated by the development of racial tolerance in other countries. From this it becomes apparent that in a society such as exists in the West Indies in which the tradition of uncritical reception of external social values persists, there will be a tendency to absorb good as well as worthless standards without question. Not the slightest attempt will be made to see whether the demands of the new society preclude the adoption of certain values which contain no particular merit or efficacy. To a large extent this is true in respect of the adoption of the entire body of values regarding, and attitudes towards, race by the West Indies. An entire community has hitherto been persuaded by means of all the devices in the power of a ruling racial group that to be born of a dark complexion is to incur exclusion from all that is finest and best in life and to be relegated to a state of perpetual tutelage. This ascendancy is not easily lost nor should it be expected to be abandoned without a struggle. The main difference between the situation today and the former position is that the determination to retain ascendancy has been compromised. It has been relinquished in the political sphere but retained in a more imperceptible form in the social and economic fields. In this form it is likely to hold many people enthralled for several years to come. This will be so, since much of their private and undeclared motivations, designs, and calculations towards fulfilling personal ambitions will have been based upon an assumption of the permanence of the status quo. Within this social context it was inevitable that every child of every race growing into adulthood should have received and applied in his own environment these accepted postulates of preferment.

A NEW APPROACH

This then is the social heritage of the West Indies, the reality of which is still present, and no amount of sweet words or wishful expressions will charm the consciousness of it out of the mind of West Indians. Those leaders of opinion who desire to show goodwill would be well advised to try another approach. The first step towards this should be to promote an identification of true West Indians with their native land. The question to be asked here is, 'Who are West Indians?' There are some persons who may be irritated by an insistence on this. They may argue that there should be local support for a growing tendency away from definitions the purposes of which are to promote a narrow nationalism. It may be said that as a new state it serves the interest of the West Indies to take advantage of this trend and so obtain the benefit of the experience gained in older countries. There are several answers to this line of argument. One of the more important of these is the danger now present of having persons in positions of influence whose real loyalties are outside of the West Indies but who pretend to instruct and advise on public matters and critical decisions. This situation is bound to create, at best, an unhappy ambivalence which cannot be in the interest of the West Indies. Whatever may be said for the contrary view, a country needs leaders, whether on the cricket field or around the conference table, who will use every faculty and skill at their command to promote its interests. And for the attainment of the necessary attitude of mind, identification is indispensable. Once this state is achieved there will be less need for the ambiguous and confusing distinctions between the West Indian and the West Indian-born so much beloved by social columnists. If the strength of a country's nationalism is to be judged by the length of time required to become a national of that country there is very little national-

ism in the West Indies. There is a commonplace that it is
almost impossible for a foreigner to become an Englishman. It takes three or more generations to achieve this
state of acceptance in the case of Europeans. For the
coloured races, on the other hand, it is a total impossibility.
Even in the cosmopolitan United States of America at
least five years must elapse before strangers are accepted.
One becomes accepted as a Trinidadian or a Jamaican
merely by claiming to be one. This gives rise to the acro-
batic feat whereby some persons find it feasible to be, for
example, Englishmen when in England and Jamaicans
when in Jamaica. Such a facility unfortunately is denied
the poor West Indian migrants to Britain. However long
they remain in the United Kingdom and however much
they try to contribute they will always be, as West Indians,
strangers.

As a concession to those who advocate a wider nationalism for the West Indies it might be admitted that this
could be, and often is, turned to the advantage of the community. There should however be one proviso. It should
be far less easy than it is now for a person whose loyalties
belong to another society to attain to a position of influence
in this country. There are individuals who acquire by
merit in every field of endeavour an international prestige.
To this unusual group of persons the West Indies has made
some notable contributions. But as it is one of the conditions precedent to the acquisition of such distinction that
the more blatant social prejudices should be abandoned,
there is little cause for fear that, as in most other instances,
an importation of skills involves an importation of racial
bias. This class of persons should therefore be excluded
from such a proviso.

RULES AND EXCEPTIONS

The development which is now most to be feared is not
merely the importation of skills which involves an importa-

tion of racial bias but an importation of racial bias without the attendant importation of any special or scarce skills. No real attempt has been made to examine whether the imported managerial and executive staff which is currently being used in a high proportion by many firms in industry and commerce possess any particular skills not available among local personnel. It must be concluded that West Indian governments either have no express policy for finding jobs for the well trained citizens of the countries or they deliberately subscribe to the view that where there is no discernible difference in skills, it is preferable to placate owners of capital by allowing them to choose freely whether they will employ foreign or local personnel. Hardly anyone is convinced that most claims to special skills can be justified on enquiry. Certainly no scheme has yet been announced outside of British Guiana and perhaps the Federal Government, whereby West Indians are to be trained for positions currently being filled by Europeans in increasing numbers. Where then do the Jamaican and other West Indian governments propose to place the products of their educational programmes? Planning for useful citizenship, it would appear, is over when the period of schooling comes to an end. After this the young people must be left to flounder around and finally to discover that the doors of opportunity are closed to them. This is amply illustrated by the advice given to a young Jamaican scholar, highly trained in a field of science at one of the leading universities in the United Kingdom. On his recent return to Jamaica he intimated to his mentor, a European in a position of authority, long resident in Jamaica, his desires to enter a particular field of industry. He was advised in all sincerity, and in the light of obvious knowledge, that such aspirations were pointless, since 'there were no opportunities for natives in industry'. Needless to remark, whenever such a suggestion is made public, there will be the usual dissembling protests. There might be, in addition, a clumsy attempt to prove the contrary by making a temporary provision for the placing of the particular person affected. In such a case the party would be well advised to decline the offer. Most exceptions merely serve to emphasize rules.

It is customary in support of assertions that there is little or no racial discrimination practised in commerce and industry to point to persons of rare ability who have achieved eminence in the Civil Service. Obviously this is not meant to be taken as a contribution to serious discussion. It was stated earlier that the Civil Service, in Jamaica at least, is perhaps the only place in which talent receives a fair recognition, and even this body still has pockets of prejudice well established in some technical departments. It is remarkable that after the hackneyed examples within the Civil Service and a few other peculiar exceptions have been named, the list comes to an abrupt end. Is this really good enough; that in a country in which admittedly over ninety per cent of the population is of discernible African descent only about half a dozen persons representing this section can be found in positions of leadership, outside of politics and the Civil Service? Can it honestly be contended that the reason for this is lack of ability? Such an inference has long been discredited.

PUBLIC TOLERANCE AND PRIVATE PREJUDICE

It should not be presumed, because the situation in the West Indies does not assume the proportions of the racial problems of South Africa, Rhodesia, or even the Southern States of the United States of America, that it can be dismissed as trifling. Those who do this stand accused of deliberately missing the point behind the current unrest. There are three distinct levels of the application of social and racial prejudice. The first and most extreme exhibition is that which has the sanction of law and is built into the legal system of the country. This type is well demonstrated in South Africa, where the association of persons of different races, except for certain well prescribed purposes and relationships, is punishable as a crime. This state of affairs was achieved in a less rigid form in certain states in the American South, until quite recently.

The second and less virulent type is currently being applied in varying forms and degrees in the Southern United States of America. It involves a more or less well defined policy of social exclusion. It limits the contact and association of races on the social plane, in public places such as restaurants, beaches, public transport and theatres, and is often not inscribed in any law or regulation, but based on an understanding between the groups involved. Any infringement by a member of the subservient group is likely to be met by a resort to group violence, such as lynching by members of the ruling race. Though the action of the members of the ruling race will be illegal in terms of the state laws, it may often go unpunished because of some alleged technicality.

The third form of discrimination is the most difficult to deal with because it can seldom be identified in each case with precision. It operates on a more personal level than the first two, and cuts across the more obvious class lines. It is nonetheless real and is probably practised and felt by most people who have grown up in a Western society. Certainly it is very active in the West Indies, and many sociologists, West Indian and other, would be startled to hear that what they have accepted as a basic datum of West Indian social structure has been airily wished away by politicians and others, to serve the purposes of a public argument. While this form of discrimination is almost intangible in its operation in most public places, it applies in each individual's choice of social friends, and of course, at present, in each employer's choice of employees. This disposition in turn works itself out in a person's association in public places. Among persons of some pretensions to culture it is all very sophisticated and well understood though never discussed in public, and seldom even in private. Among the mass of the people, their casual speech is interlarded with references, often derogatory, to other people's colour. This latter preoccupation appears to be entirely restrictive, and employed for social control.

APPLICATION AND EFFECT

All free societies make allowances for the disposition on the part of persons of similar racial type to associate for limited purposes to the exclusion of other persons. To a lesser extent freedom of association on the purely social level is also considered the normal and inalienable right of each citizen. The general exercise of this right however must be considered as limited by the peculiar circumstances of each society and the superior demands of the interests of the state. In a society where minority groups or races control preponderant economic or social influence it is possible that such a right may be abused. A minority race with economic power is likely to organise itself to retain the benefits of such power to serve its exclusive interests. The same may be said of its exercise of social influence. Where, on the other hand, a minority race is dispersed in terms of economic organisation and has no monopoly of social influence, its social inclinations, if confined within the bounds of the law, are generally of no particular interest in the eyes of the state.

The interests of the community in a good society appear to require that there should be no one minor racial group in control of vital pockets of economic power. Though individuals from any race may possess or control large capital assets, any system which seeks to ensure the retention of power by a small group, merely in order to exclude others is of doubtful merit. Yet such is the case in many aspects of West Indian life. Individual success depends largely on establishing contact and identity with social and racial groups, rather than on demonstrating ability.

The effect of this on both the holders of economic power

and on the race excluded from positions of influence is to be observed mostly at the level of individual personality. In the case of the ruling racial groups there is an amused contempt, bred from an assurance in the possession of the realities of power. On the other hand there is every indication that as a partial result perhaps of social and racial impositions, the coloured Jamaican of every educational and cultural level despises himself, his ancestry and connections. At times this self-contempt on the part of the coloured Jamaican assumes alarming proportions and an almost pathological character, as demonstrated in private and public actions, particularly regarding persons of his own racial type. It is shown, for instance, in many decisions on the part of legislators involving what appears to be an unreasoning insistence on employing imported Europeans in posts which could well be filled by West Indians either at home or abroad. This would induce the reflection that there must be a deep-felt need on the part of some, to fulfil a secret desire to give orders to Europeans. On a lower level there is the often heard sneering familiarity thrown in public places at any person of colour who appears to have achieved a measure of material success in his chosen field, or displays any of the dignity and self respect which should be common in any society. This is not quite of the same character as the defiant threats which are likely to give Europeans so much cause for alarm, but rather it would seem to indicate that concessions to dignity and respect which would be allowed to Europeans or near Europeans are withheld from persons of colour. Such a disposition is a good illustration of the way in which social attitudes, held in common throughout a wide range of cultural levels, are most clearly demonstrated at the lowest level, uncomplicated by subterfuge and pretension. It reflects, in addition, the urge to control and restrict persons of similar race within the same general cultural category, into which they have been relegated by European opinion. Here again is seen the subtle effect upon one

racial group, engendered by its acceptance of the views
and standards of another concerning itself.

THE ROLE OF GOVERNMENT

It must be presumed that political leaders who now form
Jamaica's Government are sincere in their desire to advance the interests of their people. It is they who led the
struggle for universal adult suffrage. They now stand perplexed and alarmed to find that discontent has followed
their impressive programme undertaken on behalf of the
people. They must now become aware that the saying
'Man shall not live by bread alone' is not merely directory
but more significantly the result of observation of man's
true nature. It is not enough that they have given and are
giving to the majority of the people the shadow of responsibility and a growing relief from the threat of grinding
poverty and want. It is just as necessary that they should
ensure to them in substance the self-respect without which
all the bounties of economic progress will be just a hollow
mockery. To achieve this the government may have to
abandon certain unspoken and long cherished premises.
The government of any country with a tradition of colonial rule, whatever its complexion, is likely to assume that
many rules are unalterable and part of the business of
good government. Some of these will have been learnt by
observing the behaviour of former rulers or are otherwise so engrained in the social organisation as to remain
unquestioned. It is also possible that a way to the solution
of a problem such as the present one may have occurred
to our leaders, only to be dismissed as impracticable. But
they must consider that they themselves may be affected by
inbred inhibitions which will affect their judgment concerning what is possible.

A policy of gradual liberalization of social attitudes must,
to be successful, be instituted or firmly endorsed by the
Jamaican Government. The Government will not be serv-

ing its own best interests if it continues to assume a defensive attitude. It cannot be considered either fair or good politics to group those forces seeking a wider representation of coloured persons in the economic and social life of the country, with dangerous, evil or Communist inspired influences. The issues of race which now divide the country will have to be solved by more realistic and positive policies, not by pretending that there is no problem to be solved.

But first Jamaica's leaders will have to get rid of their self-induced incapacity to read political signals. For instance, contrary to their worst fears and inhibitions, it is not necessary to have a representative who looks and behaves as much as possible like a European in dealing with foreign governments and organizations, whether European or any other. An argument or inference to the contrary is an argument from inferiority. If the fiction of racial tolerance is to become a reality the racial origin of a person chosen for any position in the sphere of industry, commerce or the government services must be a matter of complete indifference. The country's reputation abroad in this respect will then be unassailable. When this state is achieved it will be unnecessary for any leader to tell the people so. They will have observed it.

8.

Black West Indians who believed that advancement was closed to them were merely self-deluded, according to an eminent English-born Jamaican's rebuttal to the previous selection. Admitting the persistence of bias and general assumptions of racial inequality, the author contends that great advances had been made, that most existing frustrations were not specifically racial in character, and that progress was retarded mainly by lack of self-confidence among the masses and by lack of enterprise among their leaders in the labor movement and their mentors in the university. The decade since these two pieces appeared has witnessed graver racial hostilities than either author anticipated, without substantially altering the structure of Jamaican society or providing the ordinary black man with a larger share of goods and resources.

H. P. JACOBS has been a Jamaican for half a century. As an educator and journalist he has made substantial contributions in almost every realm of Jamaican life—the schools, the press, the trade unions, and culture and the arts. He is presently General Secretary of the Farquharson Institute of Public Affairs in Kingston, Jamaica.

Reality and Race: A Reply to 'Realism and Race'
H. P. Jacobs

It is useless to deny that the writer of 'Realism and Race' has presented a reasonable criticism of current attitudes on the part of the conservative elements in Jamaica—what are facetiously called the responsible elements. But he has not, I think, produced a sufficiently objective analysis of the present situation.

It seems to me that he must belong to a younger generation than mine. Those of us who remember the Dreary 'Thirties are inclined, I fear, to be too complacent. We have swept away one barrier to progress after another, and we are apt to watch with contemptuous astonishment a younger generation sitting on the ruins of privilege and prejudice and saying they cannot get anywhere. They for their part have difficulties which we did not feel or foresee. Accordingly, there must be important differences in outlook between us.

I am not attempting to establish an easy compromise: to say that the writer of 'Realism and Race' is sometimes right and sometimes wrong; that he exaggerates here and overstresses there; that if he would water down a phrase or qualify a generalisation, I could reconcile him with what he calls the Establishment. I wish to show that, ob-

West Indian Economist, Vol. 3, No. 10, April 1961, pp. 13–18. Reprinted with permission of the author.

jectively, he is wrong; therefore I ought to explain the circumstances which detract from my own objectivity.

My age has been mentioned. I should add that I am an Englishman. I have never fallen into the easy habit (which the writer of 'Realism and Race' justly finds irritating in the immigrant) of claiming to be a Jamaican: though if Jamaicans claim me as such, I am grateful to them and do not feel at all they do so from worship of everything that is not Jamaican. My first duty is to the people amongst whom I live, however, and if I had not preferred to live amongst Jamaicans I should not be here.

The author of 'Realism and Race' has constructed in his mind's eye a picture of the Jamaican people. I cannot accept the picture. He fails altogether to distinguish the different sections of society. He believes that in some way the *Lumpenproletariat* or depressed masses, the trade unionists or regularly employed persons, and the intelligentsia are all in revolt against the same thing—and that what they are in revolt against is the domination of the white man, as not only the owner of capital, but the director of its use on the spot and the manipulator of political life.

IS THERE A SOLVENT?

Of course he is aware of these different elements and he justly condemns the present Government for believing that the solvent for them, which will make them one people, is economic progress. No forward-looking group in the last century and a half has made such an astonishing assumption. The early missionaries saw Christianity as the bond of society. The great administrators of the Crown colony period saw the solvent as the acceptance by the whole society of the values of liberal West European culture. One of the greatest of them, an atheist or an agnostic, pondering on Jamaican history, was struck by the fact that the missionaries, with creeds which he felt to be erroneous, had done this country more good than anyone else: he concluded that the social values inherent in their Christianity bore a striking resemblance to his own. In fact, the notion that the terms 'Greek', 'Jew', 'Scythian', did not define the relationships of men to God, was much the same, on the social plane, as the concept of secular liberalism that all races of men were entitled to equal rights. The People's National Party saw the national idea as the solvent in 1938—the concept of a common devotion to country. In 1940 it saw the solvent as Socialism—a refusal to accept class as a barrier between men, any more than being Greeks, Jews, Scythians. There was, indeed, in the Dreary 'Thirties a tendency for some people to say that 'The problems of this country are economic and not political'. But I never regarded these gentlemen as very forward-looking.

For a century and a half, therefore, there was a growing feeling that race and colour ought not to separate men, and the vital elements in Jamaican society acted on the assumption that man was a spiritual and intellectual being and not merely a down-graded monkey. It was not until the last decade or so that its leaders coiled prehensile tails about the branches of the Tree of Knowledge, dangled head downwards, and insisted that for the first time the goal was in view.

HUMBUG AND FACT

Now obviously, in the 'twenties and 'thirties there was a good deal of humbug in the talk about racial equality. I say 'obviously' because it was obvious, if you moved around in those days, that there was much lip-service to equality. I can remember a time when the churches provided almost the only career for a black man of intellectual tastes: though a few, even then, crept into the civil service, and a considerable number achieved higher status by becoming elementary school teachers. There was supposed to be an 'educational ladder': you could win a scholarship from an elementary school, and there win a scholarship to Oxford, Cambridge, or London. Since there were only two or three University scholarships available annually, your ultimate chance of passing from a wattle-and-daub cottage to Balliol was in practice somewhat restricted.

But the existence of humbug proves that moral pressures also exist. People talked about the absence of race and colour distinction because the values of liberal West European society had been imposed on the West Indian master-and-slave society. There were few set-backs: the social order came more and more to reject colour. When the colonial system began to toy with discriminatory ideas in the public service, the colonial system itself cracked.

We have now been invited to believe that man lives by bread alone, and that man's life consists in the abundance of things that he hath. Thus cupidity replaces self-devotion as the copy-book virtue of the society. Envy then replaces emulation, and the way is open, in a society where different classes tend to differ in appearance, for men to repudiate the concept of the brotherhood of man as transcending race. We are repudiating it now.

One effect of this, however, is to dispose us to argue that in the economic rat-race the devil can be allowed to take the hindmost. Tens of thousands of people live under intolerable conditions: and I am assured that they do this from sheer reluctance to work, and an absolute preference for dirt, disease, and ignorance.

When some of us, in the Dreary 'Thirties thought that something ought to be done about the condition of Jamaica, it never occurred to us that myriads of our fellow-men could be written off like that. We found a certain disposition in some quarters to take that view: but we argued that even if people preferred to live in slums, it was best to try to change their outlook.

The other day, I looked down from the foothills above Kingston and saw a line of tall trees near the Harbour, clearly visible against the water. I asked what they were, and was told they were the casuarinas that Claude Bell and his relief workers planted on the land that they reclaimed. The trees appeared a worthy memorial to a hardhanded and unsentimental man who thought there was something in the *Lumpenproletariat:* who made surplus labour into a creative force, and helped some of his fellowmen to win back their self-respect.

THE DEPRESSED CLASS

When thousands of people are left to fester in misery, it will sometimes happen that they take refuge in hate. But why should the hate of the submerged tenth in Jamaica be directed against white people? They hardly see any. Many of them, who are in contact with white people, appear to be perfectly well conducted. If hate of the white man is increasing amongst them, it is being artificially stimulated. The particular economic sphere of Jamaican life which the writer of 'Realism and Race' depicts as dominated by white men, is precisely the sphere from which the *Lumpenproletariat* are excluded.

It is worthwhile considering, in this connection, why large sections of the masses have been so interested in the murder of Patrice Lumumba. It seems absurd that they should be interested in that while showing so little interest in Jamaican events affecting their own lives.

But who in Jamaica is interested in the things that affect the lives of the men and women farthest down? To whom do their thoughts, their grievances, their aspirations, really matter? Is what happens to them news to the press? Is it the subject of questions in the House of Representatives? Since they and their lives have no meaning to their own country and their own national leaders, they identify themselves with someone like themselves who is in the news. Lumumba was an African, but a world-figure: by lamenting his death they project themselves into the world of other men. Moreover, since Lumumba was murdered, his fate suggests to them the hopelessness of their own plight: he tried, they argue, to bring his people to freedom and was accordingly killed.

Now since many people (including some who have no prejudices in the matter) think that Lumumba's death was procured by the Belgians, it is evident that if the thoughts of the masses turn, or are directed, towards Lumumba's murder, any tendency to hate Europeans will be accentuated. I think, therefore, that when the writer of 'Realism and Race' says that 'no one has so much as threatened to destroy anything except what they regard as an iniquitous social and racial structure', he must expect that white residents of Jamaica may regard his statement as rather wide of the mark. It can hardly be taken seriously unless our author regards the black man farthest down as nobody.

If in fact the depressed masses are full of rage against Belgians, white men in general, and the few white people they see, but entertain feelings of racial amity towards the more numerous black and coloured persons with whom they have contact, it is one of the most remarkable facts of history. My limited observation does not suggest they have any fraternal affection for the police. I shall be told that they dislike the police because they regard them as agents of the white man. It would be more correct to say that they have begun to dislike white men because they think they are responsible for the police.

I have no prejudice against Garveyism. I have myself spoken on a platform with Marcus Garvey and the impression left on one in the Dreary 'Thirties was that Garvey was trying to put self-respect into the masses, not to set them against the better-off, or white people in particular. I do not believe that any genuine Garveyite preaches race-hatred. But it does seem to me that U.N.I.A. speakers may sometimes miscalculate the effect of what they say. The thinking of the masses is very different from theirs, and an audience can easily stand a Garveyite argument on its head. You may tell a hungry crowd, 'The

Chinese are well off. Why? Because they work and save. You too can be well off if you work and save'. But the crowd may understand this to mean: 'You too could be well off but for the Chinese'.

For the time being, this may be enough to cover the race-hatred of the depressed masses. It is difficult to believe that it is anything specially serious for the white man, unless it is being artfully used or unintentionally fanned. Nor does the white man's dominance (if it really exists) directly affect the condition of the masses in any objective sense. It is precisely because they have slipped out of the white man's world that they have developed singular beliefs and lost all sense of direction.

UNIONISM

It is quite different when we turn to the trade unionists and regularly employed persons. In the case of the urban workers, their economic existence is to an astonishing extent bound up with the white man. Even in the rural areas, where white faces are few, bauxite and large-scale capitalist agriculture are obviously linked with the white man.

The writer of 'Realism and Race' is curiously unsatisfactory on trade unionists. He says with justice that the Government's educational policy has made people more aware of their difficulties in other directions. This he understands to be 'an awareness of social limitations', which I take to mean a realisation that the black man must not aspire to certain positions. People feel 'frustration'.

How does this 'frustration' express itself? Our writer tells us that

workers organised in trade unions will inevitably express their frustrations in economic terms. The institutional pattern of their organisation leaves them little choice. This may explain why no amount of appeals to economic reason will placate them, since they express not economic but social disaffection. The result which is being currently witnessed in Jamaica, despite the feeble and unconvincing protests of the government spokesmen, is galloping inflation driven on by relentless wage demands.

Apart from the fact that injudicious credit is the cause of the inflation rather than the wage-demands, which are in fact linked to some extent with inflationary increases in cost of living, this may be accepted. The workers are not expressing, fundamentally, an economic discontent, although cost of living is an excuse for wage demands or an exacerbation of the social discontent which is their real cause.

However, we have still to ask how the worker comes to develop the 'frustration' which causes the social discontent. Granted, for the sake of argument, that the young black mechanic is broken in spirit because he realises that he can never rise, as in Britain or the United States, to be Works Manager or Managing Director, the question is, how does he know that?

Remember, the writer of 'Realism and Race' emphasises that there is a 'myth' to the effect that social and racial integration has been effected. In other words, propaganda tells the young black mechanic that he can become Managing Director. But the propaganda does not deceive him. Why in the world does it not? If press and radio, politicians and leaders of commerce and industry, surround the worker with an atmosphere of 'sweet-mout'' in which there is free talk of racial equality, why then does not the young man accept with docility the idea that racial equality exists, even if it doesn't? 'Realism and Race' does indeed appear to offer an explanation, that the myth is dissolving. But that does not help. It is only another way of putting my question. Why should the myth be dissolving?

The difficulty is a formidable one. The inherent improbability of the proposition cannot be urged: it is not inherently improbable that racial equality exists. In any event, inherent improbability is no obstacle to belief in our trade union circles. No proposition is more inherently improbable than:

1. Two rival trade unions are good for building up working-class solidarity;
2. Working-class movements need middle-class leaders.

Yet most unionists accept these propositions.

Of course propaganda may be counteracted by repeated blows of reality. Perhaps, then, that is the explanation. But how can the younger workers have met with repeated disillusionments? Let us assume that Jones employs 100 persons, that 20 of them are young, and that of the 20 one is white or can 'pass for white'. Jones promises to send one of his younger people abroad for training—and it is the one white employee who is selected. Such things have happened. But how often can they happen in the experience of any individual black worker in his first years as an employee?

Just think of the statistics. According to the 1943 Census, there were less than 14,000 whites in Jamaica twenty years ago. The number of whites above the age of 16 competing with young black workers for working-class jobs is therefore insignificant: the ratio of one in 100 which I have suggested in my example is impossibly high. The writer of 'Realism and Race' will admit, and even claim, that working-class white children have more prospect of entering non-manual occupations than others. The number of cases of young white workers at any given time competing for non-clerical posts must be insignificant, and if I know personally of three or four cases over the last twenty years, it is probably more than anyone else does.

The older workers, manifestly, might become disillusioned. A man born in 1900, who had seen the opportunities for the black worker steadily expanding might today look back with bitter disappointments on his working life as it closes. At this point and that point he had received some modest advancement: but when the 'fifties brought

a big demand for reliable workers, he found that his employers preferred to give the training opportunities to
younger men. But such disillusionment is not militant colour feeling.

It is of course possible that the practice of importing
persons of the foreman type as instructors may in some
cases have led the workers to believe that the 'foreign'
firm for which they work does not intend to promote
them. However, in some cases the opposite impression
has been created, and excellent relations have existed between Jamaicans of all colours and the instructors.

THE TRADITION

The trouble with our author is that, somewhat like most
sociologists, he looks at society as it is rather than at society
as it has developed. The moment we look at society since
1900 as a whole, we begin to see where he has gone
wrong. In the first place, the belief that the black man cannot rise is traditional amongst black men; in the second
place the tradition is not specifically anti-white. The black
man, according to tradition, was at the base of the social
pyramid, and the white man at the apex. In between, press-
ing more immediately and with greater weight (from
their numbers) on the base, were the people of mixed
blood.

Let us elaborate this a little further. The tradition began in real facts: it is commonly assumed that it goes back
to slavery, though there seems an extraordinary lack of
positive evidence that it existed between Emancipation and,
say, the epoch of the Crimean War and the Indian Mutiny.
As the facts diminished, the tradition would weaken,
though probably not proportionately. Manifestly, an influx of foreign capital would be accomplished by a process
of re-colonisation—more white people would enter the
country. This would be attended by a certain danger of

reviving the tradition: but on the whole it seems as if the danger ought to be greatly reduced by two factors:

1. The influx of capital has coincided with self-government, and therefore with a presumable alertness, everywhere, to the possibility of new policies of discrimination;
2. The mere widening of the scope of economic activity inevitably brings with it a widening of opportunity.

Of course this would not mean that the people without education, acquired skills, and settled habits of industry would be better off. The work done by Mr. W. F. Maunder, of the U.C.W.I. some years ago, showed that there was a definite relationship, for example, between education and the chance of steady employment. The new 'industrialisation' creates more steady jobs and leaves fewer opportunities for the odd-job man.

WHO IS WORSE OFF?

We are now in a better position to grasp the significance of racialism amongst the *Lumpenproletariat*. Their condition has deteriorated; their numbers have increased; their opportunities to get a few days' work, leading perhaps to steady employment, are diminished; the world of well-lit streets, bright shops, imposing offices and factories, is full of alien and unintelligible things; society is uneasy if they even stand and stare at the new wonders; and therefore, the force of the tradition is intensified. They are more than ever convinced that there is no real place for the black man in society except by the intervention of God through an act of deliverance (the exodus to Africa) or an apocalyptic overturning of society. When they inveigh against society, the white man is the convenient symbol of the oppressor. This does not mean that the new movements are especially anti-white. I find many people who think so. Probably my friends who so believe are also convinced, that as the hostile and oppressive society is symbolised by the Ras Tafarians as 'Babylon', therefore the Ras Tafari movement really aims at overthrowing the empire of Nebuchadnezzar.

The movement amongst the depressed masses is therefore at this stage intelligible, but the same cannot be said for the unrest among unionists. The writer of 'Realism and Race' tends to compare the two, but while he says that they are both non-rational, he does not commit himself to suggesting that they are the same, except that they are both reactions of somewhat the same kind to the grim reality (as he thinks) of white domination. However, it is interesting to note that his theory appears to be supported by the fact that some regularly employed persons identify themselves with the Ras Tafarians as a 'protest' against society.

Gabbidon is a case in point. That young man was not an idle or useless person: he threw up a job to identify himself with the course of action that brought him to the gallows. The natural career of Gabbidon would have been in the trade union movement, not in a band of gunmen. He possessed certain qualities of self-devotion and consistency which ought to have been valuable in a union. Gabbidon went to disaster, not because the white men prevented him from becoming a foreman, but because middle-class union leadership prevented him from being an active unionist of the Western type.

In fact, the unrest in the unions is a revolt against the unions just as much as against the employer class, and in so far as it is against the employer class it is not specially anti-white.

While the depressed classes reject Western Christianity, the regularly employed workers show a traditional preference for dissident forms of Western Christianity. The depressed masses look at Western technology from the outside, while the regularly employed workers are usually familiarised with it in some degree and show an increasing interest in it. Except in some rural areas, unionists cannot be regarded as anti-Western. Indeed, their unrest is largely due to the non-Western character of their unions.

The unrest amongst the depressed masses shows that the politicians have failed to do what we set out to do in the late 'thirties: to build a well-planned, well-balanced society in which employment opportunities would expand evenly and a progressive agricultural policy would slow down (though it could not reverse) the flow of the rural population to the towns.

The unrest amongst the unionised workers shows that the politicians and the unionists have failed in the alternative design which took shape after 1944—a design never put into words, and probably never clearly formulated in the minds of its promoters. This was the creation of a new oligarchy, in which the propertied classes would run the country in alliance with a group of politicians supported by a renegade unionism. The oligarchs would be the business bosses, the political bosses, and the union bosses. The unions would provide the politicians with the support which would force the business community to co-operate with them, and with a mass of organised votes: in return, the unionists would have wages far in excess of those of non-unionised workers, and of the earnings of independent artisans and small farmers. This alternative to social justice is evidently no longer available.

The writer of 'Realism and Race' evidently thinks that some at least of the ill-effects of the 'social limitations' on the workers' advancement could have been counteracted by 'social policies geared to promote an appreciation of . . . cultural values', and sees that since such an appreciation has not been developed, wider education only means 'an abnegation of the fundamental loyalties which are needed to hold any society together'. This, of course, is true, but that brings us to the third stage—a consideration of the place of the intelligentsia and its character as a race-conscious body.

THE INTELLIGENTSIA

I have spent far more time on the position of the unionists than the few lines in 'Realism and Race' would appear
to justify, yet I have not dealt with the question whether it
is a fact that the black man is regarded with prejudice by
the white man in the factory, or in agriculture. But just
as we could not finally discover the nature of the movements amongst the depressed classes until we had reviewed
the state of mind amongst the unionised workers, so, I
think, we cannot fully understand the position amongst
the unionised workers until we have had a look at the
intelligentsia.

Oddly, our author does not mention the intelligentsia
as such. He does not hesitate to refer by name to 'the Ras
Tafari movement' or to 'workers organised in trade unions'.
But the word *intelligentsia* is never mentioned, although
rather more than half the article seems to be taken up
with the special difficulties of the black intelligentsia.

Our author concentrates a good deal on the idea that
the capital employed in industry need not, because it is
supplied by a particular group, be 'administered' by that
group. In short, the top management of foreign concerns
operating here ought to be Jamaican. But I suspect that
he does not mean that leading Ras Tafarians should be
put in charge of them, nor even that union delegates
should be placed in these posts. No—he is thinking of the
intelligentsia, the people of education, who can formulate
meaningful generalisations about life.

Naturally, Union Delegate Jones, who would perhaps,
from his natural ability, become a member of the intelligentsia, may be discouraged from doing so by the
thought that he will never be Managing Director of the
company by which he is employed. But the great trade
unionists and politicians of the British labour movement
in the first half of the present century knew that they could

never fill the top posts. That did not prevent them from educating themselves: they have filled Cabinet posts with distinction. What holds Union Delegate Jones down is the fact that the labour movement neither offers him a career nor stresses cultural values. He may well say, 'Hasn't the Managing Director always been a white man?' This will comfort him by making him feel a martyr: but I am afraid he may also at times murmur about the 'brown-skin man' always likely to pop into a senior post before him.

Essentially, the problem in respect of top management, as envisaged in 'Realism and Race', is one which worries the existing intelligentsia as their problem. Naturally, the writer does not so limit his own views. He considers the future of the black intelligentsia which wider secondary education will presumably create; and I agree with him in condemning a policy of extending secondary education without having an effective system of vocational guidance. I may add at this point that I also fully agree with him that Government and employers (at any rate large employers) should have a set policy of ensuring that there is not even the appearance of discrimination. I know that there are dangers in such a policy; a man may receive opportunities, by a sort of inverted discrimination because he is black. But my own experience confirms the view expressed in 'Realism and Race' that there are subtle forms of discrimination which will defeat the best intentions of management unless management is conscious that its social duty of non-discrimination must be embodied in rigid policy.

What I do not see is how any policy can be framed in terms which will ensure that the proportion of black employees in senior posts will bear any real relationship to the proportion of black people in the population. No one can seriously argue that we should legalise the obsolete distinctions of caste based on birth, so that every citizen would be registered according to parentage. It seems equally impracticable, in view of the Mendelian theory, to classify by actual color and have two full brothers belonging to different groups. All that the talk about 'black peo-

ple' not being employed by certain firms really means, is
that if you are of African and Scots descent but look like
a West African, particular firms will not employ you, although they will employ your sister who happens to be
lighter skinned. This is unfair, and absurd: but it is not
racial discrimination.

The difficulty would solve itself if the black Jamaican,
conscious of the difficulties he was likely to encounter,
decided to prove he was better than everybody else and
qualified himself more highly. 'Realism and Race', however, assures us that this is just what black members of
the intelligentsia will not do:

> The fact is that these people do not pursue ambitions
> to qualify themselves for such posts because these posts
> are regarded as closed to them.

REJECTING THE WEST

It is this closing of certain avenues which the writer of
'Realism and Race' insists is the source of all Jamaican
malaise:

> This is the world that the greater part of modern Ja-
> maica appears clearly to have rejected. It provides their
> ambitions with the prospect of low ceilings in personal
> achievements, and that they will not have.

But the difficulty is one which affects only certain categories of the existing intelligentsia: if little Johnny is slack-
ing at school, it is certainly not because he feels that even
if he learns trigonometry he will never be manager of
Alumina Jamaica. The existing intelligentsia reject the inescapable conditions of success, and they are out of the
running. Western civilisation offers glittering material
prizes: the condition is to have certain qualities. If you
value money and position you will persist, in the teeth

of discouragement, in qualifying yourself to get them. Columbus did not sit down at Cadiz and wait for an Arawak to come for him in a canoe: it was the Arawaks who (mistakenly) waited for Columbus. If the black intelligentsia of Jamaica want the glittering prizes of Western civilisation, they must conform to the rules of the competition. You cannot hope to accept the mastery of material things inherent in Western civilisation without modifying your non-Western traditions, which in Jamaica belong to the master-and-slave society which lasted for two centuries in the Caribbean as a type of organisation in flat opposition to the growing freedom of Western society.

An American Jew has expressed something of this idea of paying the price in a poem on Moses and the Burning Bush:

> *Bond for bond, old Moses!*
> *If I set them free,*
> *Free from Pharaoh, Moses,*
> *They are bound to me.*

Our intelligentsia, of all shades of colour, cannot expect perfect hotel service with the flesh-pots of Egypt all the way to the Promised Land. Our intelligentsia, be they politicians or unionists, officials or businessmen, teachers or artists, journalists or doctors, scientists or lawyers, clergymen or poets, must stop standing on the side-lines and blaming other people for the things which the intelligentsia has done all wrong. It may be tempting for sections of it to dream of power and its concomitants dropping into their laps. It may even seem to some of them that the best thing that can happen is an explosion as a result of which the owners of vast stocks of capital will welcome the intelligentsia as their allies against the raging masses, make them the stewards of their wealth, equip them with arms to control the masses, and leave Jamaica in their capable hands. It is an idle dream.

It is argued that all the talk of racialism scaring away

investors is pointless, because capital may be loaned by international agencies. But what agency would lend us, say, the capital to develop oil wells here, if we insisted that there must be no immigration? All capital inflow implies some degree of immigration, though I agree that the capital and the personnel might come from different countries. The author of 'Realism and Race' tends to overlook the fact that it really makes no difference where the aliens come from—the black intelligentsia, if it feels inferior, will go on feeling inferior: as it already shrinks from the black intelligentsia of the other West Indian islands.

It is interesting to note that these tendencies are purely modern. The reactions of the Jamaican black man to Emancipation and to the opportunities offered by the banana industry indicated very considerable enterprise and resolution—so did the way in which the black lower middle class moved to secure secondary education for their children in the present century. The phenomena which in 'Realism and Race' seem to be regarded as normal reactions appear to me pure decadence. The intelligentsia is failing all along the line, and the black intelligentsia is in particular unable to rally the masses around it, or to give any clear lead in art, politics, or business. The failure of unionism seems to me the key to the current non-Western development of our society: and for this the intelligentsia must take the blame.

9.

Many radicals among the West Indian black masses, aware
of the disparity between nominal independence and their
own continued dispossession, express increasing animus
against favored elements of the population. In this anonymous tirade, published in a Guyanese black-power journal,
the economic and social realities of Jamaican society are
laid painfully bare. Blacks are told that both self-respect
and survival require them to take over the economic institutions and resources of the country from whites, browns,
Chinese, Syrians, and Jews who are said to control them.

The Favored Minorities*
Anonymous

1. Who are the J.L.P. and the P.N.P. helping?
Ans. The white, chinese and mulatto capitalists.

2. Who finance the J.L.P. and P.N.P.?
Ans. The white, chinese and mulatto capitalists.

3. In 1938 the black man owned more of the land area of Jamaica than in 1970. Who owns the land now?
Ans. The whites, chinese and the mulattoes.

4. Who is a comrade?
Ans. An African who has been taught to hate a labourite.
   Who is a labourite?
Ans. An African who has been taught to hate a comrade.

5. Who gave guns to the black youths in Western Kingston and elsewhere to kill their brothers?
Ans. The comrades and labourites.

6. After 26 years of rule by the P.N.P. and the J.L.P. what answer can we give to the following questions:
   Do we have a good educational system?
   Do we have roads free of potholes?
   Do we have adequate water supplies throughout Jamaica?
   Do we have a telephone system that works?

* [Editors' title]
"Songs of the Soil—A Third Party Now!" *Liberation*, Vol. 1, No. 3, November, 1970, pp. 5–6. Published by Panafrican Secretariat, Georgetown, Guyana.

How often do we have to use candles when our lights
   fail?

Are our streets free from garbage?

7. The bus service of the corporate area was taken away
from a Black company by the J.L.P. and P.N.P. in 1948.
Do we have a good service now?

8. Are black people sleeping on the sidewalks and fighting dogs for garbage in 1970 after 26 years of J.L.P. and
P.N.P. rule?

Ans.   They certainly are.

9. Has there ever been a free and fair election since 1944?

*Ans.   There has ever been a bogus voting, gerrymand-
ering of constituencies, stealing of ballot boxes and whole-
sale violence during that time.*

How many persons eligible to vote in Jamaica today
have a vote?

*Ans.   Many thousands of eligible voters are without a
vote.*

10. Are we getting our fair share from our major resource
Bauxite?

11. Has the crime rate increased since 1944?

Are Jamaicans safer in their beds at night in 1970 than
they were in 1944?

12. Who feeds us? Who clothes us? Who houses us?

*Ans.   The chinese feed us; the Syrians clothes us; the Jews
houses us.*

Do we have real power in Jamaica?

*Ans.   A people who can not feed, clothe and house them-
selves are truly powerless.*

II TUTELAGE, EXPRESSION, AND CREATIVITY

10.

The nature and implications of a British colonial educational system tied to metropolitan standards were cogently stated in 1945 by the present Prime Minister of Trinidad and Tobago. He depicted a system of schooling irrelevant to most local needs, with minimal primary instruction for the masses and a classical education unrelated to Caribbean realities for a small elite minority. Notwithstanding political independence, this system substantially endures throughout the Commonwealth Caribbean as well as in the French and Dutch West Indies.

DR. ERIC WILLIAMS is the epitome of the West Indian scholar-politician. After winning a prestigious Trinidad Government Scholarship, he took a First at Oxford and went on to teach at Howard University in Washington, D.C. At the time he wrote the book from which this selection was taken, he was the senior West Indian staff member of the Caribbean Commission, an intermetropolitan coordinating body. In 1956 Williams resigned from the Caribbean Commission to found and lead to victory the People's National Movement, which has dominated Trinidad for the past decade and a half. The author of numerous books on the West Indies, including *Capitalism and Slavery, British Historians and the West Indies, The History of the People of Trinidad and Tobago,* and *From Columbus to Castro,* Dr. Williams was until 1971 also Pro-Chancellor of the University of the West Indies.

Education in the British West Indies
Eric Williams

The features of the educational system of the British West Indies are only an exemplification of what is taking place in the colonial areas generally. As can be expected, the system is designed to serve the needs of the British West Indian intelligentsia. We shall consider it in detail under the five heads discussed in a previous chapter [of Williams' book].

(1) RURAL EDUCATION

The elementary curriculum has a predominantly literary and mathematical bias, and makes little, if any, distinction between urban and rural needs.

In criticising the existing curriculum, an Education Commission which visited the eastern group of the British Caribbean colonies in 1931 gave prominence to the views of employers. *"What they rightly demand in addition to the training of will and character is the acquisition of a sound and practical knowledge of simple English, that is, ability to understand and use the language for the ordinary purposes of industrial or commercial life, a working knowledge of the simple rules of arithmetic and mensuration,*

Education in the British West Indies, New York University Place Book Shop, 1968, pp. 29–41. Reprinted with permission of the author.

and a sharpening of general intelligence. For vocational training of a specialized kind they see no need . . . And for practically all other 'subjects' they have a profound mistrust as tending to superficiality and diverting attention to unessential, and sometimes unsuitable, objects."[1]

Agricultural education, by this touchstone, becomes an unessential, perhaps even an unsuitable, object. Educational authorities argue that agricultural techniques are no simple matter and are beyond the mental and physical capabilities of children of primary school age. They are reluctant to diminish "the not very large amount of 'cultural' education at present afforded" in primary schools, and aver that any such tendency would be strenuously opposed by public opinion.[2] School gardens, however, are a regular feature of British West Indian schools; in Trinidad, all rural schools are required to have a garden, and agricultural teaching is compulsory.

(2) THE CURRICULUM

The curriculum of the British West Indian school is not adapted to the needs of the community.

The Education Commission of 1931 reported as follows: "The real weakness of the primary school at present consists not in its neglect of garden or handwork, but in its failure to concentrate on essentials, and in the lack of adaptation of curriculum to the qualifications and capability of the staff. The time-table of the average school is littered with subjects or fragments of subjects that bear no relation to the lives of the pupils or the qualifications and ability

[1] *Report of a Commission Appointed to Consider Problems of Secondary and Primary Education in Trinidad, Barbados, Leeward Islands and Windward Islands, 1931–32,* Colonial No. 79 (London: His Majesty's Stationery Office, 1933), p. 59. (Referred to hereafter as Colonial No. 79.)

[2] *West India Royal Commission Report,* Cmd. 6607 (London: H.M.S.O., 1945), p. 113. (Referred to hereafter as Cmd. 6607.)

of the teachers." The teaching of history and geography included topics such as the Wars of the Roses and the capes of Europe and was based upon text books unsuitable for British West Indian children.[3] According to another report seven years later, education is in the main external to the real life of the people, affecting it from without rather than from within; the best education provided tends to direct the attention and ambitions of its pupils away from their true interests and those of their country.[4] The West India Royal Commission of 1938 called for "an end of the illogical and wasteful system which permits the education of a community predominantly engaged in agriculture to be based upon a literary curriculum fitting pupils only for white collar careers in which opportunities are comparatively limited . . . Curricula are on the whole ill-adapted to the needs of the large mass of the population and adhere far too closely to models which have become out of date in the British practice from which they have been blindly copied."[5]

In line with this criticism, a completely revised curriculum was introduced into the schools of Jamaica in 1939. The aim of the curriculum is "to vitalise the teaching and to make it a real thing, closely connected with the life of the Jamaican child." Caribbean Readers are in general use in the British West Indies; so also are West Indian Geographies and West Indian Histories. There are also plans in Jamaica to produce short monographs on Jamaican history and natural history.[6]

In the British West Indies a secondary school is a school

[3] Colonial No. 79, pp. 59–60.

[4] *Education in the Windward and Leeward Islands*, Report of the Education Commissioners, 1938, Colonial No. 164 (London: H.M.S.O., 1939), pp. 3, 5. (Referred to hereafter as Colonial No. 164.)

[5] Cmd. 6607, pp. 92, 120.

[6] West India Royal Commission, 1938–39, *Statement of Action Taken on the Recommendations*, Cmd. 6656 (London: H.M.S.O., 1945), p. 15.

giving a particular sort of post-primary education. The emphasis is predominantly literary, as is to be expected where the needs of the intelligentsia are paramount. As on the primary level, the curriculum is divorced from the real needs of the community and the activity and experience of the pupils, with the qualification that it might be said that the secondary school virtually makes a fetish of this unreality. Secondary education is so severely restricted to the few that the English education that it provides becomes a sign of class distinction. It is so little an integral part of any national system of education, so little articulated with the primary system, that the director of education in some British West Indian colonies is responsible only for primary education.

The curriculum of the secondary school in the British West Indies is largely academic. The British West Indies have yet to appreciate the significance of the fact that it is possible to develop types of post-primary education of high educational value on non-academic lines with a certain bearing, more or less direct, on industry, commerce and agriculture. The secondary school in the British West Indies serves two main functions—it provides training for those students who proceed to universities abroad, normally in the United Kingdom and Canada, and it trains those less fortunate students who have to be content with government service at home.

The following subjects, decreed by law for the schools of Jamaica, comprise the curriculum of the British West Indian secondary school: Latin, English, history, literature, modern languages, mathematics, arithmetic, chemistry, physics, biology, geography, hygiene or other sciences, the principles of agriculture, bookkeeping, shorthand, art, music, domestic science, manual occupations. Thus has Jamaica, in the words of a recent report, been "presented . . . with an *à la carte* menu, from which the schools select those subjects to which they are limited by the competence of their teachers or by the availability of equipment. From an educational point of view the nutritive value of the subjects is not considered."[7]

This curriculum calls for more extended examination. The most obvious omission is the reference to anything West Indian. West Indian history, geography, economics, community organisation and problems—West Indian culture, in a word—find no place. In the second place, the phrase "modern languages" is meaningless. The average secondary school in the British West Indies teaches French only; Spanish, the language of the neighbouring Caribbean republics, of Puerto Rico, of Central and South America, receives serious recognition—and even that inadequate—only in Trinidad. This is merely a reflection of the Englishman's notorious ignorance of foreign languages and the traditional predominance of French in the English secondary school. In the third place, the Jamaican curriculum listed above contains Latin only, and not Greek. This is true of many secondary schools in the whole area. It is almost as if, torn between the mounting criticism of dead languages and the weight of tradition, the schools decided that half a loaf of classics was better than no classics at all or a whole loaf of classics.

Furthermore, music, art and handwork, mentioned in the law, do not achieve the prominence in secondary schools in Jamaica or in the British West Indies that they do in the schools of England, while the law makes no mention of physical training and organised games. An official report in Barbados pleads, in extenuation, that "this narrowing of the general curriculum . . . more than compensates for any disadvantages incurred by school children working in less favourable climatic conditions."[8] If the

[7] Report of the Committee Appointed to Enquire into the System of Secondary Education in Jamaica (Kingston, Jamaica: Government Printer, 1943), p. 11. (Referred to hereafter as the Kandel Report.)

[8] The Provision for Secondary Education in Barbados, Memorandum by the Director of Education (Bridgetown, Barbados: Dept. of Education, 1945), p. 8.

British West Indian climate did not exist, it would have been necessary to invent it.

The artificiality of the British West Indian secondary school is due to a large extent to the British colonial practice of taking the external examinations of Oxford and Cambridge. These examinations are set by examiners in England, and their content determines automatically the curricula of the British West Indian schools. In the words of a recent official report in Barbados, "the whole focus of teaching . . . appears to be directed towards the benefit of the comparatively few children who are capable of reaching the standards prescribed by these Examinations."[9] Another report adds that more than half the pupils leave school having failed either to take or to pass these examinations.[10]

These external examinations reflect the interests, environment and knowledge of the examiners. On one occasion British West Indian students were asked to write a composition on "a day in winter." The English examinations require a knowledge of Roman history rather than West Indian history, of the British monarchy rather than the crown colony system, of empire geography rather than West Indian geography. Furthermore, English examiners do not and cannot have a competent knowledge of West Indian conditions. British West Indian teachers, therefore, are not encouraged to study their environment, nor is there any incentive to provide text books with materials suited to the West Indian environment. This is an illustration, to quote the Education Commissioners for the Leeward and Windward Islands, "of the strain imposed when European formal requirements (as distinct from European education

[9] *The Evaluation of Education in Barbados, A First Experiment,* Memorandum by the Director of Education (Bridgetown, Barbados: Dept. of Education, 1945), p. 12.

[10] *The Provision for Secondary Education in Barbados,* p. 5.

ideals) are brought to bear on the situation in the islands."[11]

The system of secondary education in Jamaica has recently been investigated by an insular committee headed by Professor I. L. Kandel of Teachers College, Columbia University, one of the most distinguished of modern educators. The committee's condemnation of Jamaica is a condemnation of the British West Indies. The report states: "Nowhere is there to be found any definition of the aims and objectives of education except in terms of certain subjects to be studied in order to pass certain examinations. Education is conceived of as a tree of knowledge which boys and girls are to climb from the lower to the higher branches. The adolescent, to use another figure, is looked upon as a vessel into which knowledge is to be poured in doses varying with the requirements of external examinations . . . A secondary education which is organized to serve the purposes of an external system of examinations is likely to stress the acquisition, often the unintelligently memorized acquisition, of certain subjects."[12]

The secondary school system, as we have said, performs the double function of preparing students for universities abroad and the civil service at home. The former function revolves around the island scholarships provided by the local governments on the basis of an external examination, generally the Oxford and Cambridge Higher Certificate. Where only one scholarship is provided, students in the different fields compete against one another—classics, mathematics, science. But classics are popularly regarded in the British West Indies as more suited to cramming and more dependent on text books and the teacher's ability than science. The classical student is, therefore, considered to have the advantage. Thus a student, for the sake solely of the scholarship—which means affluence and prestige—, begins to specialise in classics from the age of fifteen for a scholarship examination which he hopes to win at nineteen.

[11] Colonial No. 164, p. 12.
[12] *Kandel Report*, pp. 11, 15.

Then he leaves the British West Indies and goes to England to begin science and study medicine. Or, if he is unsuccessful, he joins the local civil service with much Latin, perhaps some Greek, and no science.

The second function of the secondary school system—the preparation of candidates for the local civil service—involves a lower examination, the Cambridge School Certificate. In Professor Kandel's words, these certificates appear to be ready-made and heaven-sent instruments which relieve appointing agencies of the task of devising their own appropriate vocational tests.[13] Many a student in the British West Indies, to get as many credits as possible in this coveted examination, has been forced to study, on his own, subjects for which no provision is made in the curriculum—for example, hygiene. That the British West Indian student who dislikes green vegetables, who lives in a community where milk needs to be boiled before consumption, who is surrounded by people riddled with hookworm, malaria and tuberculosis—that such a student should have to study hygiene in his spare time, and then from a text book written for another environment and solely for credit in an examination, is tragic. It has been said that secondary education should be able to justify aid by the genuine and many-sided development of its pupils (not the pursuit of examination successes), their ready absorption into adult occupations, their cooperation in the improvement of production and the exchange of goods and services, and their contribution as specially favoured persons to local life. By these criteria, British West Indian secondary education, as at present organised, deserves no aid whatsoever.

(3) VOCATIONAL EDUCATION

The third feature of the British West Indian educational system is that it lacks diversification. This is only another

[13] *Ibid.,* p. 17.

way of saying that it does not serve the needs of the masses.

In Barbados, less than 7 per cent of the junior and senior girls in the elementary schools receive practical instruction in housecraft, and two-thirds are taught needlework.[14] The new Jamaican curriculum includes instruction in hygiene, domestic science, manual and agricultural training for all schools. Trinidad has established twelve woodwork and sixteen domestic science centres; instruction in hygiene is taught in all schools, and mothercraft is taught to senior girls. Instruction in commercial subjects and dressmaking is provided by the Board of Industrial Training, while voluntary agencies provide limited instruction in homemaking and cookery. In the rest of the colonies, vocational instruction is given "where possible."[15] How encrusted with tradition is the educational system of the British West Indies is suggested by the success of an entirely new school in British Guiana, the Carnegie Trade School for Girls. With a capacity of 100, there is an enrollment of 131 and a long waiting list.[16]

The British West Indian intelligentsia, as we have seen, equate post-primary education with academic subjects. Vocational training in post-primary schools has, therefore, had little place. The British West Indian secondary school ignores the chief source of employment and livelihood in the Caribbean, agriculture. Where agriculture figures in the curriculum, this is no more than a paper concession to modern sentiment. Thus in the grammar school in Dominica a course in agriculture is offered as an optional al-

[14] *A Policy for Education,* Memorandum by the Director of Education (Bridgetown, Barbados: Dept. of Education, 1945), pp. 24–25.

[15] S. A. Hammond, "Education in the British West Indies," *Journal of Negro Education,* Vol. 15, No. 3 (Summer, 1946), p. 441.

[16] *Memoranda on Educational Adviser to the Comptroller for Development and Welfare in the West Indies* (Georgetown, British Guiana: Government Printer, 1942), British Guiana Legislative Council Paper No. 11, p. 55.

ternative to Latin in the two highest forms. The Education Commission of 1931 recommended that, side by side with the classical secondary school, there should be established a number of modern schools, with an agricultural and industrial bias for boys, and emphasis on domestic science for girls.[17] Proposals for the establishment of four such schools in Trinidad are at present under consideration.[18] Only in one colony, Jamaica, has agricultural training beyond the primary stage made great headway. The Hope Agricultural School occupies such a position in the British West Indian educational system that the West India Royal Commission recommended that, with its transfer to an appropriate rural site, it should serve as a centre for agricultural training below the university level for the entire area.

The legislation of Jamaica makes provision, as indicated above, for commercial courses and manual occupations in the secondary school. But the secondary school curriculum, in fact, does not include commercial subjects, except for some perfunctory attention to bookkeeping and typewriting. Here, again, the explanation is to be found in the environment. British West Indian commerce and banking are in the hands of big business from Europe and Canada. The big firms import their staff in the higher brackets, and on the lower levels deliberately select employees on the basis not of merit but skin colour and social status. Racial discrimination is rampant in private employment, banks,[19] airlines, shipping companies, importing and exporting firms, even department stores. Only the very fairest-skinned British West Indian has a chance of getting any employment for which he is qualified. Short of legislation on the Latin American pattern compelling foreign

[17] Colonial No. 79, pp. 86–87, 89.

[18] *Educational Policy and Development Programme,* Trinidad and Tobago Council Paper No. 27 of 1946, p. 7.

[19] This is true of the British West Indies and Puerto Rico only. It is not true of the French Islands, Curaçao, and the Virgin Islands of the United States.

business to employ a certain percentage of British West Indians at all levels, discrimination of this kind will continue to determine the content of secondary education.

(4) THE TRAINING OF TEACHERS

When the education is so divorced from the needs of the community, it is very difficult to give the correct training to teachers. This represents another outstanding feature of the educational system of the British West Indies.

According to the Education Commission, there is no realisation of the fact that "the vital and organic connexion between the school and the community should be constantly before the minds of those who are responsible for the training and supervision of primary school teachers."[20] Community problems and West Indian culture form no part of the training course. Whilst attention is given to agriculture and domestic science, there is, in some areas, undue emphasis on formal mathematics, the chronological development of world history, and academic literature for which there is little justification in terms of the children with whom the future teachers will come in contact. Much of the training is of an academic nature more suited to the secondary school, and is given, not infrequently, by teachers who have not the necessary equipment for imparting it.

The Education Commission estimated that not more than 16 per cent of the teachers had any sort of training.[21] Many teachers in British West Indian elementary schools are pupil teachers, young students who are theoretically doing practice teaching under supervision, but who in fact do the work and have the responsibilities of regular teachers. There were in the British West Indies (excluding the Bahamas) in 1937 a total of 5,811 teachers and 1,506

[20] Colonial No. 79, p. 65.
[21] Ibid., p. 67.

pupil teachers,[22] or one pupil teacher to every four teachers. In Trinidad, pupil teachers represented in 1943 nearly one-third of the teaching staff, while over 15 per cent of the pupils who completed the highest grade in the elementary school in 1938 became pupil teachers. In the Windward Islands there are more pupil teachers than regular teachers.[23] In British Guiana, one-sixth of the teachers in 1941 were pupil teachers, while nearly two-fifths were uncertificated.[24] Pupil teachers are used because they are cheap. The West India Royal Commission of 1938 condemned the system root and branch.[25] The Comptroller for Development and Welfare in the West Indies has, however, pointed out that the cost of abolishing the pupil teacher system would be excessive, and that, instead, it should be expanded and made into a sound working instrument and a means of continued education to the young people engaged in it.[26]

It has been readily assumed up to the present time that the mere study of an honours course at Oxford, Cambridge or London, or private study for the external examinations of London University, equipped the successful bachelor of arts for teaching on the secondary level. Ability to teach has been equated with ability to learn. Here, again, the British West Indies are behind the times. In the absence of a British West Indian University, there could have been no local institution capable of training secondary school teachers. But the responsible authorities made little

[22] Cmd. 6607, p. 97.

[23] *Ibid.*

[24] *Report of the Director of Education for the Year 1941, Annual Statistics* (Georgetown, British Guiana: Government Printer, 1942), p. 5.

[25] Cmd. 6607, pp. 99, 123.

[26] *The Cost of Education* ("Development and Welfare in the West Indies," Bulletin No. 15; Bridgetown, Barbados: Advocate Co., 1945), p. 4. See also Hammond, *op. cit.*, p. 447. My own comments on Mr. Hammond's position are to be found in "Education in Dependent Territories in America," *Journal of Negro History*, Vol. 15, No. 3 (Summer, 1946), p. 549.

effort to demand of any British West Indian student educated abroad the professional preparation provided by a
diploma in education over and above the bachelor's degree.

(5) ILLITERACY, SCHOOL ENROLLMENT AND ATTENDANCE

The inadequacies of the British West Indian educational
system must now be statistically demonstrated. In the absence of reliable census figures for all territories except
Jamaica,[27] Jamaica will be taken as representative.

Illiteracy is not only an educational problem, it is also
a racial problem. Of every 100 illiterate persons, 86 are
Negro, 9 mulatto, 4 East Indian. Of the total Negro population 28 out of every 100 are illiterate; of the mulattoes
14 out of every 100; of the East Indians 49 out of 100;
of "British Isles races" 1 out of 100; of European races
8 out of 100.[28]

The responsibility of the schools for this state of affairs
is even more direct. In the age bracket 7 to 9, 41 out of
every 100 children are illiterate. One-fifth of the children
aged 7 to 14 years are not enrolled in school. In the case of
children seven years of age, 44 out of every 100 are not in
school; in the case of those of fourteen, 35 out of every
100 are not in school. With respect to the population that is
in school, the number of Negroes and East Indians who
reach the upper level of the elementary school is less than
the average for the entire island.[29]

The situation in Jamaica is typical of the situation in the
British West Indies generally. Statistics for 1944–45 gave

[27] A comprehensive census was taken in the other British
West Indian territories in 1946, but the returns have not yet
been published, except for a few preliminary bulletins.

[28] *Census of Jamaica,* 1943 (Kingston: Government Printer,
1945), p. 108, Table 54.

[29] *Ibid.,* p. 125, Table 69; p. 132, Table 72; p. 133, Table
73; pp. 109 and 113, Table 57.

an enrollment in the primary schools of 57 per cent of the
children between five and fourteen, and an attendance for
all sessions of 56 per cent of enrollment, or 33 per cent
of the population of the island's school age, five to fourteen.[30]

There are two explanations of this situation. The first is
that education is not compulsory, except on paper, attendance is not enforced, and there are insufficient schools.
The second lies in the poverty of parents, who are forced
to send children to work at an early age or to keep them
away from school on washing days. Child labour is, in
fact, one of the fundamental causes of juvenile illiteracy
and absenteeism from school. The Education Commission
considered the evils and extent of child labour in the West
Indies exaggerated, but recommended the lowering of the
school age from 14 to 12.[31] Educate only the bright
children, advised a planter in Trinidad in 1926; for the
others leave them in the fields: "of what use would education be to them if they had it?"[32] The Jamaica census
shows that from every point of view, whether it be that of
literacy, attendance, or the duration of study, the figures
for females are higher than those for males. The boys are
working in the fields.

Today there are in all secondary schools in the British
West Indies approximately 12,000 students. In Jamaica,
according to the recent census, only 2 out of every 100
persons have had a secondary education. The separate
figures for the various racial groups are as follows: Negroes, less than 1 in 100; East Indians, 1 in 100; mulattoes,
7 in 100; European races, 29 in 100; "British Isles races,"
53 in 100. Furthermore, where only one Negro or East
Indian out of three reaches the upper level of secondary

30 *Education Statistics*, Central Bureau of Statistics (Kingston, Jamaica, 1946), Bulletin No. 4, Table 3.
31 Colonial No. 79, pp. 51, 54.
32 *Report of Select Committee of the Legislative Council on
Restriction of Hours of Labour* (Trinidad, 1926), pp. 30–31.

education, the proportion is two out of three for the British Isles races.[33] Secondary education in the West Indies is thus British not only in curriculum and in orientation but also in enrollment.

This situation is due partly to the high illiteracy rate and the low level of primary education among the Negroes, mulattoes and East Indians. But a more important factor is the fact that secondary education is not free. Fees average about $48 (£10) per annum over the British West Indian area, and in many cases are higher. In addition, there are more expensive and numerous text books, while the prestige conferred by a secondary education in the West Indies demands a higher standard of clothing. In Jamaica, in 1944, fees amounted to nearly three times the government grant;[34] in one of Jamaica's most famous secondary schools fees were doubled between 1934 and 1944.

Scholarships are invariably provided in secondary schools, but there is no stipulation that they must be awarded to pupils from the elementary schools. In Barbados, where official circles consider fees remarkably low, only one-eighth of the boys and one thirty-third of the girls enrolled are receiving a free education.[35] The British West Indian tendency to regard parental income as synonymous with scholastic ability received a rude shock when certain tests, academic in nature, were given to a selected number of boys and girls between ten and twelve years of age in the elementary and secondary schools of Barbados. The tests revealed that 114 boys and 75 girls in the elementary schools would have been likely to derive more benefit from secondary education than 69 of the 210 boys and 58 of the 171 girls actually receiving it. The report, however, was content with the mild conclusion, that the results undoubtedly called only for a wider provision of

[33] *Census of Jamaica*, p. 108, Table 54.
[34] *Education Statistics* (Jamaica), Table 6.
[35] *The Provision for Secondary Education in Barbados*, p. 7.

scholarships and for a more careful entrance examination for fee-paying pupils.[36]

Educational statistics and reports do not record the pathetic efforts made by parents to afford the high fees and so provide the secondary education that is the avenue to white-collar jobs. Rather, one would have to consult the records of people's cooperative banks and local moneylenders. In 1935 Barbados had 1,182 pupils enrolled in secondary schools; by October, 1945 the enrollment had increased to 2,505.[37] The enrollment in the secondary school for boys in Grenada doubled between 1941 and 1945.[38] In Trinidad existing schools have had to be enlarged and new schools built. Official policy, however, espouses the principle of "selective" secondary education. One of the most recent reports reads: if a small country "wishes to raise the quality of its secondary education and to keep it at a high level, it is bound to limit the number of teachers and hence the number of pupils . . . To have a good home (though not necessarily parents who are well off) is . . . an important factor in the ability of a pupil to profit by education."[39] Barbados carries the snobbery of secondary education to the extreme. Secondary schools are divided into Grade A schools and Grade B schools. The fees in Grade A schools are approximately double the fees in Grade B schools.[40]

*   *   *   *

It has been objected that the general criticisms of the content of education in the British West Indies have, until comparatively recent times, been true of the systems of education in England, Europe and the United States, and that the failure to provide an education fully suited to the needs of British West Indian society is also characteristic

[36] *The Evaluation of Education in Barbados,* pp. 26–27.
[37] *The Provision for Secondary Education in Barbados,* p. 3.
[38] *The Development of Secondary Education in Grenada* (Barbados, 1946), p. 1.
[39] *Ibid.,* pp. 1–2.
[40] *The Provision for Secondary Education in Barbados,* p. 6.

of Great Britain. Therefore, runs the argument, the divorce of British West Indian education from the realities of British West Indian life, and its predominantly literary content, cannot be ascribed to the colonial status of the area. The objection is not wholly accurate, and the conclusion is wholly invalid. Although drastic criticisms have been made in Britain, yet the system, with all its defects, was a system evolved by the British and, therefore, related to the economic and social conditions in that country. When such a system was transplanted to the British West Indies, it had most of the disadvantages and very few of the virtues. What had been an evil in Britain became a catastrophe in the British West Indies. To say that the European system was transferred to the British West Indies is, in fact, to say all that is necessary.

Another argument sometimes adduced is that the politically independent countries in the Caribbean do not enjoy higher educational standards than the British West Indies. One has to consider here, however, the conditions in the British West Indies as they are, and the possibility of correcting them. To say that in Jamaica today, in 1946, with the level of education of the people, their aspirations, their desire for self-government and self-development, to say that education should not be put into the hands of the people, because Cuba or Haiti or the Dominican Republic, which have been independent for generations, does not enjoy a higher level of education than the people of Jamaica, is to open the road to the most reactionary arguments and to deny progress altogether. When one criticises the British West Indian system, it is not for the sake of apportioning historical praise or blame. It is a question rather of seeking the roots of evils in order to correct them. There are many points that can be raised in this type of comparison between the British West Indies and Haiti—or, for that matter, Mexico. They will not help the British West Indian people advance one inch in the solution of their problems.

*   *   *   *

In addition to these general features, the educational system of the British West Indies has certain characteristics which need special treatment.

The British West Indian community is a religious community, and all proposals for educational reform have to take note of the fact that large numbers of schools are church owned. The educational system, however, must safeguard the superior right of the community as a whole to control the general trend of education. This does not in any way mean that the religious sentiments of the people should not be scrupulously respected. This is not a question of religion but an elementary democratic right.

St. Lucia has 47 primary schools; all are church owned. There are 287 primary schools in Trinidad; 244 are denominational. In the eastern group of the British West Indies, 70 per cent of the pupils are in denominational schools. Of 668 primary schools in Jamaica, 464 are denominational; of 186 in British Guiana, all but 9 are denominational.[41] These schools are subsidised by the governments with respect to salaries, buildings, books and equipment. In return the governments have some voice in appointments and dismissals, curricula, management, and inspection. In the view of the West India Royal Commission of 1938, this "financial sanction against gross inefficiency . . . does not render impossible the existence of many schools where the standard of accommodation and teaching leaves much to be desired." The Commission encountered much criticism, especially among the teachers, "That schools are housed in buildings primarily adapted for religious exercises . . . , that the denominational managers paid undue attention in matters of appointment to such educationally irrelevant considerations as the applicants' religious affiliations and their willingness to undertake church duties at the week-ends or during the week."[42] In addition, denominational rivalry, the possible subjection

41 Cmd. 6607, pp. 93, 116; *Report of Director of Education for the Year 1941*, British Guiana, p. 3.
42 Cmd. 6607, pp. 93–94.

of parents to threats of eternal damnation for sending their children to any but a school of their own faith, and the religious prejudices against co-education, have resulted in the injudicious multiplication of several weak, inefficient schools where the public interest demands consolidation.

*   *   *   *

One of the most promising developments in recent years in the British West Indies is the increase of voluntary activities for informal education outside of the classroom. This deserves all the more emphasis in that it is a spontaneous development of the British West Indian people themselves.

The first aspect of this movement is the 4-H Clubs, borrowed from the United States. The movement started in Jamaica in 1940 and has since spread slowly to the other territories. It has now received official support, and a Director of 4-H Clubs has been appointed to guide and further the work in the British West Indies. The main educational objectives of these clubs, which deal with young rural people of primary school age and up to eighteen, may be stated briefly as follows: the development of desirable ideals, technical instruction, "learning by doing," the fostering of scientific attitudes, training in cooperative action, the development of habits of healthful living, the encouragement of improved practices. The scope of the clubs is the farm and the home, and the emphasis is on purposive activity, self-help, and character-building. For girls stress is placed on the home, nutrition, and dressmaking; for boys on handicrafts, agriculture and animal husbandry.

For young people over eighteen, pioneer clubs have been developed in Jamaica, leading up to the cooperative movement. In the latter the emphasis is placed not on consumers' cooperatives or on marketing, but rather on increasing productive efficiency. As one example of the concentration on the realities of local life may be mentioned a cooperative housebuilding plan initiated by Jamaica Welfare, Limited, calling for use of local materials. The plan embraces six months of preliminary study in the use of tools and simple building techniques. The same organisation has, in its adult education programme, organized a mass education project in nutrition.

The organisation of Jamaica Welfare, Limited, a few years ago is a landmark in contemporary British West Indian development. Of this organisation Professor T. S. Simey, until lately Social Welfare Adviser to the Comptroller of Development and Welfare, has written as follows: "The main object in view was to try to lessen the unfortunate tendency of the people of Jamaica to depend on Government or other outside agencies to overcome difficulties . . . Emphasis was therefore laid from the first on the people and their own efforts . . . The chief strength of Jamaica Welfare Limited lies in the remarkable inventiveness which has been displayed in attempting to solve the social and economic problems of the colony . . . The most encouraging feature of the organisation is the fact that all the Directors except the one most recently appointed are Jamaicans . . . Jamaica Welfare Limited affords convincing proof of the vitality of the people of Jamaica, and of the fact that both the common people and their leaders are capable of finding solutions for their difficulties if they are provided with the bare essentials to make this a practical possibility."[43] The Comptroller for Development and Welfare added his own tribute: "The fact that so much has been learnt in so short a time, that the organisation is a spontaneous growth and that it is the result of the initiative, the understanding, and skill of Jamaican people, affords a large measure of hope for the future of the West Indies."[44]

[43] T. S. Simey, *Social Welfare Organization in Jamaica,* October 25, 1941, pp. 5, 7.

[44] Sir Frank Stockdale, *Development and Welfare in the West Indies, 1940–42,* Colonial No. 184 (London: H.M.S.O., 1943), p. 53.

11.

The effects of the type of schooling described in the previous selection are graphically portrayed for a Jamaican rural community by a Jamaican sociologist-turned-statesman. As the author shows, the expectations of parents themselves help to maintain the traditional educational system, including such elements as rote learning, corporal punishment, and a curriculum rigidly tied to standards long outdated in the metropolis.

EDWARD SEAGA, of Jamaican-Syrian ancestry, took a Bachelor of Arts degree in social science at Harvard University. At the time he made this study, he was associated with the Institute of Social and Economic Research, University College of the West Indies, Jamaica. Seaga's concern with Jamaican life and welfare was given more practical expression after he entered Jamaican politics, won a resounding electoral victory in an urban slum district, and became a leader in the then-ruling Jamaica Labour Party and a member of the Cabinet, most recently as Minister of Finance and Development.

Parent-Teacher Relationships in a Jamaican Village
Edward P. G. Seaga

INTRODUCTION

The material on parent-teacher relationships on which this paper is based was gathered in the process of a study on "Psycho-social Aspects of Development in the Child" carried out by the writer during a residential survey in a Jamaican village. The survey extended from March to October, 1953.

This village, or 'district' as it is locally termed, is located in the foothills which border a sugar plantation less than 30 miles from Kingston, the capital of the island. The village will be denoted hereafter by the pseudonym "Rural Ridge".

Houses are situated along the gravel road which winds from the plantation up into the hills, as well as along the four foot-paths that branch from this road at right angles. In most cases, neighbouring homes are less than fifty yards apart. The 327 inhabitants share the 84 houses of this community. Homes are constructed from concrete, cut-stone, boards, coconut branches, twigs. The last mentioned type of building is often daubed with clay. In exactly 50 per

Social and Economic Studies, Vol. 4, No. 3, September 1955, pp. 289–302. Reprinted with permission of the author and the Institute of Social and Economic Research, University of the West Indies.

cent of the households in which there was a co-habiting couple in residence, concubinage was found to be present. Twenty-two per cent of the residents over 15 years of age are unable to read or write.

The primary occupation of the residents is agricultural cultivation on small holdings, supplemented by field labour on the sugar cane estate during the crop season. There are also a few craftsmen, such as carpenters, sawyers, and dressmakers, as well as three grocers.

Trucks provide transportation between Kingston and Rural Ridge twice weekly. Two residents possess radios and two others subscribe to the island's daily newspaper. No magazines are available. Two nearby townships, however, provide such facilities as dry goods and drug stores, cinemas, postal service, railroad and bus service, dental and medical clinics, a hospital, and so on.

The three religious groups in Rural Ridge are Baptist (Nominal), Shilo Apostolic Church of God, and Zion Revival. The last named group keep a Balmyard which practises faith healing.

School is held in the Baptist Church but the Jamaican Government is responsible to the extent of 50 per cent for building and furniture expenses and for the full salaries of the teachers. The building is of concrete construction measuring 48 x 28 feet. It contains no subdivision into rooms.

Of the five teachers of this school, two are classed as A1, two as A3, and one is a probationer.[1] The school is classified as Grade C, which means that its triennial range of attendance is 80–150 students, with an average attendance of 136. Enrolment totals 222 students, of which approximately 25 per cent are residents of Rural Ridge, the others coming from neighbouring villages.

[1] A1: completed three years of training college or equivalent.

A3: completed one year of training college or equivalent.

Probationer: one who has not yet completed one year of training college or equivalent but performs teaching duties.

Classes are held from 9 a.m. to 4 p.m. from Monday to Thursday, and until midday on Fridays. Most of the teachers also hold private classes for examination candidates from 4–6 p.m. The school prepares candidates for the Jamaica Local Examinations which are held annually. These examinations are offered on basic, intermediary, and advanced levels. Papers are prepared by the Department of Education.

This article will discuss only the relationships between parents of Rural Ridge and teachers of the public elementary school, which excludes, therefore, the teacher of the private infant school of the village, as well as the parents of neighbouring villages whose children attend the former school.

The question of parent-teacher relationships must also involve the wider issue of parental attitudes towards the educational system, in which the teachers are merely tutors. The necessity of an education is generally endorsed in Rural Ridge, but with certain qualifications. Firstly, it is not considered necessary for every child to receive full scholastic training. The selection of those who are to receive full training involves a consideration of the child's mental capabilities and the particular occupation for which he is training. Those who complete the programme, that is, pass the third (advanced) Jamaica Local Examination, are expected to seek further training in the professions of teaching, nursing, or postal clerkship. These three are considered the most socially acceptable and financially successful of all the occupations generally available to the children of the village. Others who are not successful in reaching this point will seek training in, or the facilities necessary for practising shopkeeping, crafts, farming, higglering, domestic work, or unskilled field labour. Secondly, apart from the occupational opportunities offered, the standard of one's education is instrumental in defining class status. The prestige of education in this community is second only to the prestige of wealth. Consequently, in Rural

Ridge, education is primarily endorsed as an acceptable means for occupational training and upward social mobility.

In contrast to this general endorsement, however, there are a number of specific criticisms of various aspects of the educational system as well as of its teachers.

The curriculum of the school is a target for some minor criticisms. Hence, although the subjects of the curriculum are generally endorsed as instructive and useful, the inclusion of relaxation periods such as playtimes, holidays, or vacations, is often criticized unless they are on a most limited scale. This criticism is always in a semi-serious manner, however, and cannot be regarded as one of more than minor consequence. The following extract from the writer's note-book illustrates the point:

> Teacher gave five weeks instead of the customary month for midsummer holidays. The result was that a number of parents remarked to me, conversationally: "Ah don' know why teacher give dem so much holiday; better dem stay at school and learn something; all dem do now is romp and tear up dem clothes". Some even complained directly to the teacher, but not in an offensive manner.

In comparison, criticisms of the school syllabus are more extensive. The foremost complaint is a dissatisfaction with the reading texts used in this school. These texts, *Caribbean Readers,* replaced the older *West Indian Readers* to some extent, which themselves replaced the *Royal Crown* series. With each new series there has been a greater concentration on material from West Indian culture in order to present more familiar topics to the young readers; the criticism is that the material on West Indian culture included in these texts devotes substantial space to the exploits of "Anancy" (Spider King in folk-lore of the Ashanti people), "Brer Mongoose", etc. The role of these tales in local custom limits their use to festive occasions, formal or informal, or utilizes them as bed-time stories. The lighthearted character they inevitably acquire through these associations, convinces the villagers that they are unsuitable for the scholastic atmosphere. As one woman said: "Is only black people tek dem kind of story serious and is why we so idiot."

Again, both "Anancy" and "Mongoose" are figures immortalized for their cunning, which more often than not was of a dishonest nature. Hence, the moral of the stories is considered improper for the child. It is said: "It only teach dem to lie and t'ief."

Finally, these stories are one of the last reminders of the African past of the people—a past which is termed 'bungo', that is, uncivilized and regressive. Among friends then, or the family, the stories can be revived despite their associations, in the same way that other personal embarrassments might be discussed freely on these occasions. But it is not expected that they should be revealed publicly, just as private embarrassments must be excluded from public hearings.

Quoting from the note-book again:

> Miss E. is reputed to be the most belligerent and outspoken woman in the district. On the first instance that I met her she told me that Government had no interest in educating the black people. They wanted to keep them stupid so that they could trick them. That is why they won't provide anything better than Anancy stories for them to read.

> Miss P. was commenting that her son, aged thirteen years, was in fourth class and could hardly sign his name. The boy is actually one of the dullest in the school. One of the reasons for this is the fact that—"dem children nowadays learning stupidness. Look what dem give dem to read—Anancy stories!"

These criticisms, unfortunately, are generalized to a condemnation of the entire text of the *Caribbean* series, rather than restricted to the folk-lore sections. Similarly, certain criticisms are made of the recent inclusion of 'digging' songs and calypsos in the music syllabus. The former songs are used only at a 'digging sport', which is co-operative effort by friends to prepare one man's field for planting. In return, he provides a feast and a plentiful supply of rum during the labour, and the songs, which are sung in rhythm to co-ordinated digging strokes, provide an atmosphere of impulsive merriment. Calypsos, on the other hand, are associated only with the dance hall, and although the specific songs included in the repertoire are carefully chosen, it is difficult to avoid lyrics that will not in some way offend the puritanical mind by reference to sexual or other natural impulses.

In Rural Ridge there is no definite opinion on the question of whether foreign or local material should be emphasized in the studies. It is felt that both are necessary, as long as the studies of local culture avoid culturally and morally regressive material. On the other hand, there are certain items which have been excluded from the modern syllabus that Rural Ridgers feel should be reinstituted. Parents speak with pride of their own school days when clean finger nails, tidiness, honesty, 'manners', etc. were emphasized.

C, aged twenty-four, was talking to me when her eleven-year old brother came in from school for lunch. He passed behind me un-noticed but did not greet me. She immediately reprimanded him by saying: "What kind of teacher yu have dat him can't teach yu to say how-de-do."

A woman from another district, on hearing that her son had been caught stealing pencils from the teacher's cupboard, remarked, "What kind of school dat where teacher allow de pickney dem to steal?"

It is felt that the supposed moral deficiency of the present generation is due to the absence of this kind of instruction in the syllabus.

But although these opinions are extensive it would be inaccurate to state that they are intensively rooted. They attain the degree of an overt manifestation of prejudice only in a small minority. Apart from this, they exist only as passive criticisms which are not voiced unless specifically activated by enquiry or an occasional event which acts as a trigger.

Turning from the syllabus and curriculum to the methods and responsibilities of teaching, there are more serious criticisms which limit the endorsement of educational policy, and the degree of confidence in the teachers. The most prevalent of these criticisms is the opinion that sufficient discipline is not enforced in school. Discipline refers almost exclusively to corporal punishment as this is recognized by parents and teachers as the only effective means of punishment, whether used directly or implied by threats. Further, by corporal discipline parents refer specifically to 'flogging'. Other varieties exist, such as forcing the child to kneel or stand for a long period of time, but these are considered ineffective and seldom used. A short bamboo cane, a leather belt, or a switch, are the popular instruments used in floggings (or whippings), and an offender usually receives from one to a dozen hits on the palms, buttocks, or shoulders.

Parents readily offer gruesome stories of their own school days when corporal discipline was both extensive and intensive. The teacher would 'stretch out' a student and apply the strap severely, usually until welts and bruises were raised on the skin.

Although corporal punishment is still extensively practised in this school, teachers do not use the bruising violence of the past, both for fear of parental retaliation, and because present-day educational policy is far less sympathetic to corporal punishment. The severity of the old parental attitude to flogging is reflected in the motto: "Lick dem teacher, only save de eye"; but today, floggings are condoned by parents only if no bruises or disabling pains result. The smallest welt or physical disability raises the treatment from the category of punishment to 'ill-treatment', and brings a storm of parental protests that often ends in physical violence and/or judicial action.

Mrs. B., an upper-middle class[2] woman, related to me the case of her eight-year old grand-daughter whom one of the teachers forced to kneel on the ground until she learned to add certain numbers. Periodically, while kneeling, the child was 'flogged' lightly on the hands with a switch as she failed to produce the right answers on being questioned. She cried, but the teacher was determined that she should stay in that position until the correct answers were given. Most of the pain was a result of kneeling on a knee swollen by wasp stings received the day before. Whether the teacher was aware of these stings or not she did not know, but the fact that the child experienced pain for some hours after the incident convinced her that she was 'ill-treated'. She planned to go to the school the next morning or send the child's mother to "tear the teacher apart, for she is only a young gal, and not even a big somebody must handle my child dat way". She further quoted that her money helped to build the school, not the teacher's. On this occasion, she did not fulfil her threats, but on a previous occasion involving her young daughter she assaulted the teacher with insults and accusations covering all facets of the unfortunate teacher's character.

Because of parental objections, therefore, the teachers are afraid to apply severe punishments, while, paradoxically, parents complain that "teacher don' flog dem hard enough".

M.'s father came to see the head teacher on one of his infrequent visits to Rural Ridge. He requested the teacher to "give de boy more floggings for 'im too rude and don' interested enough in school work". M. stays with his grandmother since his father is a non-resident.

[2] See pp. 183–84 for a discussion of class status.

Generally, the teachers regard the need for extensive discipline in school as a result of the fact that parents tend to neglect discipline at home, with the threat to the child: "Wait till you go to school. Ah going mek teacher stretch you out and tear yu skin". The writer overheard this threat, *verbatim,* on several occasions.

Actually, not all children are judged capable of 'taking learning'. There are two categories, according to the popular belief, for "some have a quick head, and some of dem head slow". Those who are categorised as 'slow' are not expected to learn much, and consequently it is not expected that the teacher will flog them seriously except in matters of deportment, for, as a middle-aged woman who raised a dozen children told the writer "Flogging don't help if de brain slow".

On the other hand, those who have a 'quick brain' are expected to progress rapidly providing "teacher pay attention to dem and keep flogging dem to make dem learn". Hence, if a child in this category fails to fulfil expectations, it is not so much a fault of the child as it is a reflection on the teacher's ability.

Another teaching technique which is popular with parents is the chorus method. Here, the teacher instructs the pupils to repeat the lesson in a loud chorus. The popularity of this method with parents is based on the fact that the chorus can be heard in the home or field as far as two miles away. Not only is this vocal feat impressive to them but it brings an assurance that the children are really being tutored conscientiously, a matter which is not taken for granted. One of the residents once remarked to the head teacher that he always considered Mr. C. (a previous head teacher) to be excellent—"for me could stay down at de coffee piece" (about one mile away) "and hear him drill de pickney in dem A.B.C." The chorus method, as a result of contemporary educational training, is not too popular among the present teachers, although it is still practised, but with less stress on volume.

In addition to this prescribed teaching method favoured

by parents, there are also prescribed ideas on the amount and type of achievement required before a pupil is considered to have made progress.

The result of the Jamaica Local Examination is the important criterion of the pupil's scholastic progress, and hence the teacher's capabilities. If sufficient students are successful, it is to the glory of the teacher. If, on the other hand, too many fail, it reinforces the argument that "teacher not forcing de pickney dem to learn enough, for so much of dem couldn't fail".

Naturally, every attempt is made to select only those candidates who have a good chance of success in order to assure a large percentage of passes, but here the teacher is faced with two problems. On the one hand, some of those selected cannot convince their parents to risk the examination fee (5/-) while on the other hand, there are usually two or three who are convinced that they can be successful despite the teacher's advice. How the first case is handled will be discussed later when the financial inter-relationship of parents and teachers is dealt with. In the second case, however, the teacher usually gives way, if he fails to convince the parent of the improbability of the child's success. The alternative to this would be to risk the parents' disfavour and possibly the transfer of the child to another school, and with this pupil would go a potential success for some future examination.

A further problem results from the fact that there are usually one or two candidates each year who cannot be convinced to repeat examinations which they recently failed rather than attempt a more advanced course against the teacher's advice. (In meritorious cases, the teacher will permit the candidate to attempt the more advanced course.) Here again it is considered wiser to submit to the request rather than risk the loss of a potentially successful candidate.

The result of all these demands is to saddle the list of candidates with a number of entrants who have only a small chance of success and who thereby limit the percentage of passes in the school. A small percentage of passes in turn limits parental confidence in the capabilities of the teachers, or more specifically, the head teacher.

Where a teacher inspires confidence he is given great latitude with the child, for it is expected that studying under him guarantees success to a great degree. Hence, one woman sent her beloved eight-year old daughter to stay with distant relatives so that she could attend the school at which her old head-teacher now presided. She had great respect for his disciplinarian approach, despite the fact that his moral attitude towards his pupils was somewhat suspect. It was under his regime that the village achieved its few noteworthy graduates.

On the other hand, if the teacher's reputation for producing successful candidates is weak, most of the parents will resign themselves to the situation and expect little progress from the student. The very few who find it possible, will transfer their children to other schools. This attitude of resignation naturally produces little parental confidence or co-operation, and as a result daily attendance is considered unnecessary, if not wasteful. In such cases, the argument is proposed: "Better de pickney dem stay home sometime and learn to do something useful; no sense dem go every day and dem not learning nothin'".

In 1952 when the school had only two successful passes out of ten candidates, one parent bluntly attributed his daughter's failure to the head teacher and transferred the child. Others echoed this attitude but were more passive in their reaction. In 1953, five of the eleven candidates were successful and much confidence restored. The present teachers of this school are all recent trainees in the profession.

The general responsibilities of the teacher do not cease with the matter of scholastic progress. It is popularly accepted that a good teacher is one who shows a keen interest in his students. This means that interest must be invested beyond the limits of academic studies and the class room. It is expected for instance, that on school outings the teachers will devote constant attention to the pupils to guard them from any of the physical dangers which parents fear might befall the child. These dangers vary from falls or getting lost, to serious accidents such as electrocution or automobile collisions. Hence, if a teacher fails to provide complete security for the child, which necessarily involves abandoning personal interests, he or she inevitably earns a reputation of selfishness and is accused of not having sufficient interest in the child. In one case, Miss L. was overheard remarking to her young brother, "All like yu couldn't go to Light and Power House, for yu can't stand steady and if you touch anything dere it would shock you dead". The reference is, of course, to an outing to the Power Station in the capital city, one which commands little co-operation from parents.

On this matter of outings, the teachers are not only expected personally to supervise the events, but also to organize them regularly. Sometimes, these events are a personal financial loss to the teacher since the amount of patronage is uncertain and insufficient seats are sold in the trucks which have to be ordered beforehand.

In the sphere of scholastic work the same extra demands on the teacher's time and interests are made. He is expected to conduct private classes for the Jamaica Local Examination students every evening after school until 6.00 p.m. from October to June. Further, in the final few months before the June examination, tutoring is expected at nights for some of the students. Some parents, in discussing services expected of the teacher, even quoted past cases of those who devoted Saturday mornings to pupils in need of special tutoring.

Again, the teachers are expected to be leaders and organizers in the various village committees. They fill the posts of President or Secretary of all these groups, especially the Church committee, and it is expected that they will bear the greater burden of the duties. One or two nights weekly and an occasional mid-afternoon session are required in this way. In addition, they must take a regular

turn at conducting Sunday service or Sunday school at
the Baptist Church.

In matters of tutoring, there is little criticism of the present teachers in Rural Ridge, with the exception of one as-
sistant who openly expresses her dislike for this voluntary
service. But with regards to service in village committees
much criticism is directed at their inertia and lack of initiative. The head teacher is, to some extent, an exception
to this, since he is semi-active on more than one committee.
A teacher's resentment for these extra duties is rarely
openly expressed in Rural Ridge, for it is recognized that
these outlets are the quickest means of winning the co-
operation and commendation of the residents, and achieving the successful examination passes, on which future
progress in their careers will rest.

The financial inter-relationship of parent and teacher
presents still another problem. Due to a misconception
of the salary of the school staff, the villagers suspect them
of being relatively wealthy, and while no one knows the
exact incomes involved, most guesses put them as much as
50 per cent above the real figure. This impression of
wealth is largely derived from the neat dress of the teachers and relatively comfortable furnishings and accommodations of their homes. The villagers maintain—"dem live
like white people"; hence, it is not unreasonable to expect
that they should also possess some of the wealth of the
white people.

As a result the teacher is almost always the giver or
lender (rather than the receiver or borrower) in this relationship. It is not unusual to find a teacher purchasing
text books for a promising examination student or even
some essential article of clothing, either directly, or by
lending the funds to the parent. In such instances, they
entertain little hope of reimbursement. Further, the child
does not always benefit, as in the case of a man who borrowed 16/- from the head teacher to help purchase a pair
of shoes for his son, an examination candidate. The boy
had not been attending classes because at his age and sta-

tus it would have been undignified to do so without shoes.
The teacher realized that as a potential examination success, he was worth an investment of 16/-, but months later
the boy was still without shoes and the teacher without
reimbursement.

Borrowing is not extensive since it is counteracted by
the average villager's sense of pride. It occurs primarily in
instances where a pupil is involved. This child must be of
sufficient scholastic promise to invoke the parent to take
this humiliating step, and also to convince the teacher that
there is a possibility of reimbursement in the form of another successful candidate.

There are other financial obligations, in which the
teacher is again the creditor. In this category, non-payment
of the small fees charged for tutoring candidates in private
sessions is foremost; almost without exception, this obligation is neglected. Since the major part of the syllabus can
only be covered in these private sessions, the teacher has
no alternative but to conduct them without payment, if
he expects to gain the successful candidates by which his
ability will be judged. What is more usual in this matter
is that a grateful parent will occasionally send gifts of
fruits or provisions to a teacher as acknowledgement of
services.

In soliciting subscriptions for welfare or Church functions, it is expected that the teachers will be among the
foremost contributors. Actual begging, however, is absent
in parent-teacher relationships, although it is present to a
small extent in the village as a whole.

As trustees of public property, the teachers are liable to
further criticism. For instance, it is popularly assumed
that some of the notebooks granted by Government are
sold elsewhere by the teachers rather than issued free of
charge as intended. Further, the products of the school
garden are again assumed to be eaten privately by the
teachers. (Actually, these are used in the school's lunch
canteen.)

Several boys were rolling on the grass of Mrs. G.'s home. Mrs. P. from next door called to ask what they were doing. One boy replied that the head teacher had sent them for some dry grass for mulching in the garden. She replied: "Don' bother go for is only teacher belly yu fattening!"

The writer did not encounter any criticism by parents of membership of the school's Saving Club, of which the head teacher was trustee.

A teacher is very rarely the recipient of gifts (which will usually be fruits or food kind) from a parent unless he is a personal friend, or has taken a special interest in the child's welfare and progress which the parent considers additional to his expected duties, or has tutored the child for an examination.

In a different sphere of inter-personal relationships, it is noteworthy that neither teachers nor parents ever address each other by their Christian names. In fact, the teacher is usually addressed as "Sir" or "Ma'am" when involved in conversation with a parent, unless the latter is a particular friend.

The ideal teacher is the individual who not only renders extensive services to the community, but one who does so willingly. However, the amicable teacher who 'mix-up' with villagers socially, especially the opposite sex, is not respected. A teacher's social companions are expected to be drawn from the elite of the district, but casual conversation and most of all, courteous greetings are expected by every villager. Finally, a teacher is expected to live according to the villager's conception of the highest moral code, which excludes concubinage, flirtatiousness, drunkenness, obscenity, political partisanship, and religious irreverence.

It has been mentioned that the head of the school is the focus for parental attitudes towards the teachers. While, however, there is little significant differentiation among the teachers in their attitudes towards parents, there is a distinct differentiation among parents in their attitudes towards the teachers. The latter are considered to be members of the small upper class (or 'opposite sect' as it is termed) of Rural Ridge, or in the case of two junior assistants, members of the upper-middle class.[3] They are all expected to choose their social companions from the upper and upper-middle class residents. But beyond the usual cordial greetings or very occasional formal visits, fraternization with residents was (in the case under review) limited to five homes, two from the upper and three from the upper-middle class. Naturally, the members of these homes exhibited more sympathetic attitudes towards the teachers than did other residents. Other members of the upper and the middle classes who were not close friends of the teachers, usually displayed less critical attitudes in these relationships than lower-class residents, who were largely antipathetic to any deviations from the educational system of their school days, and suspicious of the teacher's positions of trust. The teachers in this case, were considered as agents of Government, and as a result, received much of the criticism repeatedly directed at Government.

One of the primary reasons for these attitudes in the various parent-teacher relationships is the surprising ignorance of parents on matters concerning the school. There is little discussion between parent and child on these matters. Home work, which could provide material for such discussion, is not favoured under present policy, because it is felt that it would provide unlimited opportunities for copying. Again, no terminal reports on the pupil's progress are issued, and finally, the Parent-Teacher Association[4] of the village is defunct. A direct exchange of information between parent and teacher or parent and child on matters of education, is consequently largely left to

[3] The class membership of each individual was decided during the survey by many residents independently, at the writer's request. They were classified voluntarily into four groups: upper, upper-middle, lower-middle and lower.

[4] See pp. 187-88 for discussion of Parent-Teacher Association.

chance or the demands of some critical situation. The parent, generally, learns of the child's affairs in school indirectly, that is, by overhearing the child reciting Anancy stories or singing Calypsos at home, etc. This leads to questioning which eventually brings out the fact that these studies are now in the syllabus. It is only in the few progressive homes that details of the syllabus or curriculum are discussed by parents with children. On several occasions, parents did not even seem to know in what class their child was graded and had to ask some other member of the family: "What book[5] 'im reading now?" Further questions on the child's progress, such as his arithmetical ability, would often bring the reply, "Teacher say 'im doing all right". The emphasis is usually on what "Teacher say".

This ignorance further extends to a misconception of the mechanics of education. It is popularly believed that a child need not attend classes daily in order to receive a substantial quota of education. Two or three days per week are considered sufficient for all except the most promising students or those who are examination candidates. This belief arises out of a lack of understanding of the arrangement of the syllabus, for on many occasions when it was remarked that the absentee child might miss an important lesson at school, the reply was: "Him can still learn it tomorrow, or some other day". This attitude that two or three days per week is sufficient for attendance, is one of the basic deterrents to daily attendance and consequently one of the primary barriers to scholastic progress.

Hence, ignorance on those two points, the content and arrangement of the syllabus, restricts parental knowledge of the educational programme to matters which are less concerned with the actual business of teaching, such as the enthusiasm of the teachers in community affairs, and the results of the Jamaica Local Examinations. Once teachers have proven their ability in these ways, parents are

[5] The first book of series of Readers used by the school is read in first class, the second book in second class, etc.

likely to feel assured that their children are progressing, in spite of the fact that they can give very little reliable information on these pupils' actual scholastic achievements.

A second reason for the existence of these particular parent-teacher relationships, is the fact that both parties assess each other on the basis of conflicting criteria. Parents consider the previous system of education, in which they were tutored, as the ideal. The prototype of this system was the authoritarian task-master with an extensive and unselfish devotion to a wide range of public services in the community. The contemporary system, however, features among other things, a non-emphasis on corporal punishment, which system, according to the teachers, is initially tried by all new staff members but is eventually discarded, for more than one reason, in favour of a compromise with the older disciplinarian approach. Similarly, the newer recruits in the profession are not interested in the extensive programme of community service since it leaves little time for personal activities. But here again, the demands of the community produce a compromise.

The teachers of this school are all new recruits, and therefore products of the contemporary training system with its different ideals. Their resolving of these ideals with community demands which are based on an obsolete system produces compromises which are not assessed by the community as a product of contemporary policy, of which they know little, but rather condemned as a dilution of the older system, of which they know much.

The present teachers of the Rural Ridge school have fallen heir to these condemnations by virtue of the unpopular contemporary educational system in which they have been tutored. To offset this, they have not yet produced the quantity of Local Examination results which is the best advertisement for their system.

It would not be accurate to imply that the antipathetic attitudes in these relationships are generally overt. Critical opinions are most openly expressed among lower-class members, but even here they rarely progress beyond a point of free discussion with those of similar sympathies. The infrequent discussions between residents with opposing attitudes towards the teachers are usually heard only among intimate friends, where the risk of information reaching the teachers is at a minimum. Finally, it is an even rarer incident when a parent directly confronts a teacher with criticism.

The same approach is less true in the case of the teachers. For, although most of their criticisms of parents are discussed in the presence of sympathetic company, there are more instances to be found here where a teacher will criticize or challenge a resident's criticisms directly.

The most general reaction of parents to conflicts in these relationships is one of resignation. This resignation has an important effect on the scholastic progress of the child through its influence on attendance at classes. For parents argue: "No sense sending de pickney dem to school regular for him not learnin' anything; de now-a-days teacher dem don' know how fe handle de pickney dem and don' know wha' to teach dem". This approach is as popular as the complementary attitude that two or three days per week is sufficient for an education, and together they help to produce a very irregular pattern of attendance among the pupils of this school.

The most usual response of teachers to conflicts in these relationships with parents, is one of compromise, combined with a resigned dissatisfaction. They are aware that compliance with community ideals of education increases parental confidence, which in turn increases insistence on more regular attendance. The latter is observed as one of the major pre-requisites for successful candidacy in the examination, and this is, apparently, the final objective of the teaching programme, and to the community, the primary signal of success in the careers of the teacher or the child.

Apparently, in Rural Ridge, some attempt was usually made in the Parent-Teacher Association meetings to rectify conflicting attitudes between parents and teachers, on a general rather than personal level. However, this Association is now defunct primarily because its meetings were, according to parents, too intellectual to be attractive, and further, there was little genuine conviction that the Association would be helpful in producing the concrete improvements by which parents identify scholastic progress, such as better Local Examination results. The teachers, on the other hand, took it for granted that the importance of the Association was understood by parents, and countered the claim of dullness in the meetings as a rationalization by parents to excuse themselves from the responsibilities of attendance.

The need for propaganda to re-encourage attendance in the P.T.A. of this village is obvious, but it would be of little value unless such efforts were directed primarily at lower-class folk, since they are less co-operative in such matters than other residents.

Members of this group are not likely to be attracted by the traditional methods of soliciting by letters, Church announcements, or notices posted in the shops. These are far less effective here than the method of issuing public invitations to entertainments, such as school concerts, or film shows, which are combined with the more serious meetings. This alternative method, known as 'marrying', is occasionally used in Rural Ridge to ensure attendance at agricultural meetings.

In addition to encouraging attendance in the P.T.A. for discussion of parent-teacher relationships, other methods, such as the institution of reports on the pupil's progress would serve to extend the area of parent-teacher contacts which is necessary if each is to understand the other's attitudes.

It would be inaccurate to imply that increased association of parents and teachers would be sufficient to eliminate conflicts in their relationships, even if such meetings were primarily devoted to discussions of conflicting attitudes. For one thing, it must be remembered that the teachers are considered tutors in a particular educational system, representatives of the Government, and members of a specific social class. Consequently, parental attitudes towards the teachers will be influenced by parents' attitudes in general towards these social institutions and others with which the latter are associated. This was observed in many instances throughout this paper, for example:

1. The influence of parental attitudes towards the syllabus reflecting on the abilities of the teacher as a tutor;

2. The over-estimation by residents of the teacher's salary, resulting primarily from the latter's attitudes towards the expected wealth of upper-class members in general;

3. The suspiciousness, primarily by lower-class residents, directed towards the teachers as trustees of public property, which largely results from the suspiciousness of these residents towards the Government as a whole.

No full treatment or resolution of the problems of parent-teacher relationships, therefore, is possible without a discussion of the wider field of attitudes held by parents and teachers towards the various social institutions of the community, as well as the attitudes they exhibit towards each other directly in their inter-personal relationships.

This paper has been concerned only with the latter, although in many instances examples of the former relationships were implicitly treated.

12.

This selection shows what happens to many rural school-children who manage to stay in school long enough to articulate their ambitions. The extraordinary gulf between what they and their parents have been taught to hope for and the jobs they can possibly get, given Jamaica's economic conditions and social structure, lead inevitably to frustration and despair.

M. G. SMITH, a social anthropologist born in Jamaica, was the recipient of an Island Scholarship; he took an undergraduate degree at McGill University and received his doctorate at University College, London. He has done extensive field research in Jamaica, Grenada, and Carriacou and also in Nigeria. Smith has been Research Fellow and Acting Director of the Institute of Social and Economic Research at the University of the West Indies, Jamaica, and Professor of Anthropology at the University of California, Los Angeles. He is currently Professor of Anthropology at University College, London.

Education and Occupational Choice in Rural Jamaica
M. G. Smith

In this essay I seek to describe the patterns of occupational preference in rural Jamaica. To do so I draw on two independent surveys for my data. One of these inquiries was a study of elementary education made by Mr. P. C. C. Evans in 1957.[1] The other was a survey of conditions affecting rural labor supply which I made in 1955. Occupational choice was investigated in both studies, and by collating their data on this topic, we can explore the correspondence of career choices amongst peasant adults and children, and relate these aspirations to local prospects. The comparison depends for its value on the validity of this procedure. Various objections are possible, and I shall discuss these before analyzing the data.

*   *   *   *

The facts presented reveal a formidable gap between reality and desire. Apparently the conditions of rural life are so depressing that peasants greatly desire that their

Social and Economic Studies, Vol. 9, No. 3, 1960, pp. 332, 350–54. Reprinted with permission of the author and the Institute of Social and Economic Research, University of the West Indies. Also in *The Plural Society in the West Indies*, Berkeley, University of California Press, 1965.

[1] I very much appreciate the generosity of Mr. P. C. C. Evans of the Institute of Education, London University, for permission to use these survey findings.

children should escape them and hope that this will be achieved by occupational means. The parents' ambitions on behalf of their children are reinforced in some ways and modified in others by the children's years at school. The most unrealistic aspirations are thus partly corrected, but the basis on which occupations are chosen remains untouched. The elementary schools can merely modify details but cannot challenge this occupational preference scale or its basis, because both are cast in the image of the school.

The school presents peasants with the idea and prospect of alternative occupations. Traditionally it has been the principal avenue of social mobility open to them in Jamaica, and in some periods perhaps the sole important one. In addition the school presents a curriculum based on others designed for urban populations in industrial countries. This disvalues the peasant way of life, inexplicitly but profoundly. In the content of the education it offers, the school directs the children's attention away from their peasant community to the preindustrial towns with their wide range of prestigious occupations and seemingly endless opportunities.

We have seen that the young folk who leave school in these districts seem to need several years in which to readjust realistically to their environment. In one sphere at least they never do adjust fully, since they heap their own frustrated ambitions on their children, to bring further frustration. The school, by virtue of its curriculum and its role as the primary instrument and channel of a social mobility which is occupational in means, may modify the particulars of this ambition, but can neither challenge nor alter its direction. The occupational values that parents and children hold in common are those that the school represents.

Before proceeding, I wish to consider certain objections that may be raised to this interpretation. First, it can be argued that children in any country have high aspirations and prefer unusual occupations. This is not quite correct, as my own inquiries into the occupational preferences of Hausa school children in Northern Nigeria indicate. Moreover, in no case do these Jamaican schoolboys wish to be cowboys, engine-drivers, sailors, or airmen; nor do the girls wish to become air-hostesses, models, or to go on the stage. There is nothing unusual about nursing, dressmaking, teaching, or mechanic's work. Even so, the important point is surely that when an English or American boy wants to be a mechanic or a doctor, or when an Australian or German girl wants to nurse or teach, they usually have good opportunities for doing so, simply because they participate in an educational system that provides these opportunities, and belong to an industrial society that values such skills.

It may be argued that the children do not fully understand the occupations which they select, and that in any case their preferences change as a normal part of the process of growing up. These arguments should be discussed separately. If the school children of 14 or 15 do not understand the nature of medicine or machinery, dressmaking, nursing, or teaching, the schools must accept responsibility. However, as we have seen, there is a fair correspondence between the children's own choices and those which they report their parents to have on their behalf. Even if the child does not know what he chooses, the parent should; and the correspondence of parental and children's choices is only matched by the divergence in the choices of adults for themselves and for their children.

It is quite true that children often change their occupational preferences as part of the process of growing up. But the shifts that take place in the preferences of these children are shifts within a limited framework of implicitly urban character. When professional aspirations are too clearly unrealistic to be retained, nursing or mechanic's work takes the lead. Only after the child has left school is there a shift toward available rural occupations. To say that the changing career preferences which accompany maturation normally involve careers that are not available would be to stretch this objection too far; but unless it is stretched that far, it does not apply in this case, since it is precisely this choice of the unavailable that is so striking in our sample.

Yet another argument might be that a certain volume of occupational frustration is inevitable, and indeed desirable, in societies that value mobility and change. Without disputing this general proposition, it is clear that the volume of frustration we have been measuring here is both excessive and self-perpetuating. To compare these conditions with occupational frustration among the Hausa, British, or Americans is absurd.

Our data show that rural school children nourish bright aspirations in school and face a grim period of disappointment when they leave. The educational system which permits or encourages these aspirations cannot avoid some responsibility for the disorientation and disillusion which is their result. Dr. Madeline Kerr, in her study of Jamaican country folk, has attributed some of the cultural confusion which she observed among rural people to their experience of elementary education.[2] The gap between occupational choice and prospects discussed in this paper represents one aspect of the confusion Kerr described.

Our data have implications for the program of social and economic development which Jamaica is now pursuing. In so far as a program of agricultural development depends on peasant support for success or seeks to improve their economic conditions, it is useful to know what their occupational orientations may be. Programs which, for their success, presuppose the farmers' interest also presuppose that the farmer wishes to remain a farmer, and typically wishes his children to do likewise. Our data have shown an impressive preference for urban-type occupations among rural folk, together with an underlying desire to escape from the peasant environment. It seems self-

[2] Madeline Kerr, *Personality and Conflict in Jamaica* (Liverpool: Liverpool University Press, 1952).

contradictory to foster an educational system that permits or encourages such pronounced urban orientations among rural folk at the same time that one subsidizes farm programs which presuppose that the peasants' heart is in his land.

Since the preceding data were collected, the government of Jamaica has initiated a program of scholarships to secondary schools, which is designed to raise the secondary school population from 10,000 in 1957 to 26,000 ten years later. By 1967 the population of Jamaica may be about 1.8 million, and the school-age population about 500,000. Thus even when this scholarship program is fulfilled, only one child in every twenty may expect a secondary education. Despite its generous intention, this scheme will do little to alleviate occupational frustration among rural Jamaicans.

Finally, it has been argued that the integration of a society is not affected by the fact that many people within it have high levels of aspiration but low expectations.[3] Without careful documentation and qualification this proposition is unacceptable. Its chief novelty is to assume social integration under any conditions whatever their measure, cause or form.

Our data reveal a considerable difference between occupational choices among rural adults and children. Since this difference is matched by others between the choices of adults for themselves and for their children, we are clearly dealing with divergent aspirations and expectations. The children's preferences and those of their parents for them express aspirations. Those of adults for themselves express expectations, in the sense that they represent accommodations to local realities. The gap between these scales is the difference between aspirations and expectations. It pro-

[3] Lloyd Braithwaite, "Social Stratification and Cultural Pluralism," in Vera Rubin, ed., *Social and Cultural Pluralism in the Caribbean* (Annals of The New York Academy of Sciences, Vol. 83, Art. 5, 1960), p. 829.

vides a useful measure of the inconsistency of the social system which promotes them in its adaptive phases.

Recent studies in America have shown that "anomia results when individuals lack access to means for the achievement of life goals."[4] Anomie, the "polar opposite" of full social integration,[5] is that condition of the social system in which the individual disorganization called anomia is widespread. The data just presented indicate a sufficiently high incidence of anomia among Jamaican peasants for anomie to be more probable than social integration.

There is little symbolism about the occupational preferences parents hold for their children. In rural Jamaica these choices express the parents' frustration and desire for their children's success by means of escape from the peasant environment. To the parents, occupational advancement alone offers social mobility. The measure of the adults' disappointment with their own lives is their aspiration on behalf of their children. The low level of expectation and high level of aspiration are two sides of the same coin, in this case bound together by the frustration which ensure their perpetuation from parent to child.

The element of motivation is missing from the argument of the integrationists. Where aspiration and expectation correspond, motivation and performance may do likewise, and the integration of the system concerned consists in the mutually reinforcing relations of these four variables. Where aspiration and expectation differ sharply, so do motivation and performance as a rule, and the lack of coherence among these variables expresses the internal inconsistency of the system of which all are part. Social systems that foster and then frustrate the chosen life-goals of their members are correspondingly incoherent and ill-

[4] Dorothy L. Meier and Wendell Bell, "Anomia and Differential Access to the Achievement of Life Goals," *American Sociological Review*, Vol. 24, No. 2 (1959), p. 190.

[5] Talcott Parsons, *The Social System* (London: Tavistock Publications, 1952).

integrated. When the volume of this frustration reaches the levels with which we have been dealing, it is pertinent to ask in what sense is the society integrated at all. This question suggests that we may have isolated an index of social integration by comparing occupational aspirations and prospects. Such an index would have obvious comparative values, and could also be used to measure certain aspects of structural change which accompany programs of economic development.

13.

Language is a West Indian dilemma as fundamental as formal education. Throughout the Caribbean, European languages—the normal modes of communication in government and business and among the elite—coexist with more or less heavily creolized folk speech, related to but different from standard European vocabulary, grammar, and pronunciation. In St. Lucia, as described here, the French folk dialect stems from a different European language than the official English tongue, as a consequence of St. Lucia's settlement and changes of sovereignty. Language differences magnify social and status gulfs between the classes, especially when the folk themselves internalize the contempt in which the elite hold the folk idiom.

MERVIN ALLEYNE, born in Trinidad, received his undergraduate degree at the University College of the West Indies and his doctorate at the Université de Lyon. One of the foremost scholars of West Indian Creole languages, he is presently Senior Lecturer in Romance Philology at the University of the West Indies.

Language and Society in St. Lucia[1]
Mervin C. Alleyne[2]

St. Lucia is a small island of 233 square miles belonging
to the Lesser Antilles group of the West Indies. It is a unit
member of the embryonic Federation of the West Indies
(formerly the British West Indies) and lies 25 miles south
of the French *département* of Martinique and 26 miles
north of its sister federal unit St. Vincent. Because of its
particular political history and its geographical proximity
to Martinique, St. Lucia has had, and maintains, very close
ties with the French island in commerce and tourism. The
almost complete identity of French creole as spoken in
St. Lucia and Martinique has preserved strong cultural
links between the two islands which at one period in the
18th century fell under one single French administration.

The island is very mountainous. The main range runs
fairly fully down its length, while transversal ridges leave
from the central range on both sides and dissect the island
into fertile valleys. The population, predominantly an
agricultural one, inhabits these valleys and earns its livelihood on large sugar and banana estates, or from small-

Caribbean Studies, Vol. 1, No. 1, April 1961, pp. 1–10. Reprinted with permission of the Institute of Caribbean Studies,
University of Puerto Rico, and the author.

[1] See the Research Note, Mervin Alleyne, "Caribbean Language Study," *Caribbean Studies*, Vol. 1, No. 1 (April, 1961),
pp. 19–20.

[2] Mr. Alleyne spent the summer of 1960 in St. Lucia on a
grant from the Institute of Caribbean Studies.

holdings in bananas, a recent feature of the agricultural economy of the island.

Of a population of about 90,000, one third lives in three towns (including the capital, Castries: 17,500) and 7 villages, situated at the outlets of valleys on the sea, and very often built on the beach itself at the mouths of rivers. It is suggested that, due to the scarcity of arable land in St. Lucia, only rather swampy or beach land could be spared for housing the black population.

The physical nature of the island makes internal communications very difficult. There is one main road which follows the periphery of the island connecting the 10 towns and villages. It frequently happens during the hurricane season that road bridges over rivers are destroyed by rains and floods, leaving some towns or villages without any access by land. The peripheral road itself is of only very recent completion. Seven years ago, that part of the road along the east coast between the capital and the village of Canaries—a distance of 10 miles—was not asphalted. There is no asphalted road leading from the coastal road to the mountainous interior. This has profoundly influenced the linguistic situation in St. Lucia by impeding the progress of English into the country. There is one village in particular—Aux Lyons—which one can see nestling in the hills as one drives along the west coast road, where the inhabitants have preserved a fair degree of internal autonomy and independence from the laws and administration obtaining in St. Lucia.

At the time of the discovery of St. Lucia at the turn of the 15th–16th centuries, the island was inhabited by the Caribs who seem to have defeated and replaced the Arawaks there as well as in other islands of the Lesser Antilles. There exists today in St. Lucia no traceable descendant of these original Amerindian inhabitants; on the other hand, evidence of their former occupation is found in the preservation of archeological artifacts[3] and in the preservation

[3] On display in the Barbados Museum (Archeological Sec-

of several Amerindian lexical items in the vocabulary of the average St. Lucian.[4]

No attempt was made by any European power to settle in the island before 1639 when a small group of European settlers landed. Within a year they were killed or driven off the island by the Caribs. In 1650, occupational rights to the island were sold to the shareholders of the French West India Company and this led to the arrival of some 40 French colonists in the following year.

There followed 150 years of struggles for the possession of the island by the English and French, during which time it changed hands 14 times. The settled European population was quite predominantly French; the English seem to have been interested in St. Lucia for its strategic importance: its geographical position and its natural deep water harbour at Castries. So that when finally the island was captured by the English Navy and ceded definitively to England by the Treaty of Paris in 1814, it was French in 'language, manners and feeling.'

The broad outlines of the development of North America and the West Indies in the 18th and 19th centuries are too well known to need much recounting here. St. Lucia was not unlike any other West Indian island in that the need for a certain type of labour on the sugar-cane plantations was met by the importation of Africans as slaves. The practice of miscegenation produced a segment of population usually described as 'coloured.'

In the contact situation created by the presence of Africans of different languages and origins and Europeans (French) a new language was also born as the need arose for a vehicle of communication, not only between Africans and Europeans, but also between Africans themselves, be-

---

tion); Gothenburg Museum, Sweden (Heye Collection); St. Mary's College, St. Lucia, c/o St. Lucia Archeological and Historical Society.

[4] Cf. *roucou* 'plant from which red dye is extracted,' used by Caribs as war paint; *agouti, zandoli, manicou* (animals); *cacao, caimite* (trees); *mapipire* (snake).

cause slave traders and owners had systematically scattered their slaves so that Africans speaking the same language should not find themselves on the same plantations. Scholars are divided as to the exact genesis of French creole. This is really part of the much larger problem of linguistic creolization, and it is not intended here to attempt to deal with it. It seems, however, that whether creole is a purely African slave invention, i.e. the vocabulary of French subjected to the syntactical patterns of African languages, or a pidgin used by Europeans to render their language more intelligible to the Africans, it soon became, as a form of expression, very typical of the African slave and was ascribed the negative evaluation given to all items of slave culture.

Up to 1803, French and French creole (or 'patois' as it is called in St. Lucia) were exclusively spoken in St. Lucia. The situation may be described as follows: the entire population was able to speak French creole; the uneducated —including black slaves and the majority of coloured people—could express themselves only in Creole. The island aristocracy of plantation owners and business men, together with their clerks, accountants, etc. of French origin were, for the most part, bilingual.

During the era of slavery, there seems to have been no objection to the use of Creole by the French inhabitants. Children of French parents were allowed to speak Creole in the colonies, but were sent to France for their education in French. In that type of society, visible marks of social identification—such as language—are not held to be as important as in seemingly free and democratic societies. The demarcation lines between classes in a slave society are not at all fluid; they are inflexible and with a low degree of permeability. In a slave society with its fixity and rigidity, the cultivation of the speech habits of the ruling class does not bring the same social rewards as in present-day free societies. Similarly, in a slave society, the practice of 'sub-cultural' forms of speech by persons belonging to the dominant culture would not be as socially harmful to them as today.

Moreover, Creole was, more than any other factor, the unifying symbol of the overseas unit vis-à-vis the continental government. It is very probable that the creole language has even known moments of great prestige, especially at the time of the Revolution and later at the time of the abolition of slavery and the emancipation of slaves, when it was one of the most distinctive means of identification for the colonist in his hostility towards the metropolitan.

Evidence of the wide use of Creole even after the handover of St. Lucia to England is found in Breen's *History of St. Lucia,* when he regrets that 'patois has superseded the use of the beautiful French language even in the highest circles of French colonial society.'

The situation today is much different. French has almost completely disappeared as a vehicle for communication. Only a very few old descendants of original French families express themselves in French in particularly nostalgic moods. The change in the structure of the society is reflected in the new language situation. The advent of English-speaking people as a political élite and their later development into a cultural and economic élite have been attended by the introduction of English as the language of social, cultural and economic prestige. The amicable relations between French and French creole in a slave society gave way to extreme hostility between English and Creole in the newly free society. Creole has, of course, been the loser in this language conflict. The present situation may be described as follows: the vast majority of people who were born and have grown up in St. Lucia can speak French creole; the 1946 census shows that less than 2.0% of the population spoke only English, while as high a percentage as 43.4 spoke only Creole.[5] However, linguis-

[5] The percentage of people not speaking English was, in 1911, 61.7; in 1921, 60.1. Figures for the present time are not available.

tic practice does not coincide with linguistic ability and only a rather small percentage of those who have ability in English and Creole do make use of the latter. The general attitude towards Creole may be summed up in one word: hostility. When one then considers that the percentage of the population which cannot express itself in English and for whom Creole is the only means of self-expression ranged, in 1946, from 9% in the capital to 56.5% in the North East districts, with an all-island average of 43.4%, one immediately realises the problems which the language situation creates.

In trying to understand the general attitude to French creole in St. Lucia, we must situate the question in the wider context of the system of values which West Indian societies have inherited from the slave society. We have seen that the origins of Creole are intimately bound up with slavery, that although it must have become an important identification mark of the overseas territory, it had quite definitely close associations with the slave culture. Creole fell into the general depreciation of all the cultural items, and of all the ethnic characteristics identifiable with the black African slave. Ascription became the basis of the system of values. And so today in the West Indies, 'a good complexion' is said of one ranging from light brown to fair; similarly 'good hair' describes a type of hair resembling the European type and differing from the wooly texture of the Negro's. 'Flat nose' or 'thick lips' are both very opprobrious and abusive terms. French creole was also ascribed a very negative evaluation, and, with the general despiritualisation of the African Negro in the Americas, expressed in inferiority complexes and self-debasements, Creole was despised even by people who could speak no other language. That explains the discrediting of creolized languages throughout the Caribbean. In the particular context of St. Lucia, attitudes to 'patois' were considerably influenced by the course of the history of education in the island.

Education in St. Lucia really starts with the Mico

Schools in 1838. Until 1842 these were the only public schools in existence. They continued until 1891 when the schools were handed over to religious denominations which, however, retained the majority of Mico-trained teachers. The interest for us is that Mico-trained educationalists were Protestant English speakers. They were trained in the Mico Training Colleges in Jamaica and Antigua where French creole was never spoken. Their complete ignorance of Creole made them reject it as an unintelligible gibberish and associate it with backwardness. English became the symbol of light and Creole of darkness. The influence of these Mico teachers, and of others who came from Jamaica, Antigua and other English-speaking islands (i.e. Barbados and St. Vincent), affected the language situation immensely. In 1904, of the 43 Head Teachers throughout St. Lucia, 30 were born and had grown up in exclusively English-speaking islands; 7 of the others were Irish. Their influence is still alive today and St. Lucians relate that the Mico Head Teacher in the village of Mon Repos would walk the village by night and flog any child whom he heard speaking patois. Today, people of Mon Repos take strong exception even to being addressed in Creole. Notices were displayed prominently in schools to the effect that school children were forbidden to speak Creole at school or in the playground.

In St. Lucian society, educational differentiation rapidly brought about the creation of a different scale of values and the prevalence of a new set of attitudes imposed from outside. In a static society like St. Lucia's, there will always be some classes of élites, the standards of which will become representative and will be silently imposed upon and accepted even by groups which are essentially subjugated by these evaluations. It is only when the society is becoming dynamic, when quick changes in stratification take place, when the sudden rise and fall of individuals in the social scale become a matter of course, that the prevalence and prestige of élite groups will be challenged.

In St. Lucia, the scale of language values is arranged

in terms of a polar distinction between English and French creole. The divisions and relations between the different linguistic groups may be represented in form of a pyramid, at the base of which are situated the rural masses and the poor uneducated people of the towns and villages. These are for the most part of African or East Indian origin and speak French creole. At the apex of the pyramid, one finds a small minority of expatriate Englishmen, headed by the Governor, whose numbers are diminishing. As one descends from the apex towards the base, one meets the class of professional men—lawyers, doctors, engineers and some high civil servants—who possess remarkable linguistic ability. They can speak Standard English, some even with an imitated or acquired Oxford (sic) intonation which they use on occasions of great importance and gravity, such as giving public lectures to audiences unfamiliar with Standard English or speaking with members of the group at the apex. They can also speak St. Lucian English, as for example on occasions of great conviviality among themselves. Although many of this group will not be prepared to admit it, the vast majority can express itself in French creole. The two important situations which can provoke utterance in Creole are 1) when addressing domestics and other menial workers and 2) when it is desired to display very popular and democratic attitudes. Further towards the base of the pyramid is a group comprised of persons who have had a good primary or secondary education and are now employed as civil servants, teachers, and in the offices of private firms and banks. They speak St. Lucian English, i.e. they make use of characteristic intonation patterns, and certain grammatical forms, a phonetic and semantic structure that differ somewhat from Standard English, yet allowing people of this group to be easily intelligible to an Englishman. Between this group and the base lies a large number of people with only the rudiments of primary education. It includes domestics, labourers, people of miscellaneous employment and the unemployed, all belonging to the towns and capital. They can be grouped together with the base in that Creole is their most fluent and successful means of self-expression. This group is developing a distinctive English vernacular which is strongly influenced by Creole phonetic, semantic and syntactical patterns.

Language differences, it is seen from the above, are social and cultural markers; the linguistic grouping coincides with a high degree of exactness with the grouping based on other social and cultural criteria.

It is very difficult and dangerous to try to speak of the attitude of any one social group, taking it as a coherent whole, towards Creole. As I have said before, the general attitude is dissociative; but language practice does not fall into a precise pattern according to social grouping and it is perhaps safer and more interesting to examine the different psychological or social situations in which a particular speech style depends on a psychological situation which stimulates a subjective impulse in an individual.

Nevertheless, identification, real or imagined, with a particular social group invites a particular fundamental attitude towards Creole and an examination of this is not without interest. There are two important groups defined primarily by their group attitude towards Creole and which cut across social divisions based on traditional criteria: birth, wealth, education. The first comprises descendants of French creole families with consciousness of their French origins and traditions, who have not become fully reconciled to English as the official language in the island. These people may use French or Creole widely in the intimacy of their families and close friends. The second group includes St. Lucians who themselves migrated or whose parents migrated from exclusively English-speaking islands. These persons have retained the original shock they must have felt on hearing Creole for the first time; and even in cases—the majority—where they have acquired a knowledge of Creole, their hostility to that form of expression has remained most intense.

The attitude of the upper middle class group of profes-

sionals, etc., is rather homogeneous. As a rule they reject Creole as the crude, ungrammatical, corrupt speech
of men without culture and education. There are, however,
cases of persons of this group who feel so socially secure
in every respect and whose identification with the group
is so clearly established by other criteria that they can
permit themselves to be heard using French creole.

In the lower classes, in the linguistic group immediately
above the base, there exists a very ambiguous attitude to
the use of Creole. Very formal, serious communication
among themselves and with people of the groups above,
demands the use of English. This policy has disastrous results in the Law Court where very often the services of an
English–Creole interpreter, always available, are refused
because the person testifying is afraid of revealing his
ignorance of English. The same situation arises in banks,
where reluctance to take advantage of a Creole interpreter
has prevented persons of the group in question from understanding the full implications of their transactions. What
is interesting is that this class not only has repugnance to
speaking in Creole but considers itself gravely insulted and
dishonoured if a person who normally expresses himself
in English condescends to address them in Creole. For the
members of this group, the image which each has of
himself stimulates the psychological impulse which determines the linguistic style used in everyday, informal
conversation. And so there are conversations carried on
by members of this group in which some speak Creole
and others English. In a particular conversation group
which met at the street corner near to my hotel, the only
persons whom I never overheard speaking Creole, although, as I afterwards found out, they had the ability to
do so, turned out to be a primary school teacher and a
policeman—both having a higher status bracketing than the
others: part-time chauffeurs, carwashers or unemployed.
In addition, the parents of the policeman had come to St.
Lucia from neighbouring St. Vincent, an English-speaking
island. The ambiguity is that, generally speaking, people

of this class have a very deep affection for Creole, an affection which they are forced to suppress by the demands of the St. Lucian society, but which every so often impels them to react against these demands. When I mentioned at an Adult Education Lecture in Castries that from a purely linguistic point of view there is no reason why Creole could not become an official literary language by the same right as French and English, whose beginnings were just as humble as those of Creole, there was enthusiastic applause from the significant section of the audience. On another occasion, the master of ceremonies at the wedding reception of a casual worker and his bride, after going through the initial formalities in English, felt the conviviality and, I might say, the genuineness of the occasion and remarked that he was going to continue in *langue mama mwen* 'the language of my mother.'

The language situation is illustrative of a very interesting form of social distantiation. Generally, the democratic character of a society is evaluated according to the degree of intimacy which the members of one class are inclined to sanction between themselves and members of another less fortunate class. In St. Lucia, people who have great facility in speaking English pay considerable attention to the preservation of this index of separation from the uneducated poorer masses. Some, we have seen, even disclaim any linguistic ability in French creole. On the other hand, for the more democratic members, speaking Creole is the primary means of shortening the social distance between themselves and the members of the lower classes. Among the latter, there is, of course, the desire to remove any mark of separation from the upper classes; whereas economic factors prevent them from identifying themselves by dress, housing and general living conditions with the upper class, they attempt to achieve that identity in speech and in some cases also insist on being spoken to in English. One observes therefore a movement towards the apex of the linguistic pyramid; some natives whose linguistic ability places them very near the apex acquire an intonation, popularly but erroneously called an 'Oxford accent,' to preserve better the distance from people below them on the pyramid and to create a new separation from those at their level. Here again, it is more a question of individual psychology, of the image each individual has of himself, because the acquisition of certain linguistic habits does not necessarily mean complete cultural assimilation with and social acceptance by the class of which these habits are characteristic. English is certainly a means of social mobility and a cultural attainment such as learning to speak this language in its 'uncorrupted' form as spoken by the cultured whites is an important social index; but it is so to a relatively small degree in this small community of St. Lucia, where everyone is more or less classified at birth and the classification well known to all other members of the community.

Let us examine the psychological situations which permit the use of French creole and also the patterns of verbal conduct characteristic of different forms of social intercourse. Creole is principally the vehicle for expressing the more elemental and vulgar aspects of life. It is the language of abuse and insult; it is used to relate jokes, particularly smutty and obscene ones; to complain about the harshness of life—there is a cartoon appearing in the leading weekly newspaper which always treats of this aspect of life, and which has its caption in Creole—the only example of Creole figuring in the press; in moments of great emotion (exclamations, swearing, etc.). Creole is also a private language, one of intimacy, so that confessions are done largely in Creole and sermons delivered to the same audience in English. Creole fulfills none of the functions of a standard language. Attempts by the church and radio to use Creole have met with opposition from people of all classes.

Whereas a member of the less privileged classes tends to object to being addressed in Creole except by one of his very intimate circle, in a situation where he loses his individuality and freedom before another person such as n the relations between servant and master or mistress of a house, Creole is the vehicle normally used. In general, people in servile and domestic employment are addressed in Creole. It must be admitted, however, that this may be a preservation from the time when people in such employment invariably could not speak or understand English.

The two languages which face each other in St. Lucia are clearly different in nature and function. Creole incorporates the entire history of the indigenous people of the island. Consciousness of this history is achieved through Creole, as this language is the depository of the folklore of the people. Creole is the vehicle for proverbs; for handing down traditional popular customs, ceremonies, rituals. Traditional techniques, by which a large percentage of the population still lives, are expressed in Creole. On the other hand, English is the vehicle for very formal and artificial occasions; it is the medium through which all official, national and inherited institutions function. Creole is used to describe the non-official, private and fundamental mores of the people; Creole is, therefore, expressive of what is usually called the 'soul' of the people, it is deeply rooted to the life and the indigenous history of the people. As one expects, Creole is a more living, more creative and more spontaneous means of expression. English as spoken in St. Lucia is very conservative and particularly among people who have no opportunity of speaking it with Standard English speakers and whose contact with English has been exclusively through the school, it is very literary. Among many people in St. Lucia, a conversational Standard English style has not developed. For example, there is no elision of the copulative verb *is* or the auxiliaries *do, can,* to the negative particle, nor of the subject pronoun to the copulative *to be.* Thus *he is* is never *he's* and *he is not* is never *he isn't.* Innovations in English tend to come from Trinidad. As a general rule, linguistic innovations are produced in greatest numbers and spread more quickly in areas and among groups in which there is least conservative restriction. In St. Lucia, the class in which linguistic innovations are born does not possess English as a spontaneous means of self-expression; it has no facility in the familiar, colloquial use of English. There is besides little permeability in the St. Lucian society. On the contrary, in Trinidad, linguistic innovations are born in the creative strata—amongst the lower classes—and penetrate easily and quickly to the upper classes. Some expressions reach St. Lucia and give to the everyday conversational language of the English speakers its only living and dynamic features. In Trinidad, this phenomenon reflects the democratization of society and culture. In St. Lucia, this process of democratization is impeded by the divergence between the two languages, and besides, as we have seen, this divergence leads to more conspicuous social distantiation. The result in St. Lucia is also that no expression of culture of the lower classes is accepted by higher social groups. Dramatic productions in Creole have been discouraged; there is no movement towards elevating any expression of folklore to represent the natural culture. Again the contrast is with Trinidad where calypsos, steel bands, limbo dancing, etc. have now become fundamental items of the national culture. The linguistic dependence of St. Lucia on Trinidad is further evidence that Trinidad is the political and cultural hub around which the Eastern Caribbean gravitates.

14.

The gulf between folk and elite speech can be as great when the same language underlies both, as in Haiti. Here a small French-speaking brown elite long kept their prerogatives, denying the Creole-speaking majority access to national institutions. Folklore studies and the growth of Haitian nationalism have instilled some appreciation of Creolese, but the masses themselves still reject the folk idiom for purposes of formal education and development.

EDITH EFRON received her undergraduate and master's degrees in journalism from Columbia University. She has been associated with the *New York Times Magazine* and *Look* and was Central American correspondent for *Time* and *Life*. This selection is a chapter from her forthcoming book *Haiti: Myth and Reality*, based on eight years of residence there. She is presently a staff editor of *TV Guide* and is the author of *The News Twisters*.

French and Creole Patois in Haiti
Edith Efron

> This obsessed Heart, which does not correspond
> To my language and my clothing,
> And upon which bite, like a clamp,
> Borrowed emotions and customs
> From Europe—do you feel the suffering
> And the despair, equal to none other,
> Of taming, with words from France,
> This heart which came to me from Senegal?
> —*Léon Laleau*

Haiti is one of the many countries in the world that has two languages, and a "language problem". The official language of Haiti is French, the tongue spoken formerly by her colonial masters; all of Haiti's official institutions use this language. Creole is Haiti's unofficial language, which has been inherited by modern Haitians from their slave ancestors. Before describing the nature of the serious conflict engendered in this country by the existence of two languages, it might be wise to indicate, at least briefly, the relationship of one to the other.

Creole stands roughly in relation to French, as French once stood in relation to Latin, although it is no more correct today to call it a corrupt French than it would be to call French a corrupt Latin. It is an independent and

Caribbean Quarterly, Vol. 3, No. 4, August 1954, pp. 199–213. Reprinted with permission of the author and the editors, Department of Extra-Mural Studies, University of the West Indies, Kingston, Jamaica.

well-integrated tongue, colorful and savory, preferring poetic imagery to abstractions, rich in proverbs and sayings, singing and musical in expression. Its basic vocabulary is French, composed of words which streamed into the slave language from early French buccaneers, planters and colonists who brought their local French dialects to Hispaniola from Normandy, Picardy, Brittany and Anjou. Indian words also enrich the language, often used to describe local fruits, flowers, and animals. A large number of African words, applying to religious beliefs and customs, to foods and cooking, to household objects, have remained in the Creole tongue. Many characteristic Africanisms are prominent in Creole, notably a repetition of words for emphasis (He runs, runs, runs; it's sweet, sweet), and a strongly developed sense of *onomatopoeia* (he fell down, *ban!* He slapped her, *v'lap, v'lap!*). From neighbouring Santo Domingo and from returning emigrants from Cuba, many Spanish words filtered into the language; and finally an American Occupation left behind it a series of English words. In general, however, the vocabulary is dominantly of French origin, many of the words and forms being archaic, and incomprehensible to the modern Frenchman.

Faced, on the one hand, by academic French, the language of the civilised White world, spoken by few citizens, and Creole, a language of Black slave origin, spoken by all citizens, Haiti has evolved a characteristic myth of language to deal with the situation. French has become the official tongue, the language of intellect, of social distinction, the language of the *élite;* while Creole has been pushed into the background, receives no formal status at all and is termed the language of the *mass*. The *élite* and the *mass* are thus not only declared to be separated by religion, by culture, by social and political status, by sexual mores, by color, &c., &c., but by the very tongue they speak. This linguistic difference is felt to create an abyss between them. Indeed, Frédéric Doret, a Haitian educator, once went so far as to speak of the "two Haitis", so tragi-

cally divided by two languages.[1] In this affirmation, there
is as little reality as in all others which visualize Haiti as
being composed of two culturally distinct groups. The two
languages actually complement each other in Haitian life,
serve a vital function in the split culture of the Haitian
people—French being the linguistic vehicle for the formal-
public-official European cover of all Haitian institutions,
and the lively and popular Creole expressing in all its rich
nuances, the living mores of the country themselves.

The significant fact that language strongly implies class
status—a total absence of French decidedly placing the
Haitian in the unschooled lower classes—intensifies the
social snobbery toward the native tongue. The uneducated
Haitian feels an immense pride in his child who goes to
school and becomes "educated", who can "really" write
and speak the French language; and conversely, the
French-speaking Haitian who has emerged from the lower
classes may feel real shame over his exclusively Creole-
speaking family, keeping them out of sight of his more
educated acquaintances. A Haitian folktale incorporates
both these prejudices into a curious story:

> A man by his first marriage, had a daughter, Gina-
> tone, who received a very elegant education in another
> country. The man remarried, and had seven daughters,
> to whom he preferred Ginatone. This excited their
> jealousy and the jealousy of their mother. They decided
> to kill her . . .
> When the husband, who was often absent on busi-
> ness, returned from a trip (he found her missing). His
> wife, reproaching the conduct of his daughter, said
> there was nobody who could speak French to her. The
> father thought this explanation true, and forgot his
> daughter, whom he believed to have returned to the
> land of her childhood . . .[2]

[1] Frédéric Doret, "Les Deux Haiti," in Dantès Bellegarde,
ed., *Écrivains Haïtiens* (Port-au-Prince, Haiti: Éditions Henri
Deschamps 1950), p. 186.

[2] Rémy Bastien in Dudley Fitts, ed., *Anthology of Contempo-*

Where purely Creole-speaking people are not able to use
French in those formal circumstances where it is felt to be
desirable they attempt to have it spoken for them. And at
the major religio-social ceremonies of lower class life,
there is often a peasant notable, or a bush priest (*pret'
savanne*), or simply a slightly more educated member of
the community, who is requested to rise, and say a few
words in French—much as one might say grace before
dining. This, it is felt, lends dignity and prestige to the
occasion. Where extreme formality and a note of genuine
chic are desired—such as in demanding the hand of a girl
in *plaçage* or marriage—a *lettre de demande*, written in
French for the lover by some French-speaking local citizen, is considered correct and elegant—in the past, it was
even compulsory—although neither the sender of the letter
nor the girl's parents who receive it are able to read a word
of the document, and must have it translated for them.
Indeed, if the peasant or working-class Haitian desires to
be truly ostentatious, he will even attempt to speak a sort
of pigeon French, feeling that only this language can do
justice to a significant occasion. In a charming passage in
Gouverneurs de la Rosée, Jacques Roumain has one of
his lower-class characters complain humorously, but a bit
boastfully, nevertheless, about the need for *parler-français*
when courting a girl:

In my time, the whole business of girls was nothing
but a peck of trouble and difficulty. You had to use
special manoeuvers, feints, *parler-français*, oh, a whole
bunch of monkey-shines. And finally you found yourself *placé* for good, and tied up like a crab, so to speak,
with a house to build, furniture to buy, not to mention
the dishes . . .
And so I began, in my Frenchiest French: "*Made-
moiselle, depuis que je vous ai vur, sous la galerie di
presbyte, j'ai un transpo' d'amou' pou' toi. J'ai déjà*

coupé gaules, poteaux et paille pou' batir cette maison de vous."[3]

As the classes rise, and the urban population is increasingly exposed to French, and as the children of the intermediary classes spend longer years in the city schools, the preoccupation with speaking French becomes even more serious and invades everyday life. On calls, when receiving visits, at parties, weddings, dances, and particularly when meeting and conversing with people who are not intimates or family members, French is felt to be obligatory, no matter how poorly it is spoken, no matter how richly Creolized it may be. Justin L'Hérisson in one of his novels describes the language of one such member of the middle classes, who has become a *bourgeoise* upon the acquisition of wealth by her husband:

And the former reader of the cards, Madame Velleda Petite-Caille, did the honors of her salon admirably. She spoke French "by routine", and apart from a few mistakes in pronunciation, one would have thought that she had received the most excellent instruction. She said, for example, *"Mercir je vous remercir"* with the most perfect aplomb. Her witty guests pardoned everything in her except this *Mercir, je vous remercir*, which she was unable to correct, despite the violent remonstrances of her husband, who, because he had a great facility of elocution, thought himself a phoenix.[4]

Sensitive to each others' snobbery of language, urban Haitians are fond of making fun of each others' mistakes in French; there is even a Haitian version of Sam Goldwyn, or a male Mrs. Malaprop—one well-known middle-class politician whose "Creolisms" in French are recounted with gusto in thousands of homes, and to whom all new and

[3] Jacques Roumain, *Gouverneurs de la Rosée* (Paris: Les Éditeurs Français Réunis, 1944), pp. 53–54.
[4] Justin L'Hérisson, "La famille des Caille," in Bellegarde, *op. cit.*, p. 252.

hilarious "Creolisms" are attributed, whether he has actually committed them or not.

Edmund Wilson has remarked of the local broadcasts
in Port-au-Prince that they "are often made in invertedly
macaronic language of Creole supplemented by French".[5]
This is actually a fairly good description of the language
spoken socially by most urban Haitians, save for a most
highly educated minority.

Some notion of the poverty of the French language as
it is used among middle-class urbanites, who attend Haiti's
public schools for only a few years, can be obtained by
the statistics of admission to the final examinations of the
students in the *cours moyens et supérieurs* of Port-au-
Prince, the primary schools: "Out of 203 candidates", reported *Le Nouvelliste*, on September 7, 1950, "only 17
were admitted to take the examinations, after the eliminat-
ing test in French".

French is spoken best in that most educated group, the
Bourgeoisie, which provides the major part of the clientèle
for the private secondary schools and the universities, and
which includes the greatest number of well-travelled people, and professionals who have often studied in France.
Men, better educated, usually speak a more cultivated and
literary French than women, although among women, the
younger generations speak better French than their
mothers and grandmothers, who were rarely educated to
any significant degree at all. Even in the *bourgeoisie*, however, purity and academic correctness of speech remain a
matter of degree. A strong Creolisation of the language
occurs regularly, in almost everyone's speech, errors in
grammar, gender, and syntax are common, and while
the educated Haitian believes the French of his class to be
extremely pure—Jules Faine writes that "The Haitian
adores to speak French and speaks it with purity, with an
elegance that almost attains a certain coquetry"[6]—this is,

[5] Edmund Wilson, in *The Reporter*, May 23, 1950.
[6] Jules Faine, "Préface," in his *La philologie créole* (Port-au-
Prince, Haiti, Imprimerie de l'État, 1937).

n the whole, far from true. Only among intellectuals, professionals, and writers, for the most part, does one find French used, at times, as a reasonably living language; and even among the writers, Bellegarde comments:

> The conflict between Creole and French is clearly mani-
> fest among certain of our writers. Their style lacks in
> spontaneity and in naturalness. It often has the air of
> a peasant dressed up in his Sunday best. French is not,
> for them, a pure and flowing expression of their ideas
> and sentiments. They do not write, they formulate.[7]

In an article on the future of the French language, in Haiti, Pradel Pompilus, an educator, has recently written:

> My researches have brought me to interest myself in
> the spontaneous development of French in our milieu,
> and in order to gather (information) . . . I do what
> any good investigator does: I spend hours in theatres,
> more attentive to the comments of the spectators than
> to the play or film; take rides on buses, with no precise
> destination; I wander, on the evenings of public con-
> certs, among groups of strollers. How many times have
> I returned to my home in consternation, asking myself
> if the domain of the patois had not been extended, in
> spite of the real progress of elementary and secondary
> education—and if the French language is not declining
> in Haiti.[8]

Despite the myth, Creole is Haiti's living tongue in all classes. In the biggest business houses, in the corridors of the National Palace, in Government bureaus, at the ele-gant family dinner table, at the *Bourgeois* cafés, one hears Creole almost constantly. "It is the language in which all the small business of Haiti is conducted", as Leyburn

[7] Dantès Bellegarde, *Haïti et ses problèmes* (Montreal: Édi-tions B. Valiquette, 1941?), p. 67.

[8] Pradel Pompilus, "Destin de la langue française en Haïti," *Conjonction*, No. 37 (February, 1952), pp. 6–7.

writes.[9] It is in Creole that the educated Haitian curses, i
is in Creole that he tells his jokes, it is in Creole that he
makes love, it is in Creole that he gossips with his friends
it is in Creole that he grumbles about the Government, i
is in Creole that he repeats the slang, the funny expressions of the era, the wise cracks and political jokes that
course through society—it is in Creole that he lives. "Who",
asks Ernest Douyon, with universal candor, "is the man
of standing, who is the society woman who in private does
not continually use Creole?"[10]

That the educated Haitian loves to speak Creole, even
positively relishes it, is obvious. One need not even listen
to his crows of pleasure over some deliciously funny turn
of phrase, some pithy Creole remark or saying which expresses so perfectly the point of some devious local situation. One need merely observe the sudden vivacity of his
facial expressions, the volatile quality of his gestures, the
gleam in his eyes when he is speaking Creole. His entire
body, his face, his voice, so rigid, restrained and expres-
sionless when he is speaking French—the correct and distinguished language—bursts into easy, gracious movement
when he speaks Creole. He is at ease, he is visibly enjoying himself. Indeed, nothing seems to touch both educated and uneducated Haitian so deeply and immediately
as to discover that a foreigner shows exceptional virtuosity
in Creole. This will be met with cries of joy among "aristo-
crats" as well as peasants.

Aggressively snobbish towards Creole in public, most educated folk feel impelled to denounce the language, declare
that it is vulgar, ugly, crude, that it hurts their ears, and
even, in some cases, maintain that they hate it or "never
speak it". Interestingly enough, women, who, by and large,
speak French far less well than men, seem more inclined
to make these charges publicly against the native tongue.
Possibly this is felt by them to be a compensation for in-

[9] James Leyburn, *The Haitian People* (New Haven, Conn.:
Yale University Press, 1941), p. 304.
[10] Ernest Douyon, "Préface" in Faine, *op. cit.*

adequate French. The collective disdain for Creole undoubtedly reaches its absolute pitch when the educated Haitian travels abroad, even for a few months, and—as so often happens—returns to Haiti, insisting to all who will listen that he has forgotten how to speak Creole! Making deliberate mistakes in this language, he constantly asks for help in remembering words which, somehow, elude him, and rolls his r's madly in that essentially r'less tongue. This failure in memory notoriously afflicts Haitians who have been to France, and return with sharp French accents—Haitians call this, mockingly, talking '*pointu*', or 'pointy'—which invade what little Creole is left to them, after their trip.

So great is the official respect for French, and the contempt for Creole, that in educated homes of the middle class and *Bourgeoisie*, children after three or four years of age are scolded, and even beaten, for speaking Creole, despite the fact that their elders use it constantly, and are disciplined into talking French. In some homes, the formal rule is established that while the parents may speak to the children in Creole, the children must reply in French, both as a token of "respect" and for "practice". One of Haiti's most brilliant intellectuals recalls that, as a child, he was obliged, one week in each month, to polish his own shoes, empty the chamber pots—and talk French! Thus, early in life, the Haitian child is systematically trained in a duality of attitude toward language! In the highest classes, as in the lowest, he speaks Creole with relish, at every opportunity; indeed, because it is often denied to him, the child of the upper classes loves it even more as a bootleg pleasure. Nevertheless, he learns to look down upon Creole as an inferior tongue. And in most cases, the upper middle class child grows up like his elders, to speak Creole constantly, to deny that he does so, and is, by adolescence, fully prepared after a trip abroad to pretend that he, too, has suddenly "forgotten" his mother tongue.

The official myth of language, is, one might even say, nothing more than an extension of this individual "forgetting" on a national basis. The official stand on language simply "forgets" that all Haitians, including the "élite", speak Creole, and maintains, in this absent-minded fashion, that French is the "national" tongue. And where the tendency to "forget" the maternal language may force Haitians into adopting individually ridiculous postures and attitudes, the official "forgetfulness" for a century and a half has precipitated the entire community into a series of entirely irrational situations.

One may find, for example, that in a majority of churches, priests are declaiming sermons in French, destined to exalt and uplift the souls of their audiences, and turn them away from the primitive faith of their ancestors—sermons which might as well be delivered in the purest of Latin, along with the rest of the Mass, for all the comprehension they evoke in most of their hearers. Leyburn remarks that he has met "priests who though they have lived in the country for a generation, have never learned the tongue used by ninety-five out of a hundred of their parishioners all the time, and by a hundred per cent of them some of the time."[11]

Where individual rural priests and pastors have been motivated by a sincere desire to bring Christianity to the Haitians in their parishes, they have, of course, learned Creole, and have even made use of a few experimental catechisms and prayer books prepared in the Creole language. Also, as the number of Haitians entering the clergy has augmented, Creole has been increasingly used—particularly by Protestant churches, who train their seminary students to deliver Creole sermons. But the majority of clergymen are still Frenchmen, serving in the towns and cities, and the social pressure of the linguistic myth relieves them of the necessity to learn Creole. Hence, in a

[11] Leyburn, *op. cit.*, p. 129.

majority of cases, the Haitians continue to receive their formal religious training and instruction in a language they can barely understand.

Several decades ago, Frédéric Doret reported with pleasure that:

> . . . a group of members of the Catholic Association of Haitian Youth of the City of Jacmel, has undertaken, in their sphere of action, to throw a bridge across the gulf that separates the two Haitis . . . They have assigned to themselves the humble role of catechists, catechists who are entirely resolved to obtain results, for they are taking the road to the hearts of their listeners, by commenting in Creole the instruction of the French Priest.[12]

Similar tiny groups of evangelists dedicate themselves, today as well, to the propagation of religious instruction in Creole, conceiving of this as a most revolutionary manner of communicating with the "hearts of their listeners". The extreme potency of the national myth of language is so great, that it occurs to few Catholics that the national religion might just as easily be conveyed to all Haitians in Creole, to begin with, and save these feeble, if generous, upper class gestures of solidarity. Evidently, even those who most strongly object to the tangible results of the language myth continue to think in its restrictive terms, and nobly throw Creole bridges across a "gulf" which does not exist, to join together "two Haiti's" which have never truly been separated, save in the official imagination of the educated.

A similarly irrational situation exists in national political life. Inheritors of the French political institutions, the Haitians have and cherish all the forms of French parliamentary democracy. A President is elected, a Constitution exists (although it is constantly changed to suit contemporary contingencies), Senators and Deputies are

[12] Doret, *op. cit.*, p. 186.

elected from the different districts of Haiti, and, in electoral periods, the People are declared to be "Sovereign"—the candidates for offices invariably going before the electorate to ask for its votes. But—due to the myth of language—political leaders, during electoral campaigns, stand before masses of wondering partisans, and make long and dramatic speeches in French, well-interlarded with quotations from the classic French poets. Although the listeners are incapable of making head or tail of anything that is being said to them, they applaud the *gros français,* the dramatic delivery, with tremendous enthusiasm.

While even the modern President, such as Vincent, Lescot and Estimé (all of whom spoke Creole incessantly in private), permits himself to make an occasional speech in Creole to a wildly delighted popular audience, all of the important announcements, discourses, and policy speeches of Haitian Governments are made in French—which the average citizen does not understand. The law makers in the Parliament also conduct their business in French. The laws, when made or changed, are published in French in the official gazette called *Le Moniteur*—which cannot be understood by the majority. The public newspapers which give political news are also printed in French. Thus, no official political institution in Haiti is in any way directly comprehensible to the vast mass of its people—for not one utilizes the language spoken by the people.

This of course does not imply that there is no national political life in which the people participate, for it has been shown already that such is not the case. Behind the façade of French Parliamentary Institutions, the true political life of the country pursues its own destiny—an underground and unrecognized institution, its "constitution" the by-laws of the intricate Master-Slave relationship, its forum the secret gossip sessions of the eternal politically discontented, and its language, of course, Creole. Open "opposition" almost never emerges through the French Parliamentary Institutions, which do not represent public opinion, but which exist, for the most part, to keep urbanites in political jobs. Since "opposition" is a private, concealed rather than official, public phenomenon, its natural language is Creole, rather than French. And furthermore, since "opposition" is the major, if not the only, political attitude of the vast majority of Haitians in all classes, the political opposition, being thus an essentially democratic, if revolutionary, movement, invariably and instinctively talks Creole.

Thus, when the political atmosphere permits it—usually after the fall of a Government when there is a period of free expression—"opposition" leaders go out to the "Masses" and deliver resounding harangues in Creole, which are meant to be understood and are understood by the people. The most notable "opposition" politician in the recent era has been young Daniel Fignolé, a leader with a tremendous popularity among *Le Peuple*. His speeches are invariably made in an earthy and resounding Creole, and when he ran for election to the Chamber of Deputies in 1950, he genuinely and democratically won his votes—democratic elections, in Haiti, being politically compatible with the Creole language alone! Nevertheless, when in Parliament, Fignolé, like everyone else, has spoken French and his partisans for the last few years have understood little or nothing of what their representative has been saying in the national tribune.

Similarly, the only time that Creole appears in the newspapers is to express an "Opposition" point of view; and during the last electoral campaign and the Constitutional Convention which preceded it, *La Nation,* the left-wing paper, ran a series of articles in Creole. One of these articles expresses so excellently the relationship between French language-and-Official Government, as opposed to Creole language-and-the-Opposition, that it is quoted here at some length, translated from the Creole:

The newspapers are full of news of what's going on at the Constitutional Convention. They're talking about the "Battle of Oratory". And what do you think this "Battle of Oratory" is? It's talking French, yes, talking beautiful French, making beautiful sentences, as if the people needed men to spout French at their heads. The people are wasting away, unemployment is in its flanks, it can't find food to eat. What are you telling the people about "Battles of Oratory" for, heh?

Talk to the people about things which can solace its misery; tell the people that the Constituents are giving it a Constitution to strangle it. But don't you dare talk to the people about "Battles of Oratory", about French sentences that are being made at the Convention. What the hell do the people care about the Constituents' good French, for God's sake! Ever since cucumbers have been fighting with eggplants, the Haitian Negro is talking French as hard as he can, and it's brought him nothing . . .

It's not talking pretty French that's going to relieve the misery of the people.

Very often you see a woman and a man holding each other's arms, walking down the street holding tightly to each other. You think they love each other so much? You're wrong. Each is holding the other up so they both don't fall down in the street, they're so hungry. There's the truth!

So now go talk to this man and woman about an "Oratory Battle", about the lovely little French that the Constituents are speaking—they'll give you a sharp kick in the pants![13]

The popular *master-slave mechanism* of politics, working through the peppery Creole language, dominates all Governments, despite their restrictive use of French. And if the "Masters" know well how to exploit by means of French, the "Slaves" know equally well how to resist and exploit in retaliation, by means of Creole. As *Le Fumiste*, a humorous anonymous contributor to the newspaper *Notre Temps*, wrote during the last elections:

[13] *La Nation*, November 24, 1950.

After a thunder of applause, the big fat candidate
jumped heavily to earth, landing upon the toes of a *chef
de bouquement* (a local political boss) who, without
moving from the spot, called out:

"Maitre, ou palé bel francé mais élections couté chè"
("Master, you speak beautiful French, but elections are
expensive!")[14]

No better example can be given of the Master-Slave mechanism at work; and no better indication to the rôle of
French, as public-master language, and of Creole as
private-slave language can be found, either!

While the problems created in religious life and in politics by the linguistic conflict are grave indeed, the myth
of language attains its highest point of unreason as it manifests itself in Haiti's French-style educational system, which
conveys "culture" to the Haitian people via the French
language. While this constitutes no problem in higher education, it creates a serious impasse in popular primary
education. In most primary schools throughout the Republic one may find ill-paid middle-class teachers proud of
their relative mastery of the French tongue, conducting
their classes in this language before a group of awestruck,
uncomprehending children of peasant, proletarian, or
lower middle class origin. No Creole texts are used by the
Haitian school system; the language of the country is un-
used, untaught. The Haitian child must be educated in
French, a language he does not speak and almost never
hears at home.

Where such men as Bellegarde deplore the "puerile
maternal patois" and the "vicious habits of speech" of the
Haitians, which conflict so unhappily with the official language of Haiti's educational system[15]—more rebellious
educators have taken an opposing point of view and criticize the use of French in the primary educational system
of a Creole-speaking country. Needless to say, the former

---

14 *Notre Temps,* September 11, 1950.
15 Bellegarde, *Haïti et ses problèmes, loc. cit.*

point of view is the one which has dominated official Haitian life for a century and a half. The minority pleading for primary education in Creole has been too small to affect, in any measure whatever, the stolid and almost holy conviction of the majority of educated Haitians that French is, by its intrinsic nature, the only possible language of education and instrument of "culture"; and that, if *Le Peuple* cannot learn French, *Le Peuple* may simply remain illiterate.

The people who have been fighting Creole education have a series of traditional justifications for their attitude. One hears most often that Haiti will be isolated from the outer world if her primary schools use Creole—as if the vast majority of Haitians are not presently even more isolated by their total illiteracy and ignorance. One hears also that Haiti's dominant claim to distinction and "originality" is her French language and "culture"—which would instantly be lost to her if her school system used the Creole language—Creole, presumably, in its unofficial state not constituting a menace to the official French "culture". Finally, and most often, one hears that education in Creole is a total impossibility, because Creole is not a "real language". Bellegarde has written:

> Creole, having neither grammar nor a written literature, cannot constitute the material of methodical teaching, unstable, subject to continual variations in its vocabulary, in its syntax and pronunciation, it has none of the characteristics of a fixed language, and can neither be transmitted nor conserved save by oral use.[16]

This is, on the whole, the notion held by the vast majority of educated Haitians about Creole. As Christian Beaulieu, an advocate of Creole education, wrote irritatedly of this concept, "To listen to these people, one might think that . . . writing comes before the creation of a language, that the spoken language is somehow the instrument of the

[16] *Ibid.*, p. 45.

written word which has pre-existed since all time—instead of being merely a graphic representation of the auditive image created by the word itself!"[17]

The United Nations report on Haiti, in 1949, agreed that French is a desirable language for secondary and higher education, and certainly for the University level—maintaining that "the fact of being integrated in the large current of the French culture is, for Haiti, an advantage of inestimable value . . . the knowledge of French not only permitting her access to the great treasures of occidental civilization, but also a perfect means of participating in the scientific and technical progress of the modern world."[18] Nevertheless, the UN explicitly recommended to the Haitian Government that Creole be immediately instituted in the primary schools. This has not yet been done. It is obvious, however, that eventually the sheer pressure of popular need, if not the sheer pressure of logic, will force some future Government to take the final leap into linguistic reality.

There is one small group of Haitians which, more than any other, has struggled painfully with the deepest implications of the myth of language in Haiti, and has wilfully plunged to the very heart of the conflict, in an effort to attain some comprehension of its inner meanings. This group has been Haiti's literary men and intellectuals—those for whom language and its subtleties are of passionate importance, those who, if they are to have any validity, must express with the greatest of fidelity the culture to which they belong.

The claim which educated Haitians have laid to the French culture, since Independence, has been based, chiefly, upon a purely literary or verbal concept. Haitians

17 Christian Beaulieu, *Les griots,* Vol. 4, No. 4; Vol. 1, No. 1 (1939), p. 589.
18 United Nations, *Report on Haiti* (New York, 1949), pp. 52–53.

who are literate, speak, read and write French, and for them this has been the principal factor of cultural identity; her writers and poets in the past have written uniquely in the French language. Haiti's best known literary spokesman for her traditional demand to be recognized as member of the French cultural community has, in the modern era, been Dantès Bellegarde, who expresses, admirably, in the following passages famous in Haiti, the intellectual essence of the official or conventional Haitian attitude toward language and culture:

> The Haitian national culture has manifested itself for more than a century in work of real value, *written in the language particular to Haitians, the French Language*.[19]
> The Haitians, by their constant commerce with the books in which the French have laid down the treasures of their intelligence and sensibility, live and evolve in the atmosphere created by the ideas, the traditions, the French beliefs.[20]
> Who could deny this influence of language upon thought? . . .
> For us to think "bantu" instead of thinking "French" we would have to put to use the innumerable bantu dialects spoken in South Africa. And since we might not possibly find enough competent professors to teach them to us, we would have no other recourse but to emigrate *en masse,* and to go and live among the Kafirs.[21]

Here, one has a supreme example of the power of the educated Haitian to "forget" both the existence of his native tongue, and the presence of the overwhelmed majority of the population which does not understand French words, and has never read any French books! Similarly it illustrates the power of the educated Haitian to "forget"

[19] Bellegarde, *La nation Haïtienne* (Paris: J. de Gigord, 1938), p. 348.
[20] Bellegarde, *Haïti et ses problèmes,* p. 15.
[21] Bellegarde, *Dessalines a parlé* (Port-au-Prince, Haiti, 1948), pp. 164–65.

the existence of his vast and complex African-Slave heritage, and concentrate only on the French-Master heritage.

On the other side of the arena, stands a small minority
of "new" intellectuals, which has emerged within the past
three decades. These have largely rejected the orthodox, or
Bellegardian point of view, in favor of a greater measure
of cultural, and linguistic realism. Looking about them at
the Americas, in which they live, rather than keeping their
eyes hypnotically fixed on *L'Académie Française*, this minority has finally perceived that Mexicans, Cubans, Argen-
tinians, &c., speak Spanish, that Brazilians speak Portu-
guese, but that none of these nations, for all that, have the
"cultures" of their original mother countries. Thus, in his
revolutionary *Ainsi Parla L'Oncle*, published in the '20's,
Dr. Price Mars distressed his Haitian reader by saying
that the French language itself, as used in Haiti, must
reflect a Haitian culture rather than that of France, and,
he pointed out, that it was perfectly possible for Haitians,
using the medium of the French language, to "bring to the
world a notion of art, an expression of the soul which
might be at once very human and very Haitian".[22]

Radical as these ideas were for the Haitian milieu, they
were to evolve still further. It has been increasingly maintained by the most modern that even Haitian French, with
all its local implications and altered meanings, does not
fully express that part of the Haitian which so freely flows
in Creole. The sociologist René Victor points out the impossibility for our novelists to render in French certain
qualities of mind as they are expressed in Creole; and the
necessity for these novelists to transcribe these expressions,
in quotes, as they stand.[23]

There is no question but that today, to quote the poet
Carlos St. Louis, "the inadequate character of French as a

[22] Jean Price Mars, *Ainsi parla l'oncle* (Port-au-Prince,
Haiti, 1928), p. 190.
[23] René Victor, *Essai de sociologie et de psychologie Haïtienne* (1937), pp. 19–20.

carrier of Haitian sentiments . . . forms, ordinarily, the subject of literary discussions among young writers. "Haitian literature", he reports, "will never be original as long as it depends (exclusively) upon the French vocabulary".[24] More and more, modern writers are using Creole in their work. And where Georges Sylvain, in translating the Fables of Lafontaine into Creole several decades ago was considered a veritable revolutionary (as was the poet Oswald Durand who wrote *Choucoune* and other poems in Creole)—today, there are few important modern writers who have not experimented with and published at least a few Creole poems, and who have not begun to use Creole expressions and sentences in their novels.

In one of Jacques Roumain's earlier novels, he puts the poet Roumer into the tale, as a prominent character, who talks exultantly about a Creolized poem he has written. From Roumer's short monologue, one gains a strong impression not only of the immense relish with which the "new" intellectuals greet the use of Creole in literature, but of their triumphant pleasure in rebelling against the conventional literary regulations which prescribe the use of this tongue in serious writing:

> For example, listen to this magnificent Alexandrine verse which is going to make our dear Afro-Latin (I almost said *Affreux-Latins*) intellectuals go wild with anger— those guys . . . whose lips more purple than the grape open only on the imperfect subjunctive! *Ta fesse est un boumba chargé de victuailles!* (Your buttock is a boumba loaded with victuals!) '*Ta fesse est*': do you hear the hissing and boiling of the hot fat falling into the bowl?; *un boumba:* oh, marvellous! that word makes you think of the explosion of a bomb, of an impetuous behind, of a voluminous and blackened casserole; *chargé de:* that's a preparatory stop; then, brusquely:

[24] Carlos St. Louis, ed., "Préface" in *Panorama de la poésie Haïtienne* (Port-au-Prince, Haiti: Éditions Henri Deschamps, 1950).

victuailles! That, oh that's perfectly sublime, that '*tchou-sille*' of the burning grease in the casserole![25]

This poem, to which he refers, heralded, in Haiti, by the tiny group of Creole experimentalists, is today recognized by most intellectuals as one of the first serious efforts to write good poetry using the native tongue alone or in combination with French. Today, while Roumer is still probably the best Creole poet in Haiti, other and younger poets—notably Morisseau Le Roy and Pierre Mayard, have written voluminously in Creole, their work being widely known and well loved by most of their fellow writers. Certainly the most imaginative experiment with Creole in the novel form was Jacques Roumain, whose *Gouverneurs de la Rosée* not only offers passages of pure Creole, but attempts to Creolize French in a systematic and stylized way, thus creating a Haitian "atmosphere" which few other novelists have yet achieved. Creole is slowly being liberated from bondage, is being recognized, today—although by a tiny group of *avant-garde* intellectuals alone—as a vital instrument of Haitian expression.

While it has required more than a century to produce a rebellious *avant-garde* "discovery" that the Haitian "soul" or personality could not be exclusively expressed by academic French—this truth has long been known to the Creole language itself! While Haiti's official institutions are describable, and can be expressed in the French language, the unofficial or private mores of Haiti are almost invariably described or expressed by Haitians in Creole. French is the carrier for the official, mythical or for the inherited *covering* of the national institutions; it is the carrier for the idealization of these institutions. But Creole is the carrier for the living mores themselves, expressing not only the

[25] Jacques Roumain, *La proie et l'ombre* (Port-au-Prince, Haiti: Chassaing, 1931), pp. 18–19.

implicit French-master ideal, but the conflict between the ideal and the reality.

It can hardly come as a surprise, therefore, that the Creole language should contain within itself as articulate a commentary on the Haitian's conflict between French and Creole as upon all other such conflicts. Eight popular Creole sayings can be quickly listed, which illustrate the Haitian's most intimate feeling about the relative functions of the Creole and French languages in his life—and which, by extension, convey his feelings about the French component of the Haitian mores:

Fai' la France: (To make like France). This is a common Creole expression, used in all classes to describe, nastily, a man who talks a lot and says nothing, who attempts to sound important, but who is not to be taken seriously; it indicates pretentiousness, snobbery, and hollow verbiage.

Créole palé, Créole comprenn' (Creole spoken is Creole understood). This is an expression which can be used in either language, French or Creole. When interpolated into a delicate, veiled, or diplomatic conversation, it signifies a great deal: "I don't have to say too clearly what I mean. You understand the implications. You perceive the *real sense* of my words". Used freely, even in a French conversation, it implies that the real meaning or sense of language exists in Creole, while it is masked, or even absent, in French. Creole, here, is the symbol of true communication.

C'est Créole m'ap palé avé-ou, oui! (Listen, it's Creole I'm talking to you!) In Creole conversation, if a listener does not seem to understand, or is pretending to misunderstand what is being told him, he may be brought up sharply with this comment. By implication, one may be permitted genuinely or deliberately to "misunderstand" in French, but one has no right to "misunderstand" in Creole. Where Creole is, presumably, the language of comprehension and of truth, French is, by implication, the language of bluff and of mystification.

Palé Français (To speak French). This is a popular term, in use by all classes, to indicate the offering of money or a bribe to someone; the actual negotiations, while perhaps being carried on in Creole, are called "Speaking French", for this is presumed to give them a more respectable allure. Here, the French language itself is used as the symbol of distinguished duplicity, and the glossing over with respectability of dishonest thoughts or acts.

L'ap mandé charité en Français: (He's asking for charity in French). This expression will be used to describe that individual who is begging, grafting, extorting money, with a steady stream of explanations, apologies, and promises intended to make his act seem less reprehensible. He may be talking fluent Creole, in the process—but, where an honest request for a gift of money without the pretense of paying it back is merely called "asking for charity", any effort to deceive the giver, to camouflage the real parasitical intention is called "asking for charity in French". In this saying, as in the one which precedes it, the French language is the symbol of a respectable or proper coating of dishonest thoughts or acts.

Finally, there are two Creole sayings of enormous cultural significance, the first used to indicate loyalty in a man: *"Si Monsieur avé-ou, l'a v'al nans Guinée avé-ou"* —(If that man is with you, he'll go to Guinea with you!) —and the second indicating a traitor: *"Sais attention, oui! C'est Français, oui!"* (Watch out for him! He's a Frenchman, he is!")

From these few sayings, in constant use in Haitian society, one perceives very clearly that, for the "Creole-thinking" Haitian, French is the language associated with bluff, camouflage, indirection, duplicity.

The insistence that French words are "hollow", that the French language has been emptied of its meaning, has lost contact with reality, that evil motives lurk behind a camouflage of French vacabulary, is to be heard and read constantly in Haiti. Indeed, when Haitians translate such

"Creole thoughts" about French into French, they invariably pen such paragraphs as:

> Unhappily, people adore, in our country, to gargle words, *sonorous words, with hollow resonances.* These are the strong points of those idiots with their petrified brains . . . *who refuse to look reality in the face.*[26]
> Political professionals who have been allowed by the citizens to run our political life, have finally *emptied those words of their content* which once served to denounce the most cruel injustices.[27]

These are, indeed, complex and profound observations. They are made only by those Haitians who are highly educated. Ironically enough, most of them are unaware, apparently, of the fact that their "primitive patois", Creole, had made these very observations long ago! Indeed, how much more subtle and appropriate is the malicious *"C'é Créole* m'ap palé avec-ou, oui!" which defies the listener to pervert the thought, which defies him to falsify the idea, than the quiet morality of Edmond Paul, Haiti's earliest sociologist, who wrote, in French, "To speak Creole in order to express a correct thought will always be worth more than to speak beautiful French in order to express a false thought."[28]

It is almost incredible that it should have taken more than a century for Haitian intellectuals to "discover" that Creole, rather than French, expressed most fully the Haitian "soul" or personality. Had they merely listened to themselves talking Creole, as Pressoir recommends, they might have discovered it in the earliest days of Independence! Actually, as the Creole language itself suggests in the strongest of terms, the official French institutions of Haiti, which form a cover and a camouflage for the local mores, *are* treacherous symbols. By their utilization of

[26] Jean Grevy, *Le nouvelliste,* October 6, 1950.
[27] *Notre Temps,* September 4, 1950.
[28] Edmond Paul, *Oeuvres,* p. 326.

French, the large majority of the Haitian people are prevented from participating in them; and in return, the very mistrust and incomprehension of them by the people, render them meaningless, hollow, empty and symbolic. They are *simulacres*, specious imitations, as Hilbert said, indirectly, in giving this title to his novel satirizing Haitian life.[29] And similarly, the French language, which expresses these symbolic institutions, assumes itself a symbolic function in a society where it is largely unknown. As Sténio Vincent has remarked, "French is, for us, a borrowed language, a language of a *representation;*" the word *representation* has no literal translation into English. It is defined by Larousse as meaning: "exhibition; the action of putting something before the eyes". And, by the means of an official, incomprehensible language, the major official institutions of Haiti are actually exhibited, put before the eyes of the outer world, and put before the eyes of her people, who can neither understand them, nor use them—and beneath whose envious adoration of them lies a profound distrust and hatred of them.

Only in the last few decades have those most sensitive, advanced, and imaginative people—Haiti's intellectuals—begun to penetrate through the oppressive wildernesses of Haiti's complex mythology of language and culture. Their major discovery, in this epoch, remains, on the whole, the discovery of the validity of the Creole language—the native language which, in its popular sayings, has always revealed a penetrating understanding of those very myths of language and culture which have caused it to be rejected!

[29] Fernand Hilbert, *Les simulacres* (*l'aventure de M. Hellénus Caton*) (Port-au-Prince, Haiti: Imp. Chéraquit, 1923).

15.

Trinidadians, like other West Indians, have been traditionally inclined to believe that metropolitan culture and institutions in general are superior to anything local or homegrown. The interplay between British-sponsored cultural forms, local folklore, and West Indian class stereotypes is examined in this selection by a Trinidadian sociologist. He shows that local intellectual and cultural deficiencies are largely a consequence of symbolic affirmations of Britishness among the elite and middle class, and he explores the impact of these attitudes on responses to such homegrown innovations as the steel band.

LLOYD BRAITHWAITE, a Trinidad-born sociologist trained in England, has long been connected with the University of the West Indies, having served as Director of the Institute of Social and Economic Research, Head of the Department of Sociology, and Dean of the Faculty of Social Science in Jamaica. He is currently Pro-Vice-Chancellor of the University of the West Indies, Trinidad.

The Problem of Cultural Integration in Trinidad
Lloyd Braithwaite

Every social system possesses some symbolic means by which the unity of the society is affirmed. In those societies which are highly stratified or in which there are several groups with sharply divergent cultures, there tend to be a variety of such means. In the case of Trinidad, we have a highly stratified society in which there is nonetheless a great deal of common cultural allegiance. It is to be expected therefore that many of the "national" ceremonies will reflect the stresses and tensions within the society.

An analysis of the Carnival, one of the distinctive features of Trinidad culture shows that it contrives to be a national festival while at the same time there exists a struggle for its control and reform waged by the upper classes. This is only one aspect of the problem of cultural integration, that is, the problem arising from the different forms of "expressive" behaviour on the part of different sections of the community. It is perhaps in this connection that Professor Simey's saying that "the West Indian needs a culture in which he can find himself at rest" has its most significant meaning.

The island society faces the problem of integrating the

Social and Economic Studies, Vol. 3, No. 1, June 1954, pp. 82–96. Reprinted with permission of the author and the Institute of Social and Economic Research, University of the West Indies.

minority sub-cultures of the Hindus and the Muslims. But this can be considered to be a special case. Even when we neglect the Indian minority we find a lower-class sub-culture which makes the problem of integration seem more difficult and interesting. We find in the society a field of expressive behaviour ranging from the British Council to those who look backwards to Africa for cultural inspiration. The difficulty in establishing a common norm is well illustrated in attitudes towards the British Council. Its activities in the island have been greeted with great enthusiasm by some, but have met with a great deal of reservation from others. In view of the prestige which Great Britain, as a metropolitan country, and Britishers resident in the island enjoy it is not surprising that there are people who enthusiastically support the importation into the island of the "best of British culture".

The British Council has been described by one of its representatives as the "projection of Britain" on the world abroad.[1] It was originally formed for the purpose of spreading knowledge of Britain to foreign nations. However, with the war, it was decided to turn the attention of the British Council towards colonial areas as well. Trinidad, like other colonial areas, became one of the scenes of operation.

The activities of the British Council were at first rather confined. The giving of scholarships, supplying of books, etc.—these were activities which appeared innocuous enough to the bulk of the population, while positively welcomed by those who benefited from them. The first real impact that the British Council had on the general population was through the visit of Mr. Harold Stannard. Unlike previous visitors, Mr. Stannard showed an immense curiosity in getting to know the country and in particular the way people felt. He addressed meetings up and down the country. Mr. Stannard had to bear the brunt of the

[1] Sir Angus Gillan, "The Projection of Great Britain on the Colonial Empire," in Sir Harry Lindsay, ed., British Commonwealth Objectives (London: Michael Joseph, 1946).

resentment which the educated radical groups felt towards those in authority. It was commonly believed in view of the unusual nature of his visit, that he was an intelligence officer, which in some sense at least he was. What was more surprising was that people became worried because they believed him to be a "spy". What exactly the term "spy" connoted in this connection was not clear. It seemed to reflect the somewhat paranoid attitude of the radical and served the function of labelling the unusual European as "an enemy" in spite of whatever evidence of goodwill he shewed.[2]

Some idea of the suspicion with which he was received can be gathered by that prolific provider of written evidence of the radical view, Dr. Tito P. Achong. In his second report as Mayor of the City of Port of Spain he devotes a special chapter to Stannard headed "Peripatetic propagandist of British culture".[3] Here he describes how he met Mr. Stannard in the Town Hall: "The function of Mr. Stannard obviously was to push down his brand of British culture into willing or unwilling throats of the people of this land." After some preliminary parrying,

> I then braced myself for direct action. We swapped brief stories on 'culture'. I told him in as clear a manner as I could that his notion of a cloistered British culture for the Trinidad community must be ruled out as a paradox. The component parts of the community had had cultures of their own long before William the Conqueror had landed in England in 1066. It would be unwise for the Chinese and Indian sections of the people of Trinidad, I said, to forsake the past glory of their ancestral homelands and to be unmindful of their

[2] This belief in Mr. Stannard as a "spy" and of the British Council as a spying organization was recently expressed in conversation by one of the most prominent coloured persons in the island community, and one, moreover, active in "progressive" work.

[3] Tito P. Achong, *The Mayor's Annual Report, Trinidad, 1942–43* (Boston: Meador, 1944).

future generations for British propagandist 'culture'. As for Afro-West Indians it was their solemn mission, I emphasized, to gather as far as practicable, the learning and culture of all lands and to synthesize them into an organic whole. This was too much for the British Council's professional propagandist. He stood up, salaamed in old-time Oriental fashion, and departed.[4]

This attitude on the part of Dr. Achong was shown at a different period of time by Albert Gomes, who was at one time the leading "literary" and "art" critic in Trinidad, and also by Lennox Pierre, the Secretary of the Trinidad and Tobago Youth Council. In private it was shared by at least one other outstanding figure in the realm of "culture" who, nonetheless, gratefully accepted a British Council scholarship when it was offered for study in England.

The section of the British Council's activities which aroused these objections was not its scholarship programme. There was no objection to people being sent to Great Britain for the purpose of absorbing British culture. In the first place, the visit to England gave the recipients of the scholarship additional status. In the second place, their visits were likely to result in promotion within the civil service and in the teaching profession, or to Government appointments if the recipients were not already employed in the Government service. Hence it was that a radical anti-imperialist Trade Unionist accepted the offer of a six-week visit to the United Kingdom in order to make a study of Trade Unionism there.

The hostility to the Council's activities developed, rather, over some of its activities within the island itself. It assumed the significance it did because of the symbolism of

---

[4] For Mr. Stannard's own evaluation of the situation in the West Indies see his chapter in Rita Hinden, ed., *Fabian Colonial Essays* (London: Allen and Unwin, 1945). At a public meeting Mr. Stannard declared that he knew how West Indians felt because he was Jewish and the Jews had been described as the "niggers" of Europe; nonetheless, he felt that the British Empire was "the greatest force for good in the world today".

class current in the society. The upper classes and the middle class of the island (including the native-born Trinidadian) have always aspired towards accepting the culture of Western Europe in general, and Great Britain in particular. A visit to the United Kingdom, to the Continent of Europe, to the United States or Canada, necessarily brought about status. It indicated that one was, first of all, in a financial position above the ordinary and secondly, it was symbolic of having been able to achieve a higher sense of values. There was an almost magical belief in the possibilities of a visit abroad which somehow transformed the individual into a new person. He was likely not only to assume a new status but to have this new status thrust upon him. The native Trinidadian, now usually a professional man, was suspected of wishing to cut his roots, to free himself from any local acquaintances who had not found themselves in this privileged class. Casual acquaintances or even friends waited for him to determine what their new relationship would be. They would often hesitate to greet the recent arrival for fear of being snubbed. From this arose the spate of jokes which in white as well as coloured society reflected the anxieties and hostilities that arose from the ambiguous position that resulted from the need to re-define the status of the individual on his return. For instance, there is the oft-repeated story of the young man who on returning from the United Kingdom visited the market and affected not to recognize the crabs for sale there. However, when one of these bit him he was pleased to recognize, in real creole speech, the creole remedy "Squeeze he eye!"

Even among the radicals this straining towards acceptance of British values existed. The Trinidad Labour Party was modelled on the British Labour Party, and its leader, Captain Cipriani, was fond of saying that what was good enough for the British Labour movement was good enough for him. The demands of the Trade Unionist and the Labour movement were for social services "as is done in England"; so that even when the British were being beaten they were beaten with a British stick. This incorporation of a British and a European scale of values in matters of taste and aesthetics, personal and social, for long went unquestioned. It was indeed very largely unconscious and unacknowledged. Thus it was that Trinidad and West Indian students in England could show appreciation of a group (which had provided them with a Christmas dinner prepared in order to show them a typical English Christmas) because, as they expressed it, their English hosts had gone out of their way to provide them with a Christmas dinner such as they were accustomed to in the West Indies.

Artistic societies—The Trinidad Musical Society, La Petite Musicale, The Trinidad Art Society, and the like—existed and even flourished. In many respects the aesthetic and artistic interests overcame some of the social barriers of class and caste. At the same time the attitude towards the popular culture of the social groups from which these individuals derived was one of tolerance mingled with contempt. If Carnival and the Calypso were indulged in, they tended to be placed in a somewhat different category from real art.

There was never at any time any effort on the part of the "cultured" to create their own art. Listening to recorded music, reproduction of plays written in and for a different culture whether they were appropriate or not; such were the activities that dominated the activity of these groups. In painting there was little original work done.

With the rise of a new self-consciousness and a new sense of belonging there developed a serious concern for "creative" work, for things that would reflect the individuality of the author and the individuality of his origin. To many it appeared, to use the categories of Sapir,[5] that the culture after which they had been striving was a spurious and not a genuine one. New writing that dealt

[5] Edward Sapir, "Culture: Genuine and Spurious," in David Mandelbaum, ed., *Selected Writings in Language, Culture and Personality* (Berkeley, Calif.: University of California Press, 1949).

with the local scene started to appear in the 1930's—
C. L. R. James' "Minty Alley", Alfred Mendes' "Black
Fauns" and "Pitch Lake" were the first indication of
this concern. The only previous novelist whom Trinidad
had produced before this was the well-known author,
W. J. Locke.[6] Since then there has appeared a spate of
poems and short stories dealing with the local scene. The
attitude of most of the educated groups was that of being
lost in a void. There was the tearing away from the orientation to European culture in the search for something distinctive, but at the same time there was nothing that could
replace it.

The problems and the attitudes of the Trinidad intellectual were well described by Willy Richardson in a poem
which took pride of place in a collection, "Best Poems of
Trinidad":

> Here is a land of flowers
> Here is a land of showers.
> Tourists say it is a lovely land
> Here is a land of brilliant sunshine
> But it is not yours and it is not mine.
>
> Here is a land that men have conquered
> Here is a land that men have owned
> Here is a land for "Auld Lang Syne",
> But it is not yours and it is not mine.
>
> We are men without a country
> We are men without a faith.
> We are men without a future.
> We are men who wait for death.
>
> Meanwhile we giggle gaily
> Meanwhile we hide our pain
> Seeking a moment's adjournment
> From the court-martial of the brain.
>
> And tomorrow the hills will be looking fine
> But they won't be yours and they won't be mine.

[6] Locke was a European who although of Trinidad birth
never wrote of Trinidad life.

In their search for roots, for some sources of inspiration, several of the "artists" of the society turned towards the despised culture of the man in the street. After all, the only song or work of art of any kind that has expressed anything of a patriotic sentiment was the Calypso composed after the Carnival riots of the 1880's:

In My Own, My Native Land

Can't beat me drum
In my own, my native land
Can't have we Carnival
In my own, my native land
Can't have we bacchanal
In my own, my native land
In my own, native land
In my own, my native land

The problem for the artist in this society was the more difficult because in so far as he created anything worthwhile he had to look outside of himself for an audience and for a market. The criticisms and appreciations which he valued were, perhaps wisely, not those of the local critic but that of the British and American world. Appreciation on the local level tended to develop into mutual admiration societies in which unless there was some question of personality or other extrinsic factor involved, one author favourably reviewed another's work in return for a like favour that he expected to be granted.

The position of the artist reflected the position of the whole society. In so far as the original cultural heritage of their ancestors (mainly African) was lost, in so far there was an easy incorporation into and participation in the life of the metropolitan area. This rendered educational and consequently political advance easier perhaps, but it shifted as a consequence the centre of gravity of the community so to speak to a position outside itself. This was the price that had to be paid.

The failure to develop any centre of intellectual life

in the colony was, however, only partially consequent upon this fact. The historical tradition in the West Indies was one of sending children abroad to be educated. Hence there has never been, until the situation was remedied recently, any provision for higher education in the area. This has served not only to limit the numbers of people who receive higher education but also to prevent the development of any intellectual centre of learning. From this point of view it must be remembered that until the recent establishment of the University College of the West Indies those who received higher education did so not as a group but as separate and scattered individuals. Whatever group-loyalty developed to any institution of higher learning was a loyalty to something in a foreign country, to something far distant where sentimental ties of a tenuous nature could replace any active organization. This was hardly likely to produce practical results. Moreover, the education which was received in the higher centres abroad tended to be of a mainly professional kind. Certainly there was very little experience of research. This was important because it is conceivable that the development of research in the social sciences (in history, psychology, sociology) or even in social work might have helped to bridge the gap between the middle-class artist on the one hand and the social reality that surrounded him.

As it was, the world of thought and imagination, trained to deal with thoughts and objects so often foreign to the individual's experience, became separated from the world of everyday living. The absence of a cultural tradition, of any possibility of what one might term, "apprenticeship" made the task of learning technique, and of developing appropriate attitudes difficult. Denied mobility and possibility for movement in the social system many coloured middle-class intellectuals went in for artistic work as a compensation and were not seriously moved by any creative impulse. There was an inordinate hankering for achievement and distinction over-night. Quick publication and favourable review in the local press gave one the dignity of being a poet and an author. And publication, in the absence of any publishing firms, was simply a matter of individual action. Over-night reputations mushroomed. Always there was the absence of impartial criticism.

For such criticism one had to go abroad and this resulted frequently in actual emigration from the island. C. L. R. James, Alfred Mendes, Eric Williams, Samuel Selvon and others, all emigrated abroad, only a few to return. Most of those who managed to make any money out of writing have done so by their sales to the English and American public; or by broadcast of their productions to the West Indies by the B.B.C.'s overseas service, "Calling the West Indies".

The social-class–caste structure of the society tended in some respects to hinder the development of any mature form of expression. Those who were technically the most competent came from the most isolated of the social groups—the upper class. Even where technical interest overcame social isolation the development took place on separate lines. Thus, the dramatic societies in Trinidad have developed along racial lines. There are white dramatic societies and coloured ones. From one point of view this division did no harm as long as the dramatic societies produced plays with European backgrounds. The appearance of a mixed racial group in such a play would probably have appeared incongruous to the audience in a society where there was such a high degree of sensitivity to the problem of racial relations. In recent years there has been only one locally produced drama written by a Trinidadian. Perhaps it is no accident that this first effort was written about the conquest of Trinidad by the British and thus did not touch on any of the tensions that exist in present-day Trinidad society.

Some of the intelligentsia became absorbed in this "reproductive" sort of activity and to this group the work of the British Council in providing facilities of one sort or another caused the Council's activities to be viewed in a favourable light. But to those who were interested in "creative" work these activities seemed to constitute a threat to their position and to what they were striving for. The "imposition" of British culture was resented and interest was directed toward "expression" among the masses.

The existence of two separate and distinct cultural expressive patterns corresponding to social class not only symbolized the difference between the classes (the lower class on the one hand and the rest of the society on the other) but helped to accentuate further the difference between them. To a certain extent there was an acceptance of much of this lower-class "culture", notably at Carnival time. But this acceptance was only of a limited nature. The people of the towns were unaware (the upper and middle classes totally, the lower classes partially) of the dances and the songs of the countryside. When, for instance, a collector of folk traditions gave an illustrative lecture in Port of Spain on the "Folk Songs and Folk Dances" in the island, most of the people attending had never seen the Limbo Dance, the Bongo Dance or the Calinda, although most of the participants were drawn from villages on the outskirts of Port of Spain.

The results of this attempt to draw on these "folk" traditions led to the creation of two dance groups—the "Little Carib" and the "Holder" dance groups. These have survived over a period of years and bid fair to become permanent features of the cultural life of the community. Some of the folk dances have also been introduced as physical education into the rural schools.

This turn in interest towards the masses has revolutionized people's attitude. Previously items such as the Shango, the Bell-air dance, were dismissed as unimportant at least, if not hostilely opposed. Periodically there would appear an outcrop of letters in the press in which the behaviour of people at "wakes" was criticized and the "wake" itself condemned. The Shango flourished in out-of-the-way country parts and on the outskirts of the city.

Even Calypsonians poked fun at the Shango and the
Shouter:

> It was in the height of Guanapo
> That I met up with a dance they called Shango
> While travelling through the vicinity
> I heard them singing melodiously
> Azangana! paratico—Oh!
>
> A group of voices singing so loud
> As if they want to buss a hole in the cloud
> —*Tiger*

On the whole the idea of most people was to differentiate themselves as much as possible from anything that
sounded "African". "African" was associated with the
primitive, the barbarous and the uncivilized, and in fact,
the idea of Africa and its inhabitants corresponded in no
small measure to the stereotype so often to be found in
the United Kingdom. With the search for some form of
national expression, and with the resentment against those
of the ethnic groups which had retained a greater portion
of their original cultural heritage (the Indian group in
particular) the attitude markedly changed.

Members of the Negro Welfare and Cultural Association and similar groups had shown some interest in African survivals. (One member of the Negro Welfare sang
at one of their concerts a Yoruba song which his grandmother had taught him.) But these were lower-class
groups. Now respectable people started advocating a revival of Africanism. A prominent lawyer, at one time active in the Parent-Teacher's Association (now defunct),
advocated the teaching of Yoruba and other African languages in the schools. (Periodically this suggestion arises
among the more extreme of the Negro Nationalist Movement, but is so impractical as never to have received any
serious attention.) There began a diligent search for folk
tunes and attendance at Shango dancing became a per-
missible activity, although actual participation was ta-

booed. Among certain circles the fact that something was of African origin made it more acceptable than it would otherwise have been.

However the search for a distinctive and national form of expression which would both symbolize and give unity to the society was not altogether easy. The areas in which the lower class seemed to have the most to contribute were areas heavily associated with the more despised forms of lower class behaviour. The singing and dancing of the lower class were associated with relative freedom and lack of inhibition. The words of the songs were frequently, by upper and middle class standards, vulgar; and the dancing struck the inhibited as being exceedingly erotic in nature. Again, the contribution which was most acceptable from the point of view of the "culture" of the community, the steel band, associated as it was with Carnival, became tabooed on account of other socially reprehensible factors associated with it. The problem of uniting the various forms of expressive behaviour into "national" patterns are so well illustrated by the steel band movement that some account of it is given here.

THE STEEL BAND[7]

The ethnologist interested in tracing cultural elements of African heritage will find few evidences of African drums still surviving in the island. In the Shango groups, and the Rada groups in the outlying districts of the island are to be found a few drums, but the variety that apparently is to be found in a country like Haiti does not exist in Trinidad. The reasons for the relative decline in the drums are numerous. The attitudes of the people towards things African, the increasing urbanization of the island, the breach with the creole culture through the substitution of English speech—all played their part. Of more interest,

[7] In giving this account I am indebted to the steel band committee.

is the effort on the part of the authorities to control the expressive behaviour of the masses. Proper historical accounts are not available; however, Osborne Innis, himself a coloured creole, but sympathetic to the suppression and reform of the lower classes, has given an account which conveys at least some of the spirit with which the reforms were carried out.[8] He refers in his reminiscences to the obnoxious practice of beating the big Bongo drums. Huge crowds would assemble in the yards and the beating of the Bongo drum would proceed throughout the night. Great difficulty was experienced in the controlling of the nuisance until Government hit upon the idea of prosecuting in an indirect way those who were associated with the criminal elements who frequented the yards where these drums were played. This was alleged to have had the desired effect.

Although there is no strict enforcement of the legislation to control, the laws on the statute book still remain:[9]

80. Every person or occupier of any home, building, yard or other place who shall:

(1) without licence under the hand of a commissioned officer of constabulary permit any persons to assemble and play or dance therein to any drums, gong, tambours, bougees, chac-chac or other similar instrument of music at any time between the hours of ten o'clock in the evening of one day and the hour of six o'clock in the morning of the next day, or

(2) permit any person to assemble and dance therein the dance known as "Bongo" or any similar dance, shall on conviction before a Magistrate be liable to a penalty not exceeding ten pounds, and it shall be lawful for any constable with such assistants as he may take to his aid, to enter any home, building, yard or place where

[8] L. O. Innis, *Reminiscences of an Octogenarian* (Trinidad, n.d.).

[9] *Laws of Trinidad and Tobago*, Ch. 25, p. 345, quoted from M. J. and F. S. Herskovits, *Trinidad Village* (New York: Knopf, 1947), p. 348.

any persons may be so assembled and stop such dance
or seize and carry away all such drums, gongs, tambours, bougees, chac-chac or other instruments of music.

Likewise during Carnival Day there is still placed upon
the streets of Port of Spain placards prohibiting, among
other things, the beating of any drum or the tooting of
any horn. These prohibitions although violated nowadays
without any prosecution must have materially helped to
bring about the disappearance of the drums. At any rate on
Carnival Day, as in the countryside for Bongo dancing,
a substitute for the drums was found. For weeks before
Carnival branches of bamboo trees could be seen being
dragged through the streets for a new type of "drum" involving the beating together of specially selected pieces of
bamboo. The Bamboo tamboo (tambour) became synonymous with Carnival. It was a cheap form of music and
Carnival began on Monday mornings with the invasion of
the streets by bamboo bands. Some idea of the emotional
significance of the bamboo band can be indicated by the
fact that one Calypsonian in recounting the loneliness of
a Trinidadian in New York sang:

> New York ain't got breadfruit
> All they have is grapefruit.
> Bamboo band and chac-chac
> Waiting for you here in Sangre Grande.

The bamboo band reigned completely for a number of
years, the only addition being the bottle and spoon—one
to a band. Gradually there were added the hubs of motor
car wheels and other metallic car parts that could produce
the required sounds. These metal instruments had gradually
replaced the bamboo when the second World War broke
out.

During the war years Carnival was banned as well as
were demonstrations in the streets. Frequently the steel
bands, which, in view of the prohibition, now "practised"

indoors, invaded the streets only to be put down by police action. For instance, when one steel band appeared at the Queen's Park Savannah to support the proletarian team "Colts" in the Amateur Football competition they were dispersed by police action.

These clashes between police and steel bandsmen increased in number when gang warfare between the rival steel bands developed. During the war this was due to poor police supervision, the social and psychological dislocation resulting from the establishment of the American Bases, and the consequent break-down of social control. The removal of the outlet of Carnival during the war years was also of great significance.

Immediately after the war there was a great revival of Carnival which automatically took place on V-J and V-E days before the holding of Carnival on the usual Carnival days became legally regularized. The steel band became popular and there was a great improvement of technique. The improvement in technique immensely increased the popularity of the steel band, but at the same time its connection with gang warfare was so acute that attitudes towards the bands continued to show a strong element of disapproval.

The hostility towards authority, and in particular towards the police, expressed by the members of the steel band to those making the steel band survey in 1949 was extreme; most of them replying to the question as to what they would do if they saw a policeman injured and in need of help by the roadside by saying that they would pass him by and would render him no aid. In part this resulted from bad handling of the situation by the police and possibly from a too severe or indiscriminate prosecution of offenders. Certainly there were other elements in the situation as well. The increasing sophistication of the steel band necessitated a great deal more practice, co-ordination, leadership and organization than before. Such development seems to have served to weld the steel band into a closely knit primary group with strong aggressive tendencies towards outsiders. At the same time the powerful beat and exulting rhythm of the steel band seems to have given confidence to its members. One steel band Calypso describes how "asleep in his cachot" he dreamt of a steel band going to fight Hitler:

> Adolf Hitler, here comes the enemy
> We are quite prepared for the Bad Man from
>   Germany
> No bayonet, no gun,
> The beating of the steel band go make him run.
> So, Hitler, Be on your guard.
> I mean, it's the steel band from Trinidad.

Whatever the sources of the hostility, its proportions became alarming, particularly when fights between rival gangs took place on the streets to the risk of life and limb of innocent bystanders; and when, too, pedestrians on the street were "bounced" (given slight cuts with a razor on the arms) just for the fun of it. The attitude of repression which first characterized the official attitude proved unsuccessful.

Fortunately there were some far-seeing individuals in the community who recognized the steel band as an indigenous expression which needed encouragement and who consequently sought to wean the steel band away from its criminal associations. Their point of view was adopted by the Colonial Secretary of the time and a Committee was appointed to carry out a sociological survey of the steel bands of the Port of Spain area; to make recommendations whereby the cultural and recreational potentialities of steel bands might be encouraged; and to suggest the future scope of the Trinidad and Tobago Steel Bands' Association.

The last term of reference indicates that in an attempt to gain control of the movement and to give it status the bands had been forced into an association. The problem of organization was rendered more difficult since the steel band had improved so much that the individual bands were able to obtain contracts to play at dances and night clubs, at home and abroad, including even the United States of America. The Association as at first conceived was one of linking up the bands in such a way that they would, in a self-governing manner, exert discipline on those recalcitrant groups which did not observe the code of behaviour to which they were committed. The new commercial possibilities made this task more difficult since it required a much higher degree of integrity in the leadership and loyalty on the part of the individual bands if they were to accept decisions which would have important financial consequences.

The struggle to wean the steel band away from crime was only partially successful. The councillor, the politician, the man of good will who devoted themselves to this task served to give "official" recognition by the upper classes of the society, of the achievement of the steel band in creating from nothing or rather from empty gasolene drums, something of an orchestra. This effort to integrate the steel band movement into the life of the society as a whole came to a head when there was a drive on the part of the steel band committee to raise funds by public subscription to send a representative steel band to Great Britain to represent the island at the Festival of Britain in 1951.

The drive received the patronage of the Governor and a large degree of enthusiastic support from the general public. The amount that it was sought to raise was $15,000 (B.W.I.)—£3,000—a large sum to be raised at such short notice and for such a purpose. About two-thirds of this amount was actually raised and the Government of the island provided the rest. Although the sum may appear small, in order that it could be reached at all a real "national" effort was needed involving radio appeals by leaders of the voluntary organizations, patronage of concerts by the leading citizens of the land, and voluntary collecting by individuals, etc. In this way the steel band movement became associated with all the symbols of Government, of upper-class society, etc., and this undoubtedly helped to remove the stigma attaching to "steel bandsmen".

The visit of the steel band to the United Kingdom was quite successful from the point of view of the island society. If, from the limited point of view of most of the inhabitants, it was expected that the steel band was "going to take England by storm", there was little disappointment if results fell short of this, since the same limited perspectives prevented them from appreciating how impossible this was of achievement.

Nonetheless the steel band movement has not yet become definitely removed from its criminal associations. Since the TASPO (Trinidad All Steel Percussion Orchestra) visit to the Festival of Britain there have been further outbursts of gang warfare, though not as serious as on some occasions. In one respect, however, some progress has been made. The association of the steel band with crime was to a large extent fortuitous. It was only in fact in Port of Spain that a great many of the bands had criminal affiliations. In the country districts this was not the case. However, the best bands were in Port of Spain and the general public were aware of the specially composed Calypsos by the Steel Band Association with their aggressive tone:

Ah, *Lord Invaders,* why you run, why you run
"Tokyo" back in Town.

Invaders too bad
They want to pelt a stone in the yard
Tell them we are young
Tell them we are strong.

Nonetheless, on account of the rhythms and the technical competence involved, several middle-class persons learned to play the steel band. One result of this has been the organization of these bands in the secondary schools and of the "Girl Pat" steel orchestra, a band composed of middle-class girls. In a sense this has solved the problem of getting some form of cultural expression of a national nature. However, it has not served to bridge the gap between the lower class and the middle class because as soon as the middle class groups learn the technique of actually operating the steel band they move away from association with the "real" steel bandsmen. How far this trend will overcome the concern and admiration for technical competence cannot be judged at the moment.

16.

No aspect of West Indian culture better conveys the complexity of West Indian life than recent Caribbean literary works, autobiographical, picaresque, and folkloristic. The extraordinary development of West Indian fiction since the Second World War is traced here by a West Indian novelist, who is unique in having left the Caribbean for a long sojourn in Africa. The need for a wider audience, he points out in this introduction to his own collection of Caribbean fiction, is a major reason most such writers have emigrated; but self-exile inevitably affects their creative style. Even though a number of the finest West Indian writers do occasionally return home to refresh and to restore their creative impulse, the nuances of the West Indian scene, the style, the flavor, and the pace of island life are inevitably diluted by distance and the fading of memory.

Guyanese-born, O. R. DATHORNE took his undergraduate degree at Sheffield University and did postgraduate work in English at the University of London. He has taught at the University of Nigeria and is presently on the staff of the Department of Afro-American Studies at the University of Wisconsin. His own novels include *Dumplings in the Soup* and *The Scholar-Man*.

Caribbean Narrative
O. R. Dathorne

* * * *

Andrew Salkey once said to me that there was no such thing as West Indian literature; Denis Williams affirmed that it is a province of English letters. They would both argue that it has still to attain a certain definite identity before it can acquire nationality. Indeed there is some truth in this. But literature does not operate in a vacuum, and it would seem to me that West Indian writing has to grow out of developing social patterns. West Indian culture is still only in the process of maturing and until this happens, West Indian literature, like West Indian life, reaches backwards towards Africa and India, and is saturated in its present with English and American elements. Ultimately, West Indian literature will merge and consolidate these differences into its cosmopolitan image of the future.

There are more immediately practical considerations. None of the few publishing houses in the West Indies has the financial backing to be able to risk a book and market it abroad. Even if the West Indian writer were to publish in Jamaica, or Trinidad, the West Indian reading public is still negligible, and unlike Canada, Australia and South Africa, cannot support its writers. The West Indian

Caribbean Narrative, London, Heinemann Educational Books, Ltd., 1966, pp. 2–16. Reprinted by permission of the author.

writer is therefore tied to the economic apron strings c
Britain and sometimes of America. Consequently it is no
surprising that this tends to influence his work. The ma
jority of the writers in this selection live in England. A
George Lamming said in a television interview in London
the West Indian writer came to England much as the Wes
Indian labourer did—to seek an employer.

But West Indian literature did not begin when Mittel
holzer left Trinidad for England, nor with Lamming and
Selvon who followed in 1950, nor with Naipaul's scholar
ship to Oxford. Indigenous West Indian literature is at leas
one hundred and fifty years old and goes back to the
eighteenth century. The authors at that time were formerl
slaves and their journey to England and subsequent aliena
tion from the West Indies and their writing, seem t
foreshadow the experiences of most of the writers of ou
own century. In 1787 Cugoano published his *Thought
and Sentiments,* an account of his own life and the unjus
practices of the slave trade; Equiano, in 1789, publishe
his *Interesting Narrative,* also part-autobiography and par
anti-slavery propaganda. Before these the *Letters* of Sanch
was published posthumously in 1782; and Phyllis Wheat-
ley, who had lived some time in the West Indies before
going to America, published her poems as early as 1773.
Apart from this there was some local writing going on,
and Edward Long mentions in his *History of Jamaica*
(1774) that there was a Jamaican schoolmaster, Francis
Williams, who had apparently published verse, which
Long says was overpraised. Indeed Long's derogatory remarks are general, which would suggest there was a certain
amount of writing by Negroes; he feels that too much praise
was given to them, and adds sarcastically that before their
'sacred name flows every fault'.

This does not of course take into account the vast
amount of imaginative prose literature which was published by English people who had either been to the West
Indies or had read about it. Both Lady Nugent's journal,
covering her residence in Jamaica between 1801 and 1805,

nd J. A. Froude's *The English and the West Indies*
1888), provide interesting background reading. But imag-
native interest in the West Indies goes back as early as
Alexander Barclay's *The Ship of Fools* (1509), was stimu-
ated by Raleigh's *Discovery of Guiana* in 1595, and was
given literary expression by Robert Greene, George Chap-
man, Shakespeare, Marlowe, Spenser, Marvell and Nash
among others. Later on when travel literature was in
vogue, Defoe's *Crusoe* (1719), *The Adventures of Jonathan Corncob* (1787), Michael Scott's *Tom Cringle's Log*
(1829–1833), and *The Cruise of the Midge* (1835), were
some of the many books of fiction that had at least part
of their setting in the West Indies. Anthony Trollope's
travel book on the West Indies (1859) was straight travel
literature. Some time before this, abolitionist literature
had brought about the revival of the theme originally
treated in Aphra Behn's *Oronooko* (1688), itself a variation of the Inkle-Yarico legend of African love in the new
world, which was mentioned in the *Spectator* of 3 March
1711. This revival was expressed in the form of novels,
poetry and drama until the mid-nineteenth century. In
our own times we have witnessed the West Indian once
more writing about himself, but the English interest continues, for example in Ronald Firbank's *Prancing Nigger*
(1924), in the macabre ending of Evelyn Waugh's *A
Handful of Dust* (1934), in Graham Greene, Colin Mac-
Innes and more recently in a television play by Kingsley
Amis.

Meantime in the West Indies people continued to write.
N. E. Cameron was able to bring out in British Guiana,
as early as 1931, an anthology of Guyanese poetry covering the period 1831 to 1931, and J. E. Clare McFarlane
published an anthology of Jamaican poetry in 1949. In
the field of prose Frederick Charles Tomlinson had published in 1903, Thomas MacDermot in 1907, and the Jamaican novelist Herbert G. de Lisser brought out *Jane's
Career* in London in 1914. Fiction was published locally
in the West Indies, some of only ephemeral interest; but

there were others of a more enduring quality lik A. R. F. Webber's *Those That Be in Bondage* (1917) which dealt with East Indian immigration. In the twentie our leading novelist was Claude McKay who publishee in America and whose world was an expansive one o black West Indians, Negro Americans and Africans. I the thirties C. L. R. James's *Minty Alley* was published and Alfred Mendes was attracting some attention with hi. short stories and his novel *Black Fauns* (1935). Abou this time too Walter Adolphe Roberts started being pub lished in America; his earliest novel is *The Mind Reader* a mystery story with a New York setting published ir 1929.

The forties saw an important development in the growth of our indigenous literature—the founding of three periodi cals, whose influence in West Indian literature can nevei be overestimated. Frank Collymore started *Bim* in 1942 in Barbados, the first issue of *Focus* came out in 1943, edited by Edna Manley in Jamaica, and Arthur Seymour began *Kyk-over-al* in 1945. In addition the Christmas num bers of local newspapers all had literary supplements, and the Department of Extra-Mural Studies of the then Uni versity College of the West Indies started *Caribbean Quarterly* in 1949. Most of the West Indian writers now writing had their early work first published in *Bim, Focus* and *Kyk,* which existed with little money, were never sub sidized, and which only progressed from one issue to the next because of a certain amount of goodwill on the part of buyers and a praiseworthy excess of zeal on the part of the editors. One must also add that some measure of praise is due to Henry Swanzy, who began editing 'Carib bean Voices' for the B.B.C. in 1946. It was only with these periodicals and 'Caribbean Voices' that Mittelholzer, Selvon and Lamming got a wider West Indian public. In 1950 the Pioneer Press was founded in Jamaica by Edna Manley and others; it published West Indian writing locally and would no doubt have developed into the foremost publishing house in the West Indies, had it not folded up.

Of the people who are now writing and about whom people usually speak when they refer to West Indian literature, Edgar Mittelholzer was the first to be published. Indeed, as Lamming has pointed out a little sceptically, it gave him a certain seniority of prestige among people who wrote in Trinidad'. He had published *Courentyne Thunder* in 1941. Vic Reid's *New Day* did not appear until 1949, Selvon did not publish *A Brighter Sun* until 1952, nor did Lamming publish *In the Castle of My Skin* until 1953, in the same year that Roger Mais's *The Hills Were Joyful Together* came out. When John Hearne's *Voices Under the Window* appeared in 1955, V. S. Naipaul's *The Mystic Masseur* in 1957 and Jan Carew's *Black Midas* in 1958, the development of West Indian literature had begun. Since then these writers, with the exception of Mais and Mittelholzer, have continued to write, and many more West Indian writers have been published. Frank Collymore listed a number of writers well-known in the West Indies—Seepersad Naipaul (Naipaul's father, now dead), Ernest Carr and Cecil Gray of Trinidad; John Mansfield, Inez Sibley, Claude Thompson, A. E. T. Henry of Jamaica; and Karl Sealy, L. E. Braithwaite and John Wickham of Barbados. Now West Indian writing appears frequently in English periodicals, two collections of stories have been edited by Salkey, some criticism has appeared in book-form by Lamming and Coulthard; and West Indians have been published in Australia, West and East Africa as well as Canada, America, England, and of course the West Indies. In addition their work has been translated into many European languages, and in paperback form it has reached many parts of the world and many levels of the reading public.

If a general point can be made about West Indian literature it is that the writers, living out of the West Indies as most of them do, usually exhaust any recognizable image of the West Indies in their first few books. This very point was made by a writer in the *Times Literary Supplement*: 'All novelists have trouble with their second

books; the West Indian has more trouble than others, if he
has transferred from the Caribbean to Europe.' Few have
had the opportunity of returning home: Mittelholzer went
back to live in Barbados for two years; Lamming, Selvon
and Naipaul have more recently returned as visitors.
Hearne is at the moment living in Jamaica, Dawes has
recently left British Guiana after a year there, and Jan
Carew has returned to England after some time in British
Guiana and Jamaica. It would seem therefore that the
realism of these writers—what one might call our recognition of the familiar—is bound to suffer, and their later
novels, as with Naipaul's, Mittelholzer's, Carew's, Salkey's,
Lamming's, and Selvon's, are either going to move completely away from the West Indian setting and deal with
Americans or Englishmen or Africans, or else they are going to deal with what after all these writers know best—
the alienated West Indian living out of the West Indies and
cut off from his roots.

This experimental engendering of recent West Indian
writing has meant that a great many of the first novels of
West Indian writers have a biographical basis. George
Lamming's is, among other things, fictionalized recollec-
tions of a Barbadian childhood; Geoffrey Drayton's
Christopher is thinly disguised biography. Selvon's and
Naipaul's first novels are about the young Indian growing
up in Trinidad, Jan Carew's *Black Midas* owes a great deal
to the real-life adventures of Herbert Scotland, one of the
people to whom the book is acknowledged, and Neville
Dawes's *The Last Enchantment* and Lauchmonen's *Guiana
Boy*, are respectively about youth in the city and the
canefield. But the realism goes further, and the West
Indian tall story, what one might call our 'gaff', is seen in
writers as different as Selvon and Naipaul. For instance,
the well-known tall story of the religious maniac who seeks
a kind of self-imposed crucifixion is dealt with in their different ways by these two writers; in Selvon a character
mentions it *en passant,* and in Naipaul it becomes the

limax to a farcical situation in a short story called *Man-Man*.

The ability to observe and utilize real-life experiences is not of course a West Indian monopoly, but I am suggesting hat what these writers use *is* West Indian. As a matter of act, it is not only the locality that makes it West Indian but the West Indian creative attitude, which is first of all nterested in certain types of farcical experiences, and West ndian expression, which lends itself well to describing hese. Lamming, for instance, gives an entertaining account of how, when he went to cover certain aspects of he funeral of George VI for the B.B.C., an amusing incident took place. Lamming and a companion, Thomasos, re in the Abbey and Thomasos sees a black man walking towards him complete with morning suit and sword:

> To Thomasos, who had now halted, this gentleman was simply playing the ass. That hilarious get-up might have been perfect on carnival day in Port-of-Spain. But not in the Abbey!

This is of course a typical West Indian response to such a situation and this is not fiction here; in this incident George Lamming relates something that actually happened. It becomes fictionalized in his short story *A Wedding in Spring* where George Lamming uses a device other than narrative bias to ridicule the morning suit. In the story a character called Beresford owns it, and his attachment to it is compared with that of

> his grandfather whose wedding could not proceed; had, indeed, to be postponed because he would not repeat the words: *All my worldly goods I thee endow.* He had sworn never to part with his cow, like Beresford and the morning suit.

When in the short-story Beresford and Knickerbocker arrive with top-hats and morning suits, a poodle attacks

them, rips off one of Knickerbocker's coat-tails and at
tempts to escape with the top-hats.

Another example of West Indian response to comic situ
ation and its later incorporation in a story, is the accoun
of Selvon's meeting with a Nigerian when he first went to
London:

> The third lodger was a Nigerian whom we called
> Mate. I'm not sure whether this was the name he gave
> or whether Selvon had chosen it. . . . Mate was a stu-
> dent whose monthly allowance had been temporarily
> suspended. . . . He always wore a suit, arranged in
> every pleat and seam with impeccable neatness. He
> brushed everything before he dressed, and he repeated
> the same chore before he went to bed. He might not
> regain his allowance; but he would never betray his
> clothes.

In one of Selvon's episodes in *The Lonely Londoners,*
Mate becomes Cap, a Nigerian who does no work but who
prospers in idle luxury.

As I have said, when West Indian writers want to write
about the West Indies after their first novel, it is as if physical severance from their setting has made them less sure of
detail. This has given way to a new kind of realism in
which I find that the writers are more concerned with
human situations in a setting that is every West Indian
island and yet none at all. Lamming invented San Cristobal,
Hearne sets his novels in Cayuna; but even where the
writers agree to give the place a known geographical name,
their evocation of what it means to them differs. Therefore
Jan Carew's Guyana is not Wilson Harris's—Carew sets
the physical affirmation of individual struggle against a
jungle, wobbling before man's assertiveness, Harris sur-
renders his community to the potency of myth and the
will of landscape. And the Trinidad of Naipaul and that
of Selvon—both humorists and what is perhaps less important, both Indians—is a very different one. In Selvon it
is the cosmopolitan associations that matter, that give his

books their comic verve; in Naipaul a slightly less authentic version of a closed racial world is the prerequisite towards understanding his books. The Negroes in Naipaul's world are therefore only on the periphery of his design, in Selvon they communicate at the core.

It is the way in which this polygenous mass of races intermingle in the West Indian novel that distinguishes it from the narrower dimensions of standard European fiction. In attempting to describe this the writers may have one of several things to do—the intention may be merely to exhibit the unique commingling of races that is West Indian, or to satirize its prejudices and failings, or to highlight its rigid distinctiveness above the apparent cosmopolitan flux. Edgar Mittelholzer sets himself such a task in *A Morning at the Office*. Another approach is to isolate a particular community and describe it. But whereas this is only incidental to Naipaul's purpose, it is a *sine qua non* of a novel like *Black Albino* by Namba Roy, where the setting of the story is among the Maroons of Jamaica, and deals with the effect on the tribe when the chief has an albino son. But I find that in both of these books by Mittelholzer and Namba Roy the intention is too obtrusively pedagogic; in Selvon's *A Brighter Sun* the young Indian couple and their Negro neighbours mix and participate in the business of living and incidentally learn about themselves and each other. But it is all done within the strict limitations of the novel-form, with no excursions into excessive didacticism.

As a racial theme in the West Indian novel, the African is perhaps the predominant one. From Claude McKay's *Banjo* (1929) in which the hero sentimentalizes upon African dialects that were 'rich and round and ripe like soft tropical fruit', to Denis Williams's hero in *Other Leopards* (1963), who finds to his horror that he is an uncommitted African in Africa, the search for roots goes on. It is an interest that is motivated by West Indian attitudes to Africa; genuine survivals extant in Haitian voodoo, the practices of the Maroons of Jamaica and so on; mili-

tant perversions that identify the African heritage with
Ethiopia, such as the Rastafarians in Jamaica, imaginatively treated in Orlando Patterson's *Children of Sisyphus*,
and the so-called Shango cult in Trinidad. Since it is only
relatively recently that the African has become articulate,
it is obvious that when the West Indian novelist writes
about Africa it is essentially a localized West Indian concept that he has in his mind, probably based on the fact
that West Indians, in the words of the South African writer
Ezekiel Mphahlele, 'were taught some nasty things about
us by their colonial masters and pseudo-historians'. A
West Indian version (which I must say is an authentic and
realistic presentation of the West Indian viewpoint) of the
African presence appears in the characters of Preacher
and Mr Cuffy in Naipaul's *The Suffrage of Elvira*. In
Andrew Salkey's first novel two views on Africa are put
forward—Miss Mellie's that 'we is a people who live on the
island of St Thomas, not Africa', and Mother Johnson's,
that 'everybody is a part of slavery days, is a part of the
climate-a-Africa'. In a recent novel by John Hearne, Marcus Heneky (Marcus Garvey?), is seen as more than a
mere racialist. His ideology is an attempt at re-ordering
history, and so he has had to change 'the lie that the black
man was faceless' so as 'to give the black man the sort of
vision of himself that would make him free. And make
the whites and the browns free, because they were shackled
to the lie too.' This, as a theme, will be soon effete unless
it is associated with the historical perspective and expanded into a more intense scrutiny of the nature of man.

The attempt at writing historical novels is not the same
thing as what I have called the historical perspective, although it can stimulate this in the writers who engage in
it, the readers who interpret, and the writers who are going to write afterwards. Therefore, it is perhaps a good
thing that we have at the beginning of our contemporary
novel movement in the West Indies, historical novels of
some significance. Herbert de Lisser's *The White Witch
of Rosehall* is, according to Philip Sherlock, based on the

true story of Anne Palmer, who lived with her husband John, from 1820 to 1828, at the Great House at Rosehall, a few miles from Montego Bay in Jamaica. Vic Reid's first novel, *New Day*, has as its background the Morant Bay uprising of 1865. More recently Edgar Mittelholzer in the Kaywana trilogy has canvassed something of even larger proportions; in *Children of Kaywana* life and death in the Guyana of the seventeenth and eighteenth century is centred round Hendrickje van Groenwegel; *The Harrowing of Hubertus* (or *Kaywana Stock*) continues the story down to the death of her grandson, Hubertus, early in 1800, and *Kaywana Blood,* the sequel, begins in 1795, and this time centres itself around Hubertus's young cousin, Dirk. Whatever may be the shortcomings of these novels, they are nevertheless a huge saga and represent an intentional but not obtrusive attempt to re-live history, at a time when it has become a commonplace to assert the absence of a West Indian tradition. What Kingsley Amis said about *Children of Kaywana* applies to the entire Kaywana trilogy: Mittelholzer has achieved 'the passionate realization of a world in historical and topographical as well as personal terms'.

What, however, I find more significant in West Indian writing is a definite striving for historical sense. In a place where, for many, history is the recollection of the incidents of two previous generations, it is more than ever imperative that we should give depth and dignity to what we do recall, to re-interpret the amalgam of influences that has contributed to our present social complexity. A novel like *A House for Mr Biswas,* though fragmentary in outline, itemises the incidents that contribute to the physical and cultural evolution of its hero in a society, which according to Naipaul in *The Middle Passage,* 'denied itself heroes'. It succeeds because it gives heroic stature to Biswas and it is out of this that the historical ambit expands. One might say that in this novel Naipaul makes the historical sense operate in character, but that in general, Naipaul, Hearne, Mais and Selvon lack the historical sense; their characters

live on the ephemeral terrain of circumvention; their attitudes and actions are contained in specific moments of
time. There is no 'backward glance'.

Another writer who I feel has a concept of the past is
Lamming; at times, as in *Season of Adventure*, his past is
a conglomeration of hazy notions of an African mystique.
However, I feel it is not totally unsuccessful, because when
the past does not operate through character, it asserts itself
best in the archetypal significance of the grandeur of myth.
This is Wilson Harris's method—his novels are made up of
the *personae* of world mythology. For example, in *The
Secret Ladder*, Poseidon, half-god, half-man, is the prototype of the wise old man. In *The Whole Armour*, Magda,
a *magna mater* figure, is the prototype of the old faithful
mother. Harris's incidents are usually contained within a
setting out from somewhere and death which operates in
his pages like an ominous accessory to life. The action of
his novels is one that lends itself, therefore, to wider inter-
pretations in terms of the significance of life and death.
His novels are a conspiracy against our organized concept
of time and place. In this way he is the most interesting
and original talent to have come out of the West Indies.

Naipaul criticized the West Indian novel because the
West Indian author's 'involvement with the white world
. . . deprives his work of universal appeal'. The historical
recognition is one way in which the West Indian writer has
circumvented this inability to appeal universally. Another
way is by dealing in large human terms with character
and incident—not necessarily by giving them the proportions of myth, but by re-shaping them into the more readily
apprehended and recognizable. This has been done, as we
shall see later, but there is a danger here that writers suc-
cumb too easily to superlatives, in the temptation to relate
what is either too readily recognizable or too excessively
surprising to the European and American reader—thereby
perverting their themes in order to domesticate the unrealistic. This causes not only what we might term the
'commercial' novel (Herbert de Lisser, Walter Adolphe

Roberts and Mittelholzer have written some) but also in artistic distortion and a dishonest association between the West Indies as it exists in the mind of the writer, and the West Indies as it exists in the minds of his European reading public. This is indeed very often a sorry compromise.

This is not the same as saying that Selvon, for example, ought not to write funny stories about the West Indies. Indeed this is where his success lies; they are funny, they are even distorted, but we can believe in them. As J. A. Ramsaran has said in his *New Approaches to African Literature* (1965), 'Selvon's *forte* is the episodic presentation of mood and impression'. It is because the mood and impression are Selvon's, and make no concession to the exotic tastes of a foreign audience, that we can *believe* in Selvon. One might add too that Selvon is very much with his characters, unlike Naipaul, whose humour has less compassion and is more embittered. Indeed it is surprising that West Indian writers who, Salkey feels, 'wear the comic mask with more assurance than the tragic', have only produced two comic writers. Mittelholzer and others have of course written some comedy; Alvin Bennett's *God the Stonebreaker* is very funny. But in general the West Indian has avoided the humorous novel. Naipaul quotes Graham Greene's observation that 'comedy needs a strong framework of social convention with which the author sympathizes but does not share' and adds that 'by this definition the West Indian writer is incapable of comedy'.

West Indian comedy seems to lie mainly in character, language and to a less extent in incident. Personal names, drawn from the inanimate or the trivial, provide a large element of the comic delineation—Selvon's characters have names like Five-past-Twelve, Mangohead, Small Change and Eraser; Naipaul's characters are called Hat, Big Foot, Bogart, Razor, and so on. Sometimes the same name occurs in both Selvon and Naipaul, e.g. Popo. Selvon often writes in a half-way variant between standard English and Trinidadian dialect; Naipaul writes an arch, precise kind of English. Selvon's characters, whether they are Jamaicans,

Trinidadians or Africans, speak in much the same way, but Naipaul has been noticeably unadventurous, as his main West Indian characters are all Trinidadian anyway. (Lamming has a much better ear for dialect as can be seen in *The Emigrants,* where there are dialects from many islands. But he lacks the comic gift.) Indeed, where Naipaul and Selvon succeed best is in creating a succession of bright eccentrics who do little, but whose eccentricity is in how they act and how they speak.

Perhaps one of the reasons why West Indian novelists have steered clear of humour in general is because they see it as their business to interpret and classify their social world—one in which politics seems to play a leading rôle. Politics, perhaps in its largest sense man's insistence on order, is the theme of most of John Hearne's novels. I would prefer to interpret Hearne's themes on this wider, and for me, more significant level. Mark Lattimer in *Voices Under the Window,* Carl Brandt in *Stranger at the Gate,* Jojo Rygin in *The Faces of Love,* Eleanor Stacey in *The Autumn Equinox* and Marcus Heneky in *Land of the Living* all move, as a critic said in a broadcast, 'towards the same dark end and defeat'. All of Hearne's heroes are defeated by their attempt at restoring order; this certainly makes the author's vision tragic, but it gives his novels a significance beyond their immediate statement and setting. They represent the imaginative diagnosis of a humanistic vision of revolution—a vision rendered all the more universal because the heroes or victims in his novels identify themselves with a profound and intensely passionate *Weltschmerz.* No other West Indian writer has quite succeeded in unobtrusively affirming the political and the animal in man. Perhaps if C. L. R. James were less a serious propagandist, he would have approached nearest to the kind of constitutional framework in Hearne's novels.

We find a deep political awareness also in Neville Dawes's novel and its connection with emerging nationalism. In *The Last Enchantment* the issues are specific—a neo-democratic party, which has secured power by the partial assimilation of English creeds (satirized by Naipaul in the *Suffrage of Elvira*) is opposed to a neo-Marxist popular party in need of dedicated and informed leadership. On the personal level the political consciousness of the novel operates through two characters—Ramsay Tull and Cyril Hanson, both Oxford educated; but whereas Tull entrenches his negroness against the inroads of anglicization, Hanson compromises. When they return to Jamaica, Tull becomes the chief spokesman of the leftist party, Hanson of the other. But, as with Hearne, order collapses, and with it Ramsay Tull and his ideals. Here the interpretation would seem to be more relevant and less universal than Hearne's—is socialism possible in West Indian society?

Lamming explores the politics of his island in two main novels—*Of Age and Innocence* and *Season of Adventure*. In *Of Age and Innocence*, Mark and Shepherd, who return to San Cristobal from Europe, help awaken the people from their political sloth. But the end is like Hearne's and Dawes's—the leader was crushed and the movement apparently defeated. With *Season of Adventure*, San Cristobal is a republic, and Lamming is now concerned with the more far-reaching problems of freedom—on the political, social and individual levels. Fola's search for her origins is a microcosm of the desire of the islanders for a new kind of freedom. The end of the novel is one of triumph and apprehension; politics in Lamming is a turning inwards, what he has himself called 'a clarification of his relations with other men, and a report of his own, very highly subjective conception of the possible meaning of a man's life'.

This expanded introspective study of self is, to my mind, one of the most exciting facts about the West Indian novel, which takes it out of the area of provincialism, and which will later on give it a larger and more significant potentiality than it now incorporates. Many West Indian novelists have attempted this; for example, Lamming in his first novel, *In the Castle of My Skin*, Selvon in *An Island Is a*

World, Mittelholzer in *A Tale of Three Places,* Vic Reid in *The Leopard* and Wilson Harris in his first four novels which make up a Guyana quartet. This has often meant that the writers have had to be fairly experimental with language, and this has caused some writers to be labelled 'pseudo-Joycean'. But if a myopic view of race or nationalism is widened into this much larger vision of existentialist self-inquiry, then the instrument of interrogation has to be magnified as well. This is the reason for Dawes's frequent changes of style in his novel, for Lamming's technique in *Castle,* for Wilson Harris's fastidious extravaganza of diction and image, so that no word is a 'passenger' but is relevant to dialogue, narrative, setting and action. In his later novels Lamming's style has tended to verge on the exhibitionist and the verbose, but I feel that some of the difficulties of communication lie in the nature of his themes. There is none of this at all in Naipaul, very little in Hearne, and I sometimes wonder if this is not the main reason for their success in England. We all write for an English reading public and in general the West Indian writer is concerned with canvassing emotions in much too overt a manner; in recent English literary tradition the reader is not usually even nudged by the author; the author is expected to respect emotions as sacrosanct. Conrad, Synge and Dylan Thomas all wrote outside this tradition.

The fact that West Indian writers are inextricably concerned with the working class is probably a redeeming feature in this case. One would balk at the idea of a Selvon who only wrote the soppy sentimentalism of "My Girl and the City", even though it is emotionally persuasive. A great deal of the heaviness of the language and the sententiousness of *Season of Adventure* is redeemed by the dialect and the uninhibited actions of the steelband men. Also I feel that the local idiom of Harris's characters enhances his novels—prevents them from straining towards too high a pitch of inaudible excess. In Jan Carew and Vic Reid these verbal excesses often add a touch of poetic truth to their descriptions; in some writers they are frequently overdone. But the heightened prose is a legacy from poetry, for most of our novelists began as poets; indeed not so much from poetry but from that artistic freedom of language that Walter Allen has written about in *Tradition and Dream*—what one might call the absence of rigid traditions that inhibit, and the presence of shifting values which stimulate experiment. In a different century, concerned more with that special technique of diction that is poetry, and less with a fashionable technology of words which is the prose of fiction—in an age that required a less frigid aesthetic, I wonder if most of our novelists would not have remained poets.

17.

The special circumstances of West Indian writing and the way these circumstances affect its quality are surveyed here by an Englishman. Economics is not the only motive for West Indian self-exile, he shows; the Caribbean cultural environment also leaves much to be desired. A social and intellectual milieu impoverished by isolation and by small-ness, the corrosive effects of class and ethnic prejudice, and the glare of publicity that attaches to any local success may all diminish the capacity for, and the character of, imaginative writing. In this milieu, those who achieve any-thing are apt to become self-conscious participants in, as well as conscious observers of, the local scene: their no-toriety as local celebrities makes it impossible to keep out of the public eye. Some West Indian writers, feeling required to be constantly up to the moment in approach and content, find it hard to maintain integrity of crafts-manship. A carapace of ironic humor shields them from self-criticism only at the cost of creative vitality.

W. I. CARR was for some years in the Faculty of Arts of the University of the West Indies in Jamaica. He is now Professor of English at the University of Guyana.

The West Indian Novelist:
Prelude and Context
W. I. Carr

The fact that a society is producing novels and poems does
not mean that it has a literature. Two hundred pages or so
of exhausted prose do not constitute a work of imagination;
a hundred and fifty lines of leaden blank verse is no sufficient guarantee of the existence of a poem. Most of us
have a self-preserving instinct for cliché and are therefore perfectly willing to see our prejudices, our conventional views of experience, presented to us between hard
covers. The simple fact of publication, we are apt to believe, is the token of achievement. Yet when we talk about
"the Victorian masters," for example, we should recognise
that what we are judging to be a developing manifestation of genius is in fact a very small proportion of the
amount of fiction published in the nineteenth century. So
at what point then, with what justification are we entitled
to decide that a particular writer belongs to a literature,
and that another is trapped in the dismal prison of contemporary fashion, and that another is merely vending
trivial, temporary or vicious assumptions?

* * * *

Caribbean Quarterly, Vol. 11, Nos. 1–2, March–June 1965,
pp. 71–84. Reprinted with permission of the author and the
editors, Department of Extra-Mural Studies, University of the
West Indies, Kingston, Jamaica.

Take the following stanza from a Jamaican poem:

> Through whispering shades do you stricken run
>   Alone, alone, beloved one?
> And are you lost in mist and rain
> The earth unknowing of your pain?
> And if you call none give reply,
> None give reply—not even I—
>   Not even I, beloved one?

A comparison with Thomas Hardy is barely plausible—
but we might look at it in comparison with a verse from
Hardy's *After a Journey*.

> Hereto I come to view a voiceless ghost;
>   Whither, O whither will its whim now draw me?
> Up the cliff, down, till I'm lonely, lost,
>   And the unseen waters' ejaculations awe me.
> Where you will next be there's no knowing,
>   Facing round about me everywhere,
>   With your nut-coloured hair,
> And gray eyes, and rose-flush coming and going.

Hardy's poem was written after the death of his wife, and
after he had come fully to realise the subtle meannesses she
had intruded into their relationship. The poem does not,
however, contain anything of the retrospectively self-
righteous, anything of posthumous condemnation. His endeavour is to try and understand what his feeling is. The
slightly awkward diction and the rhythms that move from
the poetic to the near-conversational enforce Hardy's gen-
tly ironic honesty in his attempt to understand the ambiguous nature of their mutual living. The Jamaican poem is
simply an incantatory blur of conventions. Hardy's puzzled, shifting movement involves us in an effort at truthful
understanding. This, we feel, is what coping with experience is like. The first poem offers nothing but the willing
tearfulness, the co-operative instinct for effusion, of the
sentimentalist. *After a Journey* is a poem of significant

intelligence—the other is a piece of self-indulgence. It is not a creative participant in a literature. Herman Melville's expression "the shock of recognition" may be adopted to describe a situation in which writer and reader are profoundly and enduringly available to each other. That meeting place of proffered and accepted experience is what we might describe as "a literature."

It is necessary to begin in this way in trying to describe some of the circumstances of contemporary West Indian fiction. No claim on behalf of its "greatness" can yet be responsibly made. It is possible that we will never be able to make such a claim. But it seems to me that the work of West Indian novelists since 1949 justifies reference to "a literature," even though much bad fiction has been published and will obviously continue to be. It is, however, an inescapable irony of the colonial situation that bad writing can, in an obscure and perverse way, comprise a revealing commentary on local experience, or at least of attitudes towards it. This does not mean that in discussing colonial writing there must be a suspension of critical effort. Bad writing must be clearly identified as bad writing otherwise one simply prolongs (with a high degree of meretricious and therefore destructive geniality) the experience out of which the writing has come. But the uniqueness of the West Indian situation must be grasped otherwise discussion of local writing will become evasive and futile. It must be remembered, for instance, that standards of critical judgment and critical honesty are the product of old, secure and confident cultures. Indeed in the West Indies itself the critical function has no welcomed and sanctioned presence. And no useful analogy can be drawn with the experience of post-Revolutionary America. In spite of the acutely perceptive awareness of loss on the part of (say) Fenimore Cooper, Hawthorne and Henry James, the Eastern States did, when we consider the West Indian context, constitute an embodied culture. The important American writers were not obliged to create a literature out of the impoverishment, the humiliation and

the self-doubt that are the prescribed allotment of the
West Indian. What the American writers can supply, however, is the example of a rare integrity. The West Indian
writer is peculiarly vulnerable to the prejudices of his
society, exposed to the temptation of a basic conformity of
feeling. The dread of isolation, which seems to me to
haunt the West Indian imagination, can easily overpower
personal understanding and commit the local writer to
the assumed and accepted pressures of his community. The
great American writers withstood them. Hawthorne, lan-
guishing at Salem, might appear an exception. But whatever degree of self-deprecating irony Hawthorne conveys
when he summons his Puritan ancestors he does at least
have ancestors to summon. When the West Indian writer
glances over his shoulder all he can perceive is an anonymous mass of suffering. And there is Mr. V. S. Naipaul's
grim observation in *The Middle Passage:*

> History is built around achievement and creation; and
> nothing was created in the West Indies.

Naipaul has his own appropriate private nightmare to in-
habit. Yet he is describing here at least the residual consciousness of even the most mature West Indian. At times
there is an air of rather fabricated melodrama about *The
Middle Passage*—experience seems too easily to incorpo-
rate itself into Naipaul's assumptions. But the irritation
his book aroused in the area when it first appeared (and
the hostility or suspicion the mention of his name invariably
produces) are a curious guarantee of his accuracy as an
analyst at least of an emotional atmosphere. The present
writer is frequently informed, for example, that Naipaul's
sociology is "all wrong," that he "doesn't know the society." The point is that he precisely gauges its fears about
itself. This is borne out in the tendency of many West
Indian intellectuals and artists to manufacture a known
and more or less comfortable world in which they can
try to identify the problems both of themselves and their

society. There are the powerful, confident estate owners of John Hearne's novels and the insistent ways in which his writing tries to draw attention to roots, to a past. There is George Lamming's invocation of the "peasant concept" as the determinant in West Indian writing. There is the attempt on the part of even so fine a mind as that of C. L. R. James to make a culture hero of Alexander Hamilton. There is the rather glib identification with African movement that dancers in Jamaica attempt. At a sad and frivolous level it can be summed up in an encounter at a party where a guest asserted that his family had been farming in Jamaica for three hundred years. His family came to the island, apparently, towards the end of the nineteenth century. When Henry James spoke of a society with a rich complex of manners as the necessary field for the activity of the novelist he expressed a peculiarly American need. But if we modify James' observation to mean a ribbed structure of circumstance and tradition, felt and available social materials, then the dilemma of the West Indian writer becomes clearer.

West Indian literature is a bootstrap literature. When the local writer attempts to survey his past little more can be present to him than a long and bloody history of systematic and incompetent exploitation. Greed, power and the restless individualism of sixteenth century Europe were the forces that brought his world into being. You cannot in the West Indies proffer, say, Raleigh and Hawkins with the nimbus of dedicated heroism to which an English schoolboy is usually accustomed. If one tries to account for the discrepancy between the numbers of slaves brought to the West Indies and the size of Negro populations now, or tries to understand why there are large Indian and Chinese communities in the area, then one encounters the bedrock poverty of the West Indian past. What American writers judged to be the sparseness of their society would be accumulated riches in the West Indies. The American colonists, after all, severed a political connection; they did not frustrate a natural cultural commerce. There has never been such a commerce in the West Indies. The West Indian has never been invited to join the group and consequently Europe has only been available to him on terms of a very specialised irony. (The finest awareness, in the West Indies itself, of just what this means is to be found in the poetry of Derek Walcott. "As well as if a manor of thy friend's . . .": the line from Donne is disturbingly poignant coming at the end of a poem entitled "Ruins of a Great House.") Reviewers in England, however, largely failing to realise what this means are given to rhetorical talk about "an exciting racial complex" as though this were the explicable and comprehensive dynamic. In fact the West Indian novelist does not know enough about himself or the varieties of race in his area to make a commanding imaginative statement. What is easily seen in England as the stimulus of racial mixture presents itself in the West Indies as the reflex of frequently defensive irony. What he confronts as an artist is not so much the imposed and brutalising handicap of colonialism as the absence of positive cultural resources. The distinction here may seem illusory—the one is the inevitable consequence of the other. But I am at the moment more concerned with the role of artist than with the artist simply as experiencing agent. For instance, I can think of no West Indian writer who has presented as impressive a sense of the destructive, predatory nature of colonialism as has Conrad. One remembers the warship shelling Africa in *Heart of Darkness* and the account of the operations in the mines. As a person the West Indian writer is an inextricable participant in the experience of his society and the experience of his society is not simply one of prolonged inhumanity. It is also the contemplation of barrenness, of a context as negative as Mr. Forster's Marabar Caves. It isn't simply a matter of, for example, Conrad's obvious superiority to any contemporary West Indian writer. It is a matter also, exile though he was, of the richer possibilities of Conrad's cultural circumstances, the prompt availability to him of tradition and achievement.

The novelist in England inhabits (by comparison) a dense world of critical discussion, of weekly reviews, of shared exchange. He has the great advantage of relative anonymity in a culture, or rather in a social context, which is not forced to engage in a prolonged and painful dialogue with itself. He is not obliged, by the conditions of his living, to explore the nature of his Englishness. It is present for him in the achievement of his predecessors. And at the same time the English novel is so evidently the product of a high degree of endowed social awareness. If the social structure of Victorian England had been different then so would many of the presented and examined moral interests of the Victorian novelists. I am not attempting here any crudely Marxist definition. I am suggesting only that the moral interests of the Victorian novelists bear a clear relation to the range and quality of their social experience. In the West Indies it is impossible to evoke an equivalence of texture. There are for example a number of shared middle class habits in the West Indies, a number of shared assumptions about behaviour and about personal relations. But they do not constitute a moral or social style. Social comedy, or comedy of manners, is virtually impossible, for it is an art which depends on a subtle awareness both of shades of surface and of implications. In the West Indies the texture is too thin and in any case the determining factors tend to be those of colour and affluence. I have often found in classes (to supply an instance from poetry) that one of the great difficulties in teaching Dryden and Pope is the inability of the students to grasp the significance in their satire of their relation with their audience. The confidence which springs from a relation of shared assumption, the economy of effect that comes from an instantaneous taking of point and intention on the part of an audience more or less trained to do it, do not emerge very clearly in a society which hasn't that kind of confidence in itself and has nothing even faintly resembling the inescapable social background of so much English literature. Consequently Dryden is often judged as shallow, and Pope is seen as inhibited and in some obscure way as "unpoetic." Byron obtains a more favourable response, but then Byron makes so many strenuous claims on behalf of *himself*.

I think the representative social experience of the West Indian novelist (once he has realised for himself that he is a writer) can be generalised as follows. He is a kind of Messianic spokesman (when he is taken seriously). He must speak for a nexus of claims and aspirations of which he is still himself a part. It might seem easy to argue that all he need do to free himself is saturate himself in the officially attested exuberance of his society, and reflect the vitality of its behaviour ("an exciting racial complex"). Some writers have in fact surrendered to this temptation and the fictive results are depressing. They become purveyors of the self-consciously exotic, the vendors of an immature, merely picaresque irony that at times can barely be distinguished from mere unintelligence, and will have their place in the historiography of West Indian writing insofar as they illuminate the problems by the very fullness of their failure. It isn't hard to see why this should happen. If you are trying to write in the West Indies you are in a curiously exposed position. You will habitually win uninspired and ill-directed national literary competitions (conspiracies of manufactured enthusiasm on behalf of "the arts"). Schools will demand your frequent (and voluntary) efforts. Friends will lean on your perceptions, you will find yourself invited to be an empanelled judge on subjects often outside your competence. You will find yourself the centre of a constricted world. Few societies, I would imagine, require a more conscientious effort to preserve what you regard as the integrity of your talent. Your experience will become a kind of battery unit for the experience of other people. You dread (or you ought to) the possibility of becoming a veranda lion, a party sage. Finally, you quit your island and make your way to Europe though even there you are likely to become involved in missionary gatherings designed to "explain" your society and its cultural unfamiliarities.

It is very easy to be facetious or uncharitable about this problem. But there can be few West Indian writers who have not experienced it in one form or another. The small, eager literary group that genuinely means well but soon freezes in its assumptions; the societies which have a vague connexion with International PEN; the reviews which appear (occasionally) in the local newspapers. This is where you are likely to have started from and you preserve for it an inevitable nostalgia for early charity, for your introduction to a world where the terms were known, while at the same time you recognise that your essential commitment is to something larger and more spacious—and something which is bound to entail your suffering. You will know that the people who helped you will never undergo the sense of loss and hope and achievement that will be yours. The pleasures of exile, to borrow George Lamming's phrase will be, for them, little more than a form of spiritual tourism. You will encounter them again at parties on the occasions when you return and you will probably find it difficult to understand what they are talking about.

This is a familiar prelude to the experience of the West Indian writer and its source is not provincial amateurism but the legitimate and hungry need for a solid context of endeavour. Hawthorne, after all, did have his ancestors. The West Indian writer has only the disparate fragments of his own and his society's experience and an immense burden of responsibility that is not the necessary lot of the artist. At the same time his own society is not likely to welcome his work. It might want to but it doesn't know how to. His work has the occasional and partisan support of government. If the writer himself has the appropriate social contacts he might be accorded a warm sense of belonging. But the real terms of comprehension and dialogue do not exist. The writer, for example, at public meetings is likely to be asked to comment on the extent to which he is West Indian. Because the West Indies is not merely in a tragic sense isolated from world history—it is also isolated from world literature. It easily supposes, for example, that local writing is calculatedly vicious and depraved. It confuses satire with sarcasm and supposes that irony is another name for patronage. It is willing to believe that its writers, especially those long resident abroad, are engaged in some form of conspiratorial treachery with English reviewers and publishers. It is likely to endorse the work of those writers who either endorse the cliché of a fifth form taste for romantic poetry, or who offer their writing as a weapon in an ill-understood political conflict. Significantly the only important ironist the West Indies has yet produced, V. S. Naipaul, appears to have taken up permanent residence in England and has refused to be identified as a West Indian writer. And Naipaul's irony is often elaborately defensive.

Within the society itself there is no coherent class structure with a fertilising mobility. There are simply the Maginot lines of colour or affluence; and behind those lines the self-conscious groups of intellectuals. The only West Indian novel which provides an analysis in depth of a society is Phyllis Allfrey's *The Orchid House*. The novel is set in Dominica, a society frozen into its past. With rich and careful nostalgia, and a penetrating but unobtrusive symbolism, Mrs. Allfrey establishes the society and the attempt of three young people both to understand it and break away from it. In political terms her society supplies the means of its own betrayal. And the meaning of her three central characters is only available to them abroad.

It is true that after George Lamming's first novel, or after V. S. Naipaul's *A House for Mr. Biswas*, an assertion of this kind is open to responsible challenge. Both these writers, it can be decently argued, depict a society. George Lamming, in fact, has even argued that the essential West Indian writer is Samuel Selvon, the master of the "peasant image." But what both Lamming and Naipaul have in common, unlikely though the comparison may seem, is that the societies they separately describe are shut off from any larger, more coherent world. The experience of their observed people has the suggestion of a password—a means of initiation and a means of exclusion. Neither Lamming's Barbadian villagers, nor Naipaul's horribly trapped East Indians are as remote in circumstance and implication as the two writers are probably willing to believe. Lamming's people are sensually aware that their experience should not end in itself. Naipaul's are compulsively hiding the keys to their own prisons. They meet in their need to make a whole out of a heap of fragments. The chief characters try to survive under conditions of grotesque underprivilege and are therefore obliged to make a paradigm out of the jetsam of what is available—and all of them make the mistake of equating what is available to them with what is available. Both writers have their own kinds of awareness of this and the difference between them is the quality of Naipaul's observant and compassionate irony and Lamming's inability to decide whether he is an artist or a probation officer. The meaningful resonance of an expression like "My mother who fathered me" (from Lamming's book) in the West Indies itself does not have the kind of spontaneous momentum that communicates in a different world. Sociologists in England, observing the mores of an immigrant population, may suppose they have grasped it. Their evidence is likely to be drawn from the priggishness of the English working class with whom the immigrants mainly come into contact. But the meaning of the expression in the West Indies, and its incorrigible effect upon human relations, is a different matter. Insofar as the field of the novelist is human relations this may help to explain why the bulk of West Indian readers are so willing to feel that the local writer's treatment of sexual relations is merely profane. The readership resents (or encourages for the wrong reasons) any careful examination of its own cultural patterns. It is hardly surprising then that Naipaul's predominant mode is irony and that he should prefer to see himself as an English writer. In a general way his po-

sition and viewpoint are easily understandable—especially
when one remembers again the amount of West Indian
writing that is produced abroad. But it is possible, and this
is one of the ironies of this kind of colonial writing that he
has not acknowledged (recognition is another matter) the
dual role that is forced upon his fellow writers.

Novelists in the West Indies lack the confidence of a culture either metropolitan or tribal. They are driven to a
degree of explanatory matter that is not imposed upon
the inhabitants of an old and settled culture. Much of the
naivete of dialogue in West Indian novels can be accounted
for thus, and also much of the naivete of English reviewer's
reaction to West Indian writing. They must illustrate
before they can try to explain. This is not because their
experience is unfamiliar or "exotic" but because the time
and the confidence necessary to create a view of life which
is at the same time new and attested do not yet exist. Naipaul, it would seem, has abdicated from even the possibility of an eventual tradition of West Indian writing.
He is also, in my view, the most gifted novelist in the British Caribbean. A kind of logic therefore seems obvious:
flight is an enduring guarantee of talent.

It is plain, however, that talent cannot be measured as
some kind of abstract possession. The simple fact of publication presupposes nothing but a share in royalties. There
are no writers that one does not try to evaluate in terms
of their grasp of and interpretation of the circumstances
they come out of. And these circumstances are often
created by earlier writers. For instance, in 1956, a small
volume called *A Literature in the Making* was published
in Jamaica. It was written by a poet and litterateur who had
been ceremonially crowned in a local theatre as the Poet
Laureate of the island. His own verse is largely pseudo-
Wordsworthian and his judgments can command no serious respect. The point is that eighteen years before a series
of articles by the same writer had appeared in a newly-
founded Jamaican weekly review and with effectively no
revision they make up the substance of the abovementioned

book—a book still canonised on library shelves, still proffered to occasional enquirers after "What has been written
on West Indian writing." For anyone who has read the
best West Indian writers in any bulk the inutility of a
volume on Jamaican writing is obvious. Two Jamaican
novelists were in fact ignored and so necessarily was every
other West Indian writer. Yet in the same weekly review
in 1940 two other Jamaican artists were contesting precisely the assumptions that dominate *A Literature in the
Making*. One artist, the novelist Roger Mais, argues that
if you are reading Shakespeare in the twentieth century
with the extravagant ambition of using him as an example,
in practice, you try and understand the *nature* of Shakespeare's originality. You do not imitate the varieties of
technique—absurdities are bound to follow. In experiencing the effect of a major writer, the argument ran, you
try to understand the quality of his enterprise within his
context. The West Indies is probably one of the few societies in the world where this kind of discussion can take
place (it still does). The enduring meanings of quality and
stature do not decide themselves, but they are more easily
stabilised in societies where the business of definition is an
act of imagination. In societies where they have not simply
a different meaning but virtually no meaning at all beyond
their insisted application to class and colour, the process
of humane evaluation is bound to appear more naive.

In other words the examination of a colonial literature
entails initially the comparison of possibility with possibility, of understanding with the materials that prompt and
assist it, not value contrasted with value. For value shifts
as societies change. . . . The challenge of West Indian
writing, then, is not that of deciding whether George
Lamming is turgid or whether John Hearne writes about
the wrong people. The critical question, to begin with, is
whether their writing is faithful to the reality they suppose
themselves to depict. It is not a question of special categories. To create them is to recreate in a metaphysical
form the original conditions. What is required is a fresh

understanding of the social and personal conditions of value terms so that an enduring and available meaning can be created.

The point calls for stress insofar as the chief themes of West Indian writing are easily forecast. Though in putting it this way I might seem to be annihilating the relevant core of what I want to say. The themes are "easily forecast" in that writers in a colonial or ex-colonial situation are going to be self-consciously concerned with questions about themselves and their experience that arise almost spontaneously out of the moral and political pressures of their communities. I say "almost spontaneously" because the writer will usually find himself in advance of the habituated assumption of the mercantile, professional and plantocratic classes upon whom responsibility will be imposed after the departure of the British. The local writer is naturally likely to insist that what he is really concerned with is a particular problem in human relationships. If his claim to be a novelist has any just meaning, then of course he is. But he cannot disengage his problem from its particular context—and its context is not just his society, it is the degree of his comprehension of it. This is perhaps the major problem that confronts the colonial writer. Unless the novelist is speaking to his immediate contemporaries, which in the West Indies itself is hardly yet possible, he must make common meaning out of experience which is peculiar and local. Let me suggest a relevant instance. "Time," in a colony nearing independence, or recently become independent, moves at an accelerated pace, at least for the intellectual and the artist. The emotional context in which the writer is working will alter far more swiftly and dramatically than would be possible in Europe—or in America unless you happen to be a negro. The writer may be in voluntary exile, and he may find his territory independent, and for him these two experiences are not dissimilar. His sense of the dramatic possibilities of experience will radically alter. At least twice in Jamaica alone I have heard two writers (both of them under forty) refer to the "younger

writers." As this was what I had regarded the writers themselves as being I was puzzled until I recollected that they
were addressing a University audience. The existence of a
local University, distributed among three islands with additional local Extra-Mural centres, is a guarantee of a degree of local meaning, of local confidence. It is hard to
imagine the situation before (say) 1952. Only one significant talent has yet come out of the University, but my
point at the moment is that its existence eliminates the
need for an indefinite sequence of "pioneers." Graduates
will continue to go abroad, but their experience will not
be the same as that of their predecessors. They will have
an official framework for their intent. And in the West
Indies, in the absence both of a tribal structure and a conception of manners, visible frameworks, visible meanings,
even if they happen to be official ones, are important. The
experience of "abroad" will remain crucially significant
but the graduate will never have the sense of poignant
isolation which in large measure entitles people who are
still under forty to regard themselves as a special generation.

The other sense in which essential themes are easily
forecast is harder to define clearly. To begin with one is
faced with problems of cultural impoverishment and fail-
ures in personal sensibility that cannot easily be separated.
And the precise point at which one is a consequence of
the other requires very careful examination. In colonial
societies in particular terms which do have genuine meaning are easily demoted into slogans. The slogans can be
embodied with more than a huckster's assertion, but it is
fatally simple for experience of a special order to do easy
and ready substitute for a mature grasp of the experience
itself. Exasperated Englishmen in the West Indies have
often said to me, "This business of the search for an
identity—it becomes a sort of tarpaulin cliché for anything
anybody thinks they feel, or ought to feel." Naturally. If
these are merely provisional terms for definition in societies
which have for so long been without them, then the charla-

tan has a hopeful future. In the main the society lacks
both the time and the inclination to make sharp discriminations within and about itself. And when, as an Englishman, you are faced with what you judge to be a totally
fraudulent reputation your task is not an easy one. You
can indulge in an unwitting cruelty simply because you
fail to understand that the inability to make a true imaginative comment on the part of this or that writer may be the
consequence of a complex of circumstances that you yourself profoundly deplore. The failure is not necessarily the
result of imaginative coarseness or emotional insincerity.
In locating what you regard simply as a failure in sensibility you may be dealing with the historical and emotional
conditions which help to make the failure inevitable. After
all, what about the writers you really think are saying
something important?

No doubt I seem to be contradicting myself, or raising
a previous issue, or possibly both. The issue is not so much
about what is cheap and fraudulent and what is not—it is
never so very hard to make up one's mind about that.
The issue is about the experience which underlies different
kinds of failure, and the varying capacities of individual
understanding. There is, for instance, a Jamaican novel
which consists of little more than invective, illuminated
by temporary moments of compassionate understanding.
These moments need to be carefully distinguished from
self-pity, for to be black is not to be automatically welcome
in the West Indies. But the novel seems to me to be directed almost entirely by a naive, retributive malice rather
than by any creative desire to explore the context and the
pressure of humiliation and underprivilege. Though the
West Indian novelist has little more to fall back on than
purely subjective reactions, highly vulnerable to the immediate pressures of local insistence, without the helpful perspectives that a larger confidence can supply. Irony and
satire, as I have said, have an air of the abnormal in the
West Indies.

In putting it this way I must appear to be making a

large concession to patronage and to an irritating kind of tolerance. And neither of these can be of any advantage to a nascent literature. But I think that I am really anxious to direct attention towards a special kind of difficulty.

A novelist like James Baldwin, for example, can annexe himself to a creative tradition that has nothing as such to do with the intimate and challenging problem of being a negro in a society marked by barely credible lack of privilege. Indeed, the tradition deepens its fictive possibilities. To the extent to which Baldwin can grasp and use the experience of earlier American writers he is better able to record his understanding, as an artist, of the tragedy of his people. This comes out very forcibly in the essay in *Notes of a Native Son* in which he describes his visit to a conference of African writers held in Paris. He felt himself to be an American—perhaps in spite of the acrid ironies that must attend that conviction in America itself. The West Indian writer, living in a society which by official intention and in some measure by practice gives the black man a dignity which is not available to him in America, is culturally far worse off. It seems clear, then, that questions of "value" must not be watered down to suit colonial convenience. There is an original problem.

Another predictable theme in West Indian writing is colour and the scale of prejudices which go with it. And in the main, the fictive treatment of colour by the local novelist is disappointing. I mean simply that too much fiction is either manifestly bad, or merely states the self-evident. It is true that the West neither has, nor probably needs, a novelist like James Baldwin. But whereas in Baldwin's case it can be responsibly argued that his experience as a negro gives him an original kind of awareness there is no West Indian novelist with an equivalence in sensibility. The quality of British colonialism is in important measure to blame for this. It is not the instinct of the British to share their identity with the societies they either take over or invent. The British impose a degree of moderately efficient bureaucracy, instil some convictions about law, and leave it at that. They do not attempt to persuade the colonial that he has a place, that he has significant membership within, the metropolitan culture. (It took the British working class long enough to inform its rulers that it had a right to the implications of Civis Brittanicus Sum. In fact it took it so long that it constitutes a major impediment in racial understanding now.) This kind of institutionalised impoverishment is immensely exacerbated in the West Indies—a society whose original inhabitants have almost entirely disappeared to be replaced by enforced expatriates, i.e. slaves and their descendants and those occasional beneficiaries of the termination of slavery, the Indians and the Chinese. No other complex of societies for which the British have been responsible can offer equivalent experience. It is not simply the fact of oppression, nor of an induced sense of inferiority. The means of cultural definition were never encouraged to exist. They were never felt to be necessary. Some of the consequences of this are predictable. Jamaica, for instance, is making a fairly sustained attempt, with the encouragement of Government, to discover the culture of the Arawak Indians who were the original inhabitants of the island. But the enterprise is necessarily factitious partly because the Arawaks, as far as is known a simple, gentle people, were extirpated entirely by the colonial masters, and partly because there is nobody in Jamaica who can claim anything more than a museum relationship with the Arawaks. The meaningful legacies in Jamaica's history are the slave chains and the mantraps preserved in the Folk Museum. Arawak remains, as so far uncovered, amount to little more than burial pits and refuse dumps. These are presumably of some interest to the archaeologist but they are hardly sufficient for an original cultural re-orientation and definition. On the other hand colour and the historical and contemporary indecencies which go with it are essential facts of West Indian life. No writer can finally manage to avoid them.

And yet in a way they are avoided, partly because of a

factitious quest for origins, and partly because of emphatic recourse to cliché. A number of writers indulge in what can only be described as anthropological assertion with nothing behind but the limit of possibility. The symbolic integrity of, for example, V. S. Reid's *The Leopard* makes novels like Sylvia Wynter's *The Hills of Hebron* or Frank Hercules' *Where the Hummingbird Flies* look like prescribed fantasies. When we are told that simple Jamaican cultists feel the historical loss of the spear and the coal-pot, the developed ritual of West African tribal life, we are dealing finally with the author's subjective requirements and not with the rewarding detail of genuine observation. It is clearly dangerous for an Englishman to offer strong disagreement with the implications of this kind of manufactured background. But my point is that the background is little more than a circle of stage fire. It is emotional decor rather than the felt substance of experience. And at the level of sociological observation it hardly fits the facts of Jamaican cultist behaviour. We are dealing here with an enduring irony in the context of West Indian writing—the tendency of history to rearrange itself at the behest of whim and limitation. Talent alone is insufficient when the society itself lacks the advantage of a traditional coherence. There is not even an agreed matrix—desperate loyalties exist among the writers themselves. It is therefore easy for the writer to take refuge in illicit inventions about experience, fantasies which gain a degree of legitimate currency because of the density of unspoken aspiration which lies behind them. This is not a healthy situation for the production of a literature and it seems reasonable to suppose that permanently major talent in West Indian writing will consolidate itself on the debris of ephemeral reputations.

The basic challenge, then, confronting anyone who attempts to comment on the achievement of West Indian fiction so far is to recognise an at least temporary ambivalence in the use of value judgments one had previously taken for granted. Or, if not an ambivalence, at least an elasticity of interpretation. This is partly a consequence of some of the circumstances I have attempted to describe, and partly a consequence of a reading of those circumstances. It doesn't mean that "value" must undergo a process of tolerant adaptation. It means that we have first to come to terms with the available roots of value. One parts company here with the experience and perception of Henry James—at any rate as an inevitable companion in the West Indian scene. We have to realise that James was exceptionally well-endowed in ways that are not available to the West Indian writer. This was partly a matter of James' own family background, but more importantly James could go to Europe and absorb himself in a culture which welcomed him, so to speak, in advance. The white American was never colonised imaginatively and James could meet (say) George Eliot, not as an equal perhaps but certainly as a fellow-practitioner. The West Indian writer, even when his verse is read in Dover Street, cannot do this. George Lamming's account (in *The Pleasures of Exile*) of a literary evening with the ICA reads rather like a deliberate refusal to indulge in special pleading, and therefore it is a mode of special pleading. But at least it gets across a reaction which is both understandable and valid. James never manifests that curious blend of self-complacence and inferiority. The West Indian has not so much been taught to feel inferior. Simply, it was the atmosphere in which he and his people were born and developed. In England he is apt to be haunted by a consciousness that addresses him in dissonant accents. More is at stake for him than his role as artist; who he is and what he looks like are enforced roles. He will not be explicit about this in his own territory—at least not if he intends to remain in it. He is much more likely to cohabit with the re-iterated slogans that make up its political life that emanate from its centres of power. Or he will dominate the small, self-conscious network of middle class personal relations that abound in a small society. This is one of the reasons, in fact, why the pleasures of exile are likely

o be more or less indefinite. The comparative anonymity
of English life can have the pull of a magnetic attraction.
Living in the West Indies is apt to have the effect a sunray
lamp might have on a lizard—you can bask in the glow
without realising that you are being shrivelled. The uses of
imagination, it would seem must be learnt abroad. In this
peculiar way the overlord culture can be forced to yield
up what it never supposed mattered.

18.

The problems of West Indian creativity are set forth in concrete detail by the St. Lucian poet-playwright Derek Walcott. He explores his own growth toward self-expression in the context of middle-class life in a small colonial society dominated by complacent philistinism—a social environment deadening to creativity. Yet, for him, the West Indies provide sources of strength as well: vivid and strongly marked physical landscapes, insular self-containment enriched by an awareness of an entire archipelago, a pervasive sense of elemental mysteries, a penchant for the mythic and fabulous, all overlaid and energized by familiarity with the world's great classics, reinterpreted in local terms. Walcott sees the exuberant indulgence and sheer physical expressiveness that stem from these and other West Indian circumstances as contributing to both the strengths and the defects of West Indian artistic creativity.

Born in St. Lucia and now resident in Trinidad, DEREK WALCOTT has captured many West Indian moods in his drama and poetry. His best-known plays include *Malcauchon* and *The Dream on Monkey Mountain;* much of his verse is collected in *The Castaways and Other Poems* and *In a Green Night.*

Meanings
Derek Walcott

My mother, who was a school-teacher, took part in amateur theatre. My father was a civil servant, but also wrote
verse and was an excellent draughtsman. He was also a
good portrait painter in water-colour. Our house was
haunted by his absence because all around the drawing
room there were his water-colours and water-colour por-
traits. He had a meticulous style with an innate humility,
as if he were a perpetual student. He must have plotted his
own development carefully, proceeding from drawing to
full-bodied painting when death interrupted it. He died
quite young. In another situation I think he would have
been an artist. He evidently had a great influence on his
friends. One of them, under whom I later studied painting,
went on to become a professional painter. I have an immense respect, in fact, an awe, for that kind of spiritual
strength; I mean here was this circle of self-civilizing, courteous people in a poverty-ridden, cruelly ignored colony
living by their own certainties. So to begin as a poet was,
for me, a direct inheritance. It was natural. I feel that I
have simply continued where my father left off.

I go back as far as this because it is almost death to the
spirit to try to survive as an artist under colonial conditions, which haven't really changed with our independent
governments. The fall-out rate among artists and actors,

Savacou, No. 2, 1970, pp. 45–51. Reprinted with permission of the author and *Savacou*.

in fact, all creative people, is considerable. They either abandon their talents or emigrate, which is the same thing.

I really became involved in theatre when my brother suggested I write a play about the Haitian revolution. He had read a book about it and gotten excited. So I said, all right, I'll try one, and I wrote a play, *Henri Christophe*. This was in Saint Lucia, where I was still living. We formed a group there called The Arts Guild—mainly school-boys, and we performed this play. Then I began to write more plays for them. We performed them in Castries, my home town; the whole island's population must be about eighty thousand. The plays may have been seen by a few hundred people in all. But The Arts Guild still exists. My twin brother, who also writes plays, continued it. At the university in Jamaica, we formed another group. Then I got a Rockefeller Fellowship to go to America in '58.

While I was in America I was supposed to study scene design as well as directing, but because I was so isolated I felt very alone in the United States. I knew I did not want what was going on. Not on Broadway, but in a way, not off-Broadway as well. I think the pressure of that loneliness made me realize I had to do something which was true to the kind of company I wanted to have. I used to go to José Quintero's classes and to the Phoenix Theatre.

The first real experience I had of writing a stylized West Indian play was in New York. It was a West Indian fable called *Ti-Jean and His Brothers*. For the first time I used songs and dances and a narrator in a text. That was the fastest play I'd ever written. I wrote it on my first trip to New York—before I got the Rockefeller—in four or five days. It astonished me. I probably wrote the damned thing because I was afraid to go out. Out of that play, I knew what I wanted.

Then I came back from New York to take up the Fellowship and I began to study Japanese films. I had seen the dancers of the Little Carib Company in Trinidad and I felt that what would spring from our theatre need not be a literary thing—not the word, not the psychology—not the *detailed* psychology of character so much as a mimetic power, in the dance particularly. I had a company in mind who would be both dancers and actors . . . a dance company mixed with an acting company. Then the Little Carib and the workshop separated, so what happened was that an actor had to try to be a dancer.

Sooner or later, I had to decide whether to go back to the West Indies at all. Luckily, my brother was still with The Arts Guild. They went to Trinidad, and he asked me if I would come and help him, so I went down there. I used it as an excuse. I didn't finish my Fellowship. I was very tired and was feeling very depressed about New York theatre and about any chance I might have of ever doing anything there. Plus, of course, at that time in '58, plays about the West Indies, or black actors—well, there wasn't much of a chance of getting anything going. There was no such thing in New York as a company of black actors. So I went back to Trinidad and began the Trinidad Theatre Workshop. Most of the people who came to this Company had some experience in amateur theatre or with other companies in Trinidad. But we began very modestly. I didn't do any work on production at first. Having gone through the American experience of seeing improvisations and directing, watching American actors and 'the method', I knew that initially I had to get discipline. I had to work for three or four years doing improvisations, letting the actors lead themselves with all of us exploring together before we finally could put on a play. It was seven years before we really decided we were fit to produce something. We chose two very modest plays—modest in scale: *The Zoo Story* and *The Sea At Dauphin*, a play I had written earlier about a fisherman.

When the improvisations began, I saw that there was something extra about the West Indian because of the way he is so visibly, physically self-expressive. If that were combined with the whole self-annihilating process of who you are and what you're doing, which you get from method acting—if those two were fused together, you could get a terrific style. So that's what we aimed at. And once improvisations began to go well, then I would know in what direction the company could move. So I was after . . . and am still after . . . a theatre where someone can do Shakespeare or sing Calypso with equal conviction.

In 1966, we did our first production in a very small abandoned bar called The Basement Theatre. We only had seats for sixty people. We thought we would just be on for two nights, but we went on for a week. We were amazed. The response was so good that we decided that we were now a producing company, and we put on other West Indian plays which got equally good report. The theatre itself was very crude: a platform very loosely made and some lights. Then we put on our first repertory season, which ran successfully for 26 nights. We did *The Blacks,* and a West Indian play called *Belle Fanto,* and *The Road* by Soyinka. By that time the actors were working very hard—working by day at eight-to-five jobs and coming back at night to perform. So there is a terrific energy that exists in the Company.

From then on we began to do a lot of plays. I can't remember them all now. I try to keep a balance in the repertory between classic or great contemporary plays and West Indian material. There are things I want to do, but not yet. Eventually, we are going to do some kind of Shakespeare, but it must have its own style—not just exotic. I am talking about a real, true style—true to our own experience. It would be very cheap to do certain things—a black *Hamlet*—just for that kind of effect. I know I have a good Hamlet in the Company, but I don't want that kind of thing.

At this time, I began to revive my own plays because I now had the company to express them. *The Dream On Monkey Mountain,* for example, I had begun in the States in '59. We were going on tour; we had just completed our first repertory season and needed a new play. I remember I wrote the second act very rapidly because we had to have a play, and I always fiddle around a long time with my

plays. Now, a strange thing happened: I had a prepared
text, but there was one figure at the back of my mind, a
death figure from Haitian mythology, that wasn't written in. There was an actor, Albert Le Veau, who had just
finished doing *The Zoo Story* and *Dauphin*. We were going
on tour, but there was no part in it for him. So I worked
in the figure from the center of the play's design, and the
part radiated through the whole text—the part of Basil. I
think that this figure tightened, webbed its structure. It's
one of the beautiful accidents that can happen when you
have a good company.

Our sin in West Indian art is the sin of exuberance, of
self-indulgence, and I wanted to impose a theatre that observed certain rules. The use of choruses required precise
measure; the use of narration required precise mime.
There was one dance step that, when it was arrested,
seemed to be exactly what I wanted—powerful, difficult,
precise. It came out of the bongo-dance. It is a male challenge dance played at wakes, obviously derived from warrior games, and I saw in that moment the discipline of
arrest, of revelation from which a mimetic narrative power
could spring like some of the *mies* in Japanese theatre.

Furthermore, I do a lot of drawing for my plays. In fact,
I visualize them completely in terms of costume and stag-
ing, even certain group formations, before I go into production and while I am writing the play. In New York, I
came to the Chinese and Japanese classic theatre through
Brecht. I began to go to the texts themselves and, because
I draw, I used to look very carefully at the woodcuts of
Hokusai and Hiroshige. There was then a very strong popular interest in Japanese cinema—in Kurosawa, and films
such as *Ugetsu, Gate of Hell, Rashomon*, etc. I had written one play which was derivative of *Rashomon*, called
Malcauchon. It was the story of a woodcutter and people
gathered together under a hut. This was a deliberate imi-
tation, but it was one of those informing imitations that
gave me a direction because I could see in the linear
shapes, in the geography, in the sort of myth and super-

stition of the Japanese, correspondences to our own forests and mythology. I also wanted to use the same type of figure found in this material, a type essential to our own mythology. A woodcutter or charcoal burner.

To me, this figure represented the most isolated, most reduced, race-containing symbol. In addition, I have my own associations of our forests, of rain, of mists, plus of course, the inherent violence or despair in a person of that type—the mad woodcutter. In the kind of play I wanted to do, it was natural to have someone who was narrating the text since, in a sense, that is Oriental as well as African. What I wanted to do was reduce the play almost to an inarticulateness of language. I would like to have had a play made up of grunts and sounds which you don't understand, like you hear at a Japanese film. The words would be reduced to very primal sounds.

But in writing the play another more literary tradition took over, so that I made the figures voluble. In a sense, I feel that is still what I am going after. I am a kind of split writer: I have one tradition inside me going in one way, and another tradition going another. The mimetic, the narrative, and dance element is strong on one side, and the literary, the classical tradition is strong on the other.

In *The Dream On Monkey Mountain*, I tried to fuse them, but I am still after a kind of play that is essential and spare the same way woodcuts are clean, that dances are clean, and that Japanese cinema is so compressed that gesture does the same thing as speech. That is where our kind of conflict is rich. I think the pressure of those two conflicts is going to create a verbally rich literature, as well as a mimetic style. This happens in Wole Soyinka. It happens as well in the kind of plays that we are writing at home.

When we first did *Monkey Mountain*, I told the actors exactly what I was after. It was easy to communicate with them because I knew what was being generated in the actors' minds. All of these actors move well. They don't dance in the ballet or modern idiom; they are not abstract dancers. They can do dances which are spontaneous yet precise and have more to do with acting than with dance. Any one of them in the Company, for instance, can do a bongo step, and the bongo step was the step which, as I said, crystallized the kind of movement I was after; it is a kind of Russian thing, low-stepping, leg-crossed, and it's just one of those associations that generated a style for me.

The bongo is a wake dance, a spiritual celebration at death of the triumph over death. I suppose two warriors would challenge each other to divert the attendant grieving people from the death. It is a very foot-asserting, earth-asserting, life-asserting dance in contradiction of the grief that has happened through the death. In that dance, when the legs are crossed, and the dancer is arrested for a second, there is all the male strength that I think has been absent for a long time in Western theatre. The emphasis is on virility. This ancient idea of the actor in a theatre where women are not allowed to take part or are uninterested was true of colonial society in the West Indies and in Africa, whether in Soyinka's Company or in mine. Very few women took part in our theatre when we began, so initially all of our plays had more male characters than women. Still, it's good. I think that in a theatre where you have a strong male principle, or where women aren't involved at the beginning, a kind of style will happen; there will be violence, there will be direct conflict, there will be more physical theatre and there will be less interest in sexual psychology. From this step, the bongo step—came a private mythology associated with the warrior-figure—the African warrior, or the Japanese samurai. In that sense, it is more like early medieval plays or early Shakespeare plays where the conflict is always a male conflict.

This is in some part affected by our being an island culture. I think that an archipelago, whether Greek or West Indian, is bound to be a fertile area, particularly if it is a bridge between continents, and a variety of people settle there. In the West Indies, there are all these conditions— the Indian heritage, the Mediterranean, the Lebanese and

Chinese, etc. I don't want to look too far ahead, but I think there will be a playwright coming out of the Indian experience and one out of the Chinese experience; each will isolate what is true to his own tradition. When these things happen in an island culture a fantastic physical theatre will emerge because the forces that affect that communal search will use physical expression through dance, through the Indian dance and through Chinese dance, through African dance. When these things happen, plus all the cross-fertilization—the normal sociology of the place —then a true and very terrifying West Indian theatre will come. It's going to be so physically strong as to be something that has never happened before.

On any island, when the night comes in—and it's true for the Japanese peasantry too—we gather around the story-teller, and the tradition is revived. A style is also emerging, because you've got the story-teller at the fire, and you've got the hero whose quest is never done. This quest figure, who is a warrior, a knight, endures experiences that resolve what he is. There is a geography which surrounds the story-teller, and this is made physical by things like mist or trees or whatever—mountains, snakes, devils. Depending on how primal the geography is and how fresh in the memory, the island is going to be invested in the mind of the child with a mythology which will come out in whatever the child grows up to re-tell.

In the West Indies, from a slave tradition adapted to the environment, the slaves kept the strength of the stories about devils and gods and the cunning of certain figures, but what was missing in the folklore was a single heroic warrior figure. We had the cunning of certain types, representative of the slave outwitting his master, like Br'er Rabbit or Tar Baby, done in West Indian dialect.

My Makak comes from my own childhood. But there was no king, no tribal chief, no warrior for a model in those stories. So the person I saw was this degraded, humble, lonely, isolated figure of the woodcutter. I can see him for what he is now, a brawling, ruddy drunk who would come down the street on a Saturday when he got paid and let out an immense roar that would terrify all the children in the street. When we heard him coming we all bolted, because he was like a baboon. He is still alive, and there is no terror anymore—except in the back of my mind. This was a degraded man, but he had some elemental force in him that is still terrifying; in another society he would have been a warrior.

There is another strange thing for me about the island of Saint Lucia; its whole topography is weird—very conical, with volcanic mountains and such—giving rise to all sorts of superstitions. Rather like what Ireland was for Yeats and the early Irish poets—another insular culture.

Whether you wanted to accept them or not, the earth emanated influences which you could either put down as folk superstition or, as a poet, accept as a possible truth. I think that is why a lot of my plays remain set in Saint Lucia, because there is a mystery there that is with me from childhood, that surrounds the whole feeling of the island. There was, for example, a mountain covered with mist and low clouds to which we gave the name of La Sorcière, the witch.

Does an island tradition impose limitations on a company such as ours? This goes back to the whole question of provincial, or beyond that, colonial experience, and of how we can broaden the base of the arts in the West Indies, and through that reach the larger audiences we should like. To me the only hope is in communal effort, just as I think some form of socialism, evolved from our own political history, is the only hope for the archipelago. When people like me ask the state for subsidy, we aren't asking the state to support the arts; we are informing the state, which is as poor and as spiritually degraded as we have been, of its true condition. The state is being asked to share the condition of its artists, to recognize its experience. The indifference is the same as it was under colonialism, but without that charming, avuncular cynicism of the British.

Yet I feel absolutely no shame in having endured the colonial experience. There was no obvious humiliation in it. In fact, I think that many of what are sneered at as colonial values are part of the strength of the West Indian psyche, a fusion of formalism with exuberance, a delight in both the precision and the power of language. We love rhetoric, and this has created a style, a panache about life that is particularly ours. Our most tragic folk songs and our most self-critical calypsos have a driving, life-asserting force. Combine that in our literature with a long experience of classical forms and you're bound to have something exhilarating. I've never consciously gone after this in my plays, nor do we go after this kind of folk-exuberance deliberately in my theatre company. But in the best actors in the company you can see this astounding fusion ignite their style, this combination of classic discipline inherited through the language, with a strength of physical expression that comes from the folk music.

It's probably the same in Nigeria with Wole Soyinka's Company. It's the greatest bequest the Empire made. Those who sneer at what they call an awe of tradition forget how old the West Indian experience is. I think that precisely because of their limitations our early education must have ranked with the finest in the world. The grounding was rigid—Latin, Greek, and the essential masterpieces, but there was this elation of discovery. Shakespeare, Marlowe, Horace, Vergil—these writers weren't jaded but immediate experiences. The atmosphere was competitive, creative.

It was cruel, but it created our literature.

SELECTED READINGS

ACWORTH, A. W., *Treasure in the Caribbean: A First Study of Georgian Building in the British West Indies*, London, Pleiades Books, 1949.

BARRETT, LEONARD E., *The Rastafarians: A Study in Messianic Cultism in Jamaica* (Caribbean Monograph Series, No. 6), Río Piedras, Institute of Caribbean Studies, University of Puerto Rico, 1968.

BENNETT, LOUISE, *Jamaica Labrish*, Jamaica, Sangster's Book Stores, 1966.

BERGHE, PIERRE L. VAN DEN, *Race and Racism: A Comparative Perspective*, New York, John Wiley, 1967.

CAMPBELL, A. A., *St. Thomas Negroes: A Study of Personality and Culture* (Psychological Monographs, Vol. 55, No. 5), Washington, D.C., American Psychological Association, 1943.

CASSIDY, F. G., *Jamaica Talk: Three Hundred Years of the English Language in Jamaica*, London, Macmillan, 1961.

CASSIDY, F. G., and LE PAGE, R. B., *Dictionary of Jamaican English*, Cambridge, Cambridge University Press, 1967.

CÉSAIRE, AIMÉ, *Cahier d'un retour au pays natal* [1939], Paris, Présence Africaine, 1956.

COLLYMORE, FRANK A., *Notes for a Glossary of Words and Phrases of Barbadian Dialect*, Bridgetown, Barbados, Advocate Press, 1955.

COMITAS, LAMBROS, *Caribbeana 1900–1965: A Topical*

Bibliography, Seattle, University of Washington Press for the Research Institute for the Study of Man, 1968.

CORZANI, JACK, *Splendeur et misère: l'exotisme littéraire aux Antilles* (Groupe Universitaire de Recherches Inter-Caraïbes, Études et Documents, No. 2), Pointe-à-Pitre, Guadeloupe, Centre d'Enseignement Supérieur Littéraire, 1969.

COULTHARD, G. R., *Race and Colour in Caribbean Literature,* London, Oxford University Press for the Institute of Race Relations, 1962.

COURLANDER, HAROLD, and BASTIEN, RÉMY, *Religion and Politics in Haiti,* Washington, D.C., Institute for Cross-Cultural Research, 1966.

CRONON, EDMUND DAVID, *Black Moses: The Story of Marcus Garvey and the Universal Negro Improvement Association,* Madison, University of Wisconsin Press, 1964.

FANON, FRANTZ, *Black Skin, White Masks,* New York, Grove Press, 1967.

FERMOR, PATRICK LEIGH, *The Traveller's Tree: A Journey through the Caribbean Islands,* New York, Harper, 1950.

GORDON, SHIRLEY C., *A Century of West Indian Education: A Source Book,* London, Longmans, 1963.

———, *Reports and Repercussions in West Indian Education, 1835–1933,* London, Ginn, 1968; New York, International Publications Service, 1968.

HEARN, LAFCADIO, *Two Years in the French West Indies,* New York, Harper and Brothers, 1923.

JAHN, JANHEINTZ, *A Bibliography of Neo-African Literature from Africa, America, and the Caribbean,* London, Andre Deutsch, 1965.

JAMES, C. L. R., *Beyond a Boundary,* London, Hutchinson, 1963.

———, *Party Politics in the West Indies,* San Juan, Trinidad, privately published, 1962.

JAYAWARDENA, CHANDRA, *Conflict and Solidarity in a Guianese Plantation,* London, University of London, Athlone Press, 1963; New York, Humanities Press, 1963.

KERR, MADELINE, *Personality and Conflict in Jamaica,* London, Collins, 1963.

KESTELOOT, LILYAN, *Aimé Césaire*, Paris, Pierre Seghers, 1962.

LAMMING, GEORGE, *The Pleasures of Exile*, London, Michael Joseph, 1960.

LEIRIS, MICHEL, *Contacts de civilisations en Martinique et en Guadeloupe*, Paris, UNESCO/Gallimard, 1955.

LE PAGE, R. B., and DECAMP, DAVID, *Jamaican Creole*, London, Macmillan, 1960.

LOWENTHAL, DAVID, *West Indian Societies*, London and New York, Oxford University Press for the Institute of Race Relations and the American Geographical Society, 1972.

MITTELHOLZER, EDGAR, *A Swarthy Boy*, London, Putnam, 1963.

——, *With a Carib Eye*, London, Secker and Warburg, 1958.

NAIPAUL, V. S., *An Area of Darkness*, London, Andre Deutsch, 1964.

——, *The Middle Passage*, London, Andre Deutsch, 1962.

NETTLEFORD, REX M., ed., *Manley and the New Jamaica: Selected Speeches and Writings 1938–1968*, London, Longman Caribbean, 1971.

——, *Mirror Mirror: Identity, Race and Protest in Jamaica*, Jamaica, William Collins and Sangster, 1970.

NETTLEFORD, REX M. and HA YACONA, MARIA, *Roots and Rhythms: Jamaica's National Dance Theatre*, London, Andre Deutsch, 1969; New York, Hill and Wang, 1970.

OXAAL, IVAR, *Black Intellectuals Come to Power*, Cambridge, Mass., Schenkman, 1968.

——, *Race and Revolutionary Consciousness: A Documentary Interpretation of the 1970 Black Power Revolt in Trinidad*, Cambridge, Mass., Schenkman, 1971.

PRICE-MARS, JEAN, *Ainsi parla l'oncle: essais d'ethnographie* [1928], New York, Parapsychology Foundation, 1954.

Proceedings of the Conference on Creole Language Studies, London, Macmillan, 1961.

RAMCHAND, KENNETH, *The West Indian Novel and Its Background*, London, Faber and Faber, 1970; New York, Barnes and Noble, 1970.

RUBIN, VERA, and ZAVALLONI, MARISA, *We Wish to Be*

Looked Upon: A Study of the Aspirations of Youth in a Developing Society, New York, Teachers College Press, 1969.

SIMPSON, GEORGE EATON, *Religious Cults of the Caribbean: Trinidad, Jamaica, and Haiti* (Caribbean Monograph Series, No. 7), Río Piedras, Institute of Caribbean Studies, University of Puerto Rico, 1970.

SINGHAM, A. W., *The Hero and the Crowd in a Colonial Polity*, New Haven, Yale University Press, 1968.

SMITH, M. G., *Dark Puritan*, Kingston, Department of Extra-Mural Studies, University of the West Indies, 1963.

SMITH, M. G., AUGIER, ROY, and NETTLEFORD, REX, *The Ras Tafari Movement in Kingston, Jamaica*, Kingston, Institute of Social and Economic Research, University of the West Indies, 1960.

SOBERS, GARFIELD, and BARKER, J. S., editors, *Cricket in the Sun: A History of West Indies Cricket*, London, Arthur Barker, 1967.

Trinidad Carnival Issue, Special number of *Caribbean Quarterly*, Vol. 4, Nos. 3 and 4, Jamaica and Trinidad, March–June, 1956.

WILLIAMS, ERIC, *Education in the British West Indies*, New York, University Place Book Shop, 1968.

——, *Inward Hunger: The Education of a Prime Minister*, London, Andre Deutsch, 1969; Chicago, University of Chicago Press, 1971.

FICTION AND POETRY

ABRAHAMS, PETER, *This Island Now*, London, Faber and Faber, 1966; New York, Macmillan, 1971.

ALLFREY, PHYLLIS SHAND, *The Orchid House*, London, Constable, 1953.

ANTHONY, MICHAEL, *The Games Were Coming*, London, Andre Deutsch, 1963; Boston, Houghton Mifflin, 1968.

——, *Green Days by the River*, London, Andre Deutsch, 1967; Boston, Houghton Mifflin, 1967.

——, *The Year in San Fernando*, London, Andre Deutsch, 1965; New York, Humanities Press, 1970.

BARRETT, NATHAN, *Bars of Adamant*, New York, Fleet Publishing, 1966.

BENNETT, ALVIN, *God the Stonebreaker*, London, Heinemann, 1964.

BRATHWAITE, EDWARD, *Islands*, London and New York, Oxford University Press, 1969.

——, *Masks*, London and New York, Oxford University Press, 1968.

——, *Rights of Passage*, London and New York, Oxford University Press, 1967.

CAREW, JAN, *Black Midas*, London, Secker and Warburg, 1958.

——, *The Last Barbarian*, London, Secker and Warburg, 1961.

——, *The Wild Coast*, London, Secker and Warburg, 1958.

CARPENTIER, ALEJO, *Explosion in a Cathedral*, Boston, Little, Brown, 1962.

CLARKE, AUSTIN C., *Amongst Thistles and Thorns*, London, Heinemann, 1965.

——, *The Meeting Point*, London, Heinemann, 1967.

——, *The Survivors of the Crossing*, London, Heinemann, 1964.

COULTHARD, G. R., editor, *Caribbean Literature: An Anthology*, London, University of London Press, 1966; New York, International Publications Service, 1970.

DAMAS, LÉON-G., *Black-Label*, Paris, Gallimard, 1956.

DATHORNE, O. R., editor, *Caribbean Narrative: An Anthology of West Indian Writing*, London, Heinemann Educational Books, 1966.

DAWES, NEVILLE, *The Last Enchantment*, London, MacGibbon and Kee, 1960.

DOHRMAN, RICHARD, *The Cross of Baron Samedi*, Boston, Houghton Mifflin, 1958.

DRAYTON, GEOFFREY, *Christopher*, London, Collins, 1959.

FERMOR, PATRICK LEIGH, *The Violins of Saint-Jacques: A Tale of the Antilles*, New York, Harper & Brothers, 1953.

FIGUEROA, JOHN, editor, *Caribbean Voices: An Anthology of West Indian Poetry*, London, Evans Brothers, 1971.

GLISSANT, ÉDOUARD, *La Lézarde*, Paris, Éditions du Seuil, 1958.

——, *Le quatrième siècle*, Paris, Éditions du Seuil, 1964.

HARRIS, WILSON, *The Far Journey of Oudin*, London, Faber and Faber, 1961.

——, *Heartland*, London, Faber and Faber, 1964.

——, *Palace of the Peacock*, London, Faber and Faber, 1960.

HEARNE, JOHN, *The Autumn Equinox*, London, Faber and Faber, 1959; New York, Vanguard Press, 1970.

——, *Stranger at the Gate*, London, Faber and Faber, 1956.

——, *Voices under the Window*, London, Faber and Faber, 1955.

HERCULES, FRANK, *Where the Humming-bird Flies*, New York, Harcourt, Brace and World, 1961.

The Independence Anthology of Jamaican Literature, Kingston, Arts Celebration Committee of the Ministry of Development and Welfare, 1962.

JAMES, C. L. R., *Minty Alley* [1936], London, New Beacon Books, 1971.

KHAN, ISMITH, *The Jumbie Bird*, London, MacGibbon and Kee, 1961.

——, *The Obeah Man*, London, Hutchinson, 1964.

LAMMING, GEORGE, *In the Castle of My Skin*, London, Michael Joseph, 1953; New York, Macmillan, 1970.

——, *Of Age and Innocence*, London, Michael Joseph, 1958.

——, *Season of Adventure*, London, Michael Joseph, 1960.

LAUCHMONEN (Peter Kempadoo), *Old Thom's Harvest*, London, Eyre and Spottiswoode, 1965.

LOVELACE, EARL, *The Schoolmaster*, London, Collins, 1968; Chicago, Henry Regnery, 1968.

——, *While Gods Are Falling*, London, Collins, 1965; Chicago, Henry Regnery, 1966.

MACINNES, COLIN, *Westward to Laughter*, London, MacGibbon and Kee, 1969; New York, Fawcett World Library, 1971.

MAIS, ROGER, *Black Lightning*, London, Jonathan Cape, 1955.

——, *Brother Man*, London, Jonathan Cape, 1954.

——, *The Hills Were Joyful Together*, London, Jonathan Cape, 1953.

MARSHALL, PAULE, *The Chosen Place, The Timeless People*, New York, Harcourt, Brace and World, 1969.

MCDONALD, IAN, *The Humming-Bird Tree*, London, Heinemann, 1969.

MITTELHOLZER, EDGAR, *The Life and Death of Sylvia*, London, Secker and Warburg, 1953.

——, *A Morning at the Office*, London, Hogarth Press, 1950.

——, *Shadows Move Among Them*, London, Peter Nevill, 1952.

MORRIS, JOHN (Morris Cargill and John Hearne), *Fever Grass*, Jamaica, Collins and Sangster, 1969; New York, G. P. Putnam, 1969.

NAIPAUL, SHIVA, *Fireflies*, London, Andre Deutsch, 1970; New York, Alfred A. Knopf, 1971.

NAIPAUL, V. S., *A House for Mr. Biswas*, London, Andre Deutsch, 1961.

——, *The Mystic Masseur*, London, Andre Deutsch, 1957; New York, Vanguard Press, 1959.

——, *The Suffrage of Elvira*, London, Andre Deutsch, 1958.

NICOLE, CHRISTOPHER, *Off White*, London, Jarrolds, 1959.

——, *Ratoon*, London, Jarrolds, 1962.

——, *White Boy*, London, Hutchinson, 1966.

PATTERSON, ORLANDO, *An Absence of Ruins*, London, Hutchinson, 1967.

——, *The Children of Sisyphus*, London, New Authors, 1964.

PUISSESSEAU, RENÉ, *Someone Will Die Tonight in the Caribbean*, New York, Alfred A. Knopf, 1958.

RAMCHAND, KENNETH, *West Indian Narrative: An Introductory Anthology*, London, Nelson, 1966; New York, Barnes and Noble, 1970.

REDHEAD, WILFRED, *Three Comic Sketches* (Caribbean Plays No. 6), Trinidad, Extra-Mural Department, University College of the West Indies, 1956.

REID, V. S., *New Day*, New York, Alfred A. Knopf, 1949.

RHYS, JEAN, *Wide Sargasso Sea*, London, Andre Deutsch, 1966.

RICHER, CLÉMENT, *Ti-Coyo and His Shark: An Immoral Fable*, New York, Alfred A. Knopf, 1951.

ST. OMER, GARTH, *A Room on the Hill*, London, Faber and Faber, 1968.

——, *Shades of Grey*, London, Faber and Faber, 1968.

SALKEY, ANDREW, *Escape to an Autumn Pavement*, London, Hutchinson, 1960.

——, *A Quality of Violence*, London, New Authors, 1959.

SALKEY, ANDREW, editor, *Breaklight: Poetry of the Caribbean*, New York, Doubleday, 1971.

——, *Stories from the Caribbean: An Anthology*, London, Elek Books, 1965.

——, *West Indian Stories*, London, Faber and Faber, 1960.

SCHWARZ-BART, SIMONE, and SCHWARZ-BART, ANDRÉ, *Un plat de porc aux bananes vertes*, Paris, Éditions du Seuil, 1967.

SELVON, SAMUEL, *A Brighter Sun*, London, Allan Wingate, 1952.

——, *An Island Is a World*, London, MacGibbon and Kee, 1955.

——, *The Plains of Caroni*, London, MacGibbon and Kee, 1970.

——, *Turn Again Tiger*, London, MacGibbon and Kee, 1958.

SHERLOCK, PHILIP M., *Anansi, the Spider Man: Jamaican Folk Tales*, London, Macmillan, 1962; New York, Crowell, 1954.

——, *The Iguana's Tale: Crick Crack Stories from the Caribbean*, New York, Crowell, 1969.

THOBY-MARCELIN, PHILLIPPE, and MARCELIN, PIERRE, *All Men Are Mad*, New York, Farrar, Straus and Giroux, 1970.

——, *The Pencil of God*, Boston, Houghton Mifflin, 1951.

UNDERHILL, HAL, *Jamaica White*, New York, Macmillan, 1968.

VERCEL, ROGER, *L'Île des revenants*, Paris, Éditions Albin Michel, 1954.

WALCOTT, DEREK, *The Castaway and Other Poems*, London, Jonathan Cape, 1965.

——, *The Gulf and Other Poems*, London, Jonathan

Cape, 1969; New York, Farrar, Straus and Giroux, 1970.

——, *In a Green Night; Poems 1948–1960*, London, Jonathan Cape, 1962.

WAUGH, ALEC, *Island in the Sun*, New York, Farrar, Straus and Cudahy, 1955.

WOUK, HERMAN, *Don't Stop the Carnival*, New York, Pocket Books, 1965.

WYNTER, SYLVIA, *The Hills of Hebron: A Jamaican Novel*, London, Jonathan Cape, 1962.

WEST INDIAN PERIODICALS

Bim. Bridgetown, Barbados. Semi-annually.

Caribbean Quarterly. University of the West Indies, Extra-Mural Department. Kingston and Port-of-Spain. Quarterly.

Caribbean Review. Hato Rey, Puerto Rico. Quarterly.

Caribbean Studies. Institute of Caribbean Studies, University of Puerto Rico. Río Piedras, Puerto Rico. Quarterly.

Jamaica Journal. Institute of Jamaica. Kingston. Quarterly.

Parallèles. Fort-de-France. 3 or 4 times a year.

Savacou. Caribbean Artists Movement. Kingston and London. Quarterly.

Social and Economic Studies. University of the West Indies, Institute of Social and Economic Research, Kingston. Quarterly.

Voices. The Book Shop. Port-of-Spain. Tri-annually.

INDEX

328

ANCHOR BOOKS

AFRICAN AND AFRO-AMERICAN STUDIES

ANCHOR BOOKS

SOCIOLOGY

16Bb

SOCIOLOGY (cont'd)